ANN CLWYD

REBEL WITH A CAUSE

WITH JOANNA MASTERS

Biteback Publishing

First published in Great Britain in 2017 by
Biteback Publishing Ltd
Westminster Tower
3 Albert Embankment
London SE1 7SP
Copyright © Ann Clwyd 2017

ISBN 978-1-78590-093-8

10 9 8 7 6 5 4 3 2 1

A CIP catalogue record for this book is available from the British Library.

Set in Baskerville

Printed and bound in Great Britain by
CPI Group (UK) Ltd, Croydon CR0 4YY

CONTENTS

Dedicated to my late husband Owen Dryhurst Roberts who convinced me to go into politics and nagged me to write this book!

And to all who fight and have fought for human rights all over the world.

PROLOGUE

Fifty years is certainly a long time in politics. It has been a roller-coaster of a half-century.

Over the years family and friends have asked me when I was planning to write a book. When I regaled my late husband Owen with dramatic tales of my trips to Kurdistan, Owen would say, 'write a book'. I have been at it off and on for twenty years but, finally, it is done.

There were many things I wanted to capture; for example, how difficult it was for women to elbow their way into British politics even in the late 1970s! Having arrived there, I have stayed with the backing of the faithful voters of the Cynon Valley. I enjoy representing my constituency and the company of the people of the Cynon Valley, who are feisty, independent and funny.

I wanted to pay tribute to the indomitable spirit of the South Wales miners and their families. I first became associated with their cause as a journalist campaigning for compensation for pneumoconiosis (dust disease) and went on to become an MP for a mining constituency during the 1984–85 miners' strike. One of the few highlights was to keep Tower Colliery open for twelve years longer than Margaret Thatcher intended.

I have served under eight leaders of the Labour Party; climbed the greasy pole, and slipped back down it numerous times! I have been a member of the shadow Cabinet and have lobbied from the back-benches. I undoubtedly have an independent streak; I do what I think is right regardless of tribal loyalty, and that has made me a thorn in the whips' side.

I like to think that I have made a difference, whether that's on international human rights issues or campaigning domestically, such as introducing legislation for regulation of cosmetic surgery and to ban female genital mutilation. But I have learnt that change is difficult and an agonisingly slow process. There are still too many cosmetic cowboys out there who manage to persuade us that we're still too thin, too fat, too ugly. It, like so many issues I've campaigned on, is ongoing, not resolved.

I have been privileged to have met so many inspiring people, from Nelson Mandela and Jalal Talabani, to ordinary people bearing extraordinary burdens with great dignity.

There have been intensely emotional moments when confronted by man's capability for brutality. And long periods of frustration at the international community's inability to prevent genocide. It would be impossible to survive it all without the support of family and friends.

Many of the issues I have been involved in have been recurring. I have had a close association with the NHS, serving on the Welsh Hospital Board and then as the youngest member of the Royal Commission on the NHS. My increasing concern over the treatment of patients came painfully close to home when my husband died in harrowing circumstances. I produced a report on hospital complaints in England for David Cameron and continue to campaign for improved care.

I was elected in the first direct elections to the European Parliament in 1979 – as an anti-EC candidate. First-hand experience changed my mind. I am horrified that the Brexit view prevailed in the referendum, fed on what I believe was false and misleading information like the bus with its promise of £350 million a week extra for the NHS.

Human rights are a cause very close to my heart. I was appointed Special Envoy on Human Rights to Iraq by Tony Blair, following years of hard campaigning as Chair of CARDRI (Campaign Against Repression and for Democratic Rights in Iraq) and then INDICT (collecting evidence of Iraqi war crimes and crimes against humanity).

Time after time I have highlighted the hypocrisy of the British establishment in dealing with regimes with dubious human rights records. In Indonesia, Iraq, and now Saudi Arabia, the British government has been exposed for pursing arms export contracts in contravention of any ethical concerns.

In January 2017 *The Observer* newspaper wrote of the execution in 1990 of its reporter, Farzad Bazoft. Now declassified documents have revealed why the then Tory government was so reluctant to intervene to save him: Margaret Thatcher's government knew of Saddam's 'ruthless' regime, but trade and our arms sales came first. So lessons are learnt? Not if we look at our trade and our arms sales to Saudi Arabia, wreaking death and destruction in the Yemen.

So the campaigns go on – and so do I!

CHAPTER ONE

SELECTION

I have always been good at making a noise when needs be. When I was a child it would get me into trouble, now it was what was expected of me. I buzzed happily along the narrow lanes of North Wales in my little Mini with the radio on full volume. As I came to each village, I would turn the radio off and the loudspeaker strapped to the car roof on. 'This is Ann Clwyd, your parliamentary Labour candidate,' I would yell – at the sheep most of the time. I was thirty-three years old and as full of energy as I had ever been.

It was June 1970 and I had been chosen to represent the Labour Party to fight Denbigh in the general election. I was not expected to win. There was little or no party machine and I was on my own. Luckily I had family in the town, so I had a good meal, sympathy and a comfortable bed at the end of each day. My Auntie Mary was the best auntie in the world. She looked after me and made me a packed lunch every day. She stayed out of the public gaze though, unsure of how to explain her socialist niece to her Tory bridge club friends. Uncle Trevor, my father's brother, was a local GP and surgeon, a position of some stature in this prosperous market town. I guessed he was an old-school Liberal, but he gamely climbed on to a public platform and spoke in my support. He was shy and slightly nervous, never having done anything of the sort before, but the audience greeted him warmly.

There was no tradition of politics in the family. During my schooldays at Queen's School, Chester, I had stood as the Plaid Cymru candidate in the school's mock election. I had astounded everyone by running such a full-on campaign that I won, despite the school being in England and many of the pupils unsure of what Plaid Cymru even was. Then, during my university years at Bangor, I had been elected to various student posts but that was the sum of it. Now, after years of campaigning journalism, I wanted to be in the middle of the action rather than reporting on it. My husband Owen, a one-time member of the Labour Club at Oxford, had encouraged me. He was Head of News at HTV Wales and had to be impartial; I think I was his surrogate conscience!

I had not been a member of the party – again that journalistic reluctance to be seen as anything but impartial – but a year or so earlier I had found myself talking to Huw T. Edwards, boss of the Transport and General Workers Union in North Wales, at the annual Welsh cultural festival, the National Eisteddfod. He was a friend of Owen's and I had got to know him quite well. We were both from Flintshire and had lots in common. He asked me whether I was interested in going into politics and I told him that I honestly hadn't given it much thought. We talked about my interests and he told me the Labour Party was looking for a candidate to fight the Denbigh seat. I was from North Wales, actually born in Denbighshire. I was Welsh-speaking, I was a woman and I was young. 'You fit the bill,' he said.

Next thing I knew Emrys Jones, Secretary of the Welsh Labour Party, got in touch. I thought about it, decided it would be a great experience, and allowed my name to go forward. I was interviewed by the local party, who presumably liked what they saw, and that was it. I was the Labour candidate for a safe Tory seat with a 25,000 majority.

I think it was Emrys who introduced me to Gwilym Prys-Davies, chairman of the Welsh Hospital Board. He was looking for new blood at the time, someone young and inquiring; so, in 1970 I started a four-year stretch on the Board. And then, through that, I became the only Welsh representative on the prestigious Royal Commission on the NHS, appointed by Barbara Castle.

When Harold Wilson surprised everyone by calling an early election in May 1970, I wrapped up what I was doing and set off for Denbigh in my Mini. I loved every minute of the campaign. Denbighshire was a mixed constituency; there were the market towns of Denbigh, Llangollen and St Asaph; the coastal towns of Rhyl and Colwyn Bay; and then the villages and isolated farmhouses. There were plenty of indigenous Welsh speakers but also English people who had retired to this beautiful part of the country and others with holiday homes. The key drivers of the local economy were farming and tourism, and the main issue, Britain's economic decline. North Wales felt out on a limb, forgotten and neglected by Westminster. The media would have you believe that the fate of the England football team in the World Cup was also an issue in the election, but I can't say anyone tried to engage me on that one.

All in all it was not traditional Labour territory. So I made a noise. I felt that if I didn't no one would even know I was there. Leaving what party workers I had to stuff the envelopes and man the phones, I took off by myself in the Mini and loudspeaker and zigzagged across the constituency canvassing support. Wherever I saw a few people gathered, outside shops or in the livestock markets, I would stop and chat. I don't know how many doors I knocked on but it felt like thousands. I spoke to anybody and everybody and on the whole people were very polite. Some would even say to me, 'I usually vote Conservative, but I like your style, so I'll vote for you!'

I might not have had a big party machine behind me, but what it lacked in quantity it certainly made up for in quality. I was taken under the wing of Eirene White. She'd been an MP for neighbouring

East Flintshire for twenty years but was now in the House of Lords. Unlike me she had been born into a political family: her father, Tom Jones, had served as Deputy Cabinet Secretary for four Prime Ministers, from Lloyd George to Stanley Baldwin. She was a socialist and a feminist, very keen to see more female representation in Parliament. What I lacked in experience, Eirene had by the bucketsful. She was a formidable political campaigner and I was grateful that she was on my side. She pulled the voting record of the sitting Tory MP Geraint Morgan and used his poor attendance in the House of Commons against him. Eirene had a formidable grasp of detail, knew all the issues backwards and had an extensive network both in and out of the party. I watched and learnt.

My proudest inspiration though was the suffragette, Leonora Cohen. She was well into her nineties by then, but still bright as a button. She had a mop of beautiful white hair and dressed in a full-length black dress with a waspy belt. She had been a key member of the suffragette movement. She was Emmeline Pankhurst's bodyguard, marched alongside her, had been sent to prison and had been on a hunger strike that nearly killed her.

She told me her stories about the struggle for women's suffrage, how she had taken an iron bar to the case containing the crown jewels in the Tower of London in protest and left a message claiming responsibility. Leonora later retired to Colwyn Bay. Feminism was back on the agenda and Leonora wanted to play a part. She would climb on to a platform and unleash the most powerful speeches on social justice and feminism. I have no idea what the people of Denbigh made of her, but to me she was a star.

Election day dawned on 18 June 1970. I had no idea how I was going to do and it was a long day. There was nothing more I could do now so I had to content myself with going for a walk and preparing for the count. That evening my uncle accompanied me to the Town Hall in Denbigh where the count took place. My husband, Owen, was back in Cardiff working on HTV's election coverage. We were joined by my small band of supporters and waited nervously for the results. Then, for the first time, I was called on to the platform with all the other candidates, big red rosette pinned on my jacket. Of course, Geraint Morgan had retained the seat for the Conservatives, but I claimed second place from the Liberals with a swing of nearly 11 per cent, the only swing to Labour in Wales. I kept smiling, shook hands with all my opponents and left. Party celebrations were muted, as nationally Harold Wilson had lost unexpectedly to Ted Heath's Conservatives; the outcome generally blamed on the trade deficit as well as England's ignominious early departure from the World Cup.

I went back to Cardiff fired up. I knew what I wanted to do for the rest of my life: politics, it seemed, was in my blood. After Denbigh, Emrys Jones and others in the party kept telling me that now I had got my first election under my belt I would find it easy to get nominated. Little did they know. Looking back it's hard to explain what a great struggle it was for a woman to break through, especially in South Wales, Scotland and the heart of England.

I had fought Denbigh as the only female Labour candidate in the whole of Wales. Nine years later at the general election Welsh Labour again fielded a single candidate in an unwinnable seat. Most parliamentary seats with large majorities were in South Wales and most in mining valleys. Each valley had its superstitions, women and birds being the two most unpopular omens. Just seeing a woman on the way to work was enough to make some miners turn pale and go home for the day. So, in the 1970s, miners and their sons found it difficult to accept women working outside the home, let alone accepting them as their equals. As one big-hearted trade union man said to me: 'There's only one thing wrong with you – you're a woman.' I think he was trying to be kind.

The women were not much better. Back in my early working days as a market researcher I would knock on doors to ask people their opinions on the political issues of the day. Invariably the women would say: 'Come back tonight, love, when my husband's in.' Later on, while out canvassing another said to me: 'I'm all for women. But I'm not sure they can do the job as well as a man.' It wasn't just politics. I researched and argued the issue of inequality extensively: less than 2 per cent of bosses in Wales were women; out of sixty-eight full-time union officers only nine were women; not a single woman professor in Wales.

The constituency parties were little fiefdoms of their own. Emrys Jones spoke openly of his frustration at constituencies' tendency to draw up shortlists consisting of their preferred candidate drawn from their own ranks and a few no-hopers. It was difficult for any outsider, however talented, to break through and if you were a woman as well, forget it.

I was then asked by a Labour friend to apply for Gloucester for the October general election of 1974. Gloucester's selection process was unusual but very testing. As part of the selection process they invited all the contenders to a social event to see how we interacted with people. It worked for me and I became the Labour candidate. It was an interesting seat. It had been a Labour seat since 1945, with Jack Diamond holding it from 1957 until a shock defeat to Conservative Sally Oppenheim in 1970. She had then defended it successfully in February of 1974. But with a majority of under 5,000 votes it was not a lost cause.

Of course, with two women as the main candidates the local media had a field day. It was labelled 'Battle of the Blondes', 'the Petticoat Battle' and that sort of trivia. Scrutiny focused on how we looked and what we wore rather than policy and I found it sexist and extremely annoying; I expect Sally did too. But times have changed and women candidates are now treated seriously and as equals to their male counterparts, well, most of the time anyway. There is still a media fascination with how we dress; look at the ridiculous preoccupation with Theresa May's shoes. Male MPs don't get that on the whole, Michael Foot and his donkey jacket. At least the coverage has improved enormously since the 1970s. Back then I wore a smart new denim suit to canvass in Gloucester City Centre. When I returned to the local headquarters someone whispered: 'Just a tip, Ann. I wouldn't wear that again, you don't look like an MP.'

It is almost funny how often the subject of dress came up in politics back then. When I first applied for the Cynon Valley in 1972 – or Aberdare as it was then – I made the shortlist and on the way into the selection a relative gave me a rabbit's foot brooch for luck. I didn't get the nomination. Years later I asked why and was told it was 'because of the funny clothes you wore'. I can still remember exactly what I wore to that selection meeting: an emerald green jacket over cream flannel trousers. They were perceived as 'funny clothes'.

At Gloucester my opponent, Sally Oppenheim, was quite a challenge. She was an intelligent, educated woman and in winning her seat she had defeated a respected government minister. Since then she had consolidated her position. She was a multi-millionaire and seemed to run the whole place. She was President of the cricket club, the bowls club, the gardening club – everything you could think of. The editor of the local newspaper, the *Gloucester Citizen*, lived on her estate, for goodness' sake. So I had my work cut out to draw attention to myself and get into the press. I had a wonderful agent: John Morgan, a Welshman who worked for the Co-op. He had great drive, enthusiasm and humour and we had a lot of fun on the campaign trail. I was game for most things that would draw attention whether it was photo-calls up a ladder with a paintbrush or riding around the city on a bike. We shook the place up.

Come the evening of the count I think Sally was getting nervous. She was pacing up and down, looking angrily at the piles of votes on the tellers' tables. It looked as though it was going to be neck and neck. In the end she hung on by just over 3,000 votes, I had managed a 4 per cent swing to Labour. She was not happy, had a face like a thundercloud and when I offered my hand after the announcement she stormed off. When I eventually got to the House of Commons ten years later I would occasionally see her in the corridors and she remembered me. Then, recently, she was walking along the corridor with someone, I forget who, and she stopped for a chat. She then turned to the woman she was with and, pointing to me, said: 'She was my most formidable opponent.' That felt good!

Quite naturally, I was disappointed not to win at Gloucester, but I was happy with my performance and hoped for better things next time. To be honest, I never minded losing in a straight fight. What made my blood boil was when the fight was fixed.

A couple of years later I travelled to Birmingham to try for Roy Jenkins' old seat at Stechford. After a nightmare journey trying to find my way off Spaghetti Junction, I finally arrived at the Labour Club and was asked to join the other candidates. The interview was to take place in the bar and all the candidates, and there were a lot of us, had to wait in the smoke-filled atmosphere until we were called in one by one. We made awkward conversation to pass the time and one man got fed up and wandered off to play the fruit machine, winning the jackpot. Everyone watched as the coins pumped out. It was none other than Robert Maxwell.

When I applied for Caerphilly in 1977 I was backed by the NUM. They were very keen to get women into Parliament and I had established a good relationship with them while working on stories about miners' compensation. In the event I got the second largest number of nominations but did not make the shortlist. To say I was frustrated is an understatement. There were no women MPs in South Wales and it looked increasingly as if there were never going to be any. The NUM were furious too. They carried a lot of clout in the Welsh Labour Party and were not used to being ignored. They walked out of the process and the story blew up, making the front page of the *South Wales Echo*. But nothing changed and I was again left looking for a seat.

In 1979 I tried for the Ogmore constituency. It took a lot of work to get the nominations you needed to even be considered as candidate. You had to go round canvassing local Labour Party members and introducing yourself – a bit like a mini version of the American primaries. Anyway, I was up against Ray Powell, secretary of the Ogmore Constituency Labour Party Social Club and constituency secretary and agent for the outgoing MP. He was an extremely devious man who had his knife in me from that time on.

There was murk surrounding Ray from the beginning. As constituency secretary he was automatically secretary of the Social Club Committee, and with only seven of the nineteen-strong committee elected by the membership he controlled it with a rod of iron. A condition of club membership was that applicants belonged to the Labour Party, which gave the club ten precious delegates to the General Management Committee. Ray had the local party sewn up. But he was not a popular man and there were several unsuccessful attempts to dislodge him and make the club's activities more transparent. One such attempt was made by a well-known local spiritualist preacher and disabled ex-serviceman called Bill Martin. He stood for election to the committee, but when he topped the ballot the election was declared null and void. The election was re-run and Bill dramatically slumped to ninth on the list. He accused committee members of corruption and demanded a recount. Conveniently, the papers had been lost. Legal action followed and after a bit of digging around by solicitors the papers were found, stuffed behind a filing cabinet in the club secretary's office. The resulting brouhaha eventually calmed down enough for Ray to try for the newly vacant seat, but as I went round talking to party members many warned me to be wary of him.

It was an interesting selection list which featured, as well as Ray, two future MPs in Ron Davies and Gwynoro Jones. I had the second largest number of nominations so I was surprised, to say the least, when I did not appear on the shortlist. Apparently there had been some skulduggery.

Ray's supporters on the constituency executive, seeing me as his main rival, had voted to keep me off the shortlist. My supporters retaliated in kind and neither he nor I made the shortlist. Next thing we knew they decided to put all the aspiring candidates on the shortlist. That is why, on an evening when I should have been on Concorde flying to New York with the Royal Commission on the NHS, I was standing on the Labour Club stage at Ogmore with eleven other people. Confusion reigned and no one quite knew how, but after a mammoth nine-hour selection conference, Ray Powell was declared the candidate on the fourth ballot with sixty votes to my forty-three.

One of my backers was Russell Smart, an economics lecturer at the Polytechnic of Wales. He had formerly been secretary of the Litchard branch of the constituency only to be barred from the social club and removed as a constituency officer for proposing changes in the way the social club was run. He became one of Ray's most vociferous critics and after the election he sent me the voting list with the breakdown for each round. Ron's name should have been dropped after the first round. Had it happened his votes would have most likely transferred to me and I would have won. I was well and truly stitched up and there was nothing I could do about it!

Things have improved enormously for women candidates since then, but it is still more difficult for women to be selected. When I was elected to the European Parliament in 1979 less than 4 per cent of MPs were women. By 1992 it was still under 10 per cent. It was clear that something had to be done. All the main parties tried to address the situation, but the following year Labour took affirmative action in the form of all-women shortlists. You can imagine the controversy and it was not universally welcomed by women MPs. I had fought in its favour alongside other members of the shadow Cabinet such as Helen Jackson and Harriet Harman, although I did have my reservations. It appeared to be unfair to discriminate against men to counteract discrimination against women. However, European law stated that it was perfectly legal to discriminate in favour of those who had previously been discriminated against. I really was not sure what the suffragettes would have made of it but desperate times require drastic measures and on balance I felt such action to be justified. The main criticism was that women selected in this way would not be selected on merit, but then, looking around the house, I felt there were more than enough men who were not there on merit. The 'old boys' network' had dominated for long enough and while we waited for a new generation of politicians to radically change the way politics operated, positive discrimination in favour of women seemed the only answer.

The policy had an enormous impact at the 1997 general election and has continued to do so. In the space of five years the number of women MPs doubled from sixty to one hundred and twenty, a hundred of whom were my Labour colleagues. Unfortunately, they were quickly dubbed 'Blair's babes', fuelled by an ill-conceived photo-call of us all dressed in red, gazing adoringly at our leader. Well, not all. I was uncomfortable with the whole thing and turned my head away so that I am not recognisable in the photograph! The number of women candidates and the resulting focus on issues that mattered to women such as women's health, domestic violence and childcare were a big factor in winning that election. Further vindication of the policy's success was the election of Jacqui Smith from an all-woman shortlist; she went on to become the UK's first female Home Secretary. Back in the early 1970s we could only dream of such representation.

The only good thing to come out of those nomination fiascos was that when the European election came along I received a call from the Llanelli Constituency Labour Party. They wanted to nominate me for the Mid and West Wales seat because they were embarrassed by the goings-on at Caerphilly and Ogmore. I decided to forget Westminster and try for the new European Parliament instead.

CHAPTER TWO

TEARAWAY

If I were a child today I would probably have had an ASBO served on me! I was a fighter, a truant, a tomboy and rebel; the bane of my mother's life.

Born Ann Clwyd Lewis in 1937, my early years were idyllic. We lived in the North Wales countryside in the village of Pentre Halkyn at the bottom of Halkyn Mountain. This was no chocolate-box Snowdonia but the fringes of industrial Flintshire. The untamed rugged beauty of the mountain, scarred by lead mining since the Romans, was a paradise for a young child, and from the top of the mountain we would look out across the Dee and Mersey estuaries towards Liverpool. From our garden we could climb into the fields and be off with friends on bike or on foot. We would dam streams, build dens, leave messages in an old oak tree and generally live in our own adult-free world among woods carpeted with blue scabious and primroses. We grazed on nuts and blackberries and even today the sound of woodpigeons brings it all back to me.

During term time I would have to walk the mile or so to the village school whatever the weather. It was a small school with basic facilities. In winter we had an open fire so you were either roasting next to it or shivering in the back. There was no running water or flush toilets. Every day each child would be handed a small bottle of milk to drink, warmed in front of the open fire behind a big black fireguard. I absolutely hated it and would do anything to get out of drinking it. That did not stop me robustly opposing Margaret Thatcher when, as Education Secretary, she abolished free milk for Britain's schoolchildren. 'Margaret Thatcher, Milk Snatcher' was a phrase that would haunt her for the rest of her life.

I suppose I was a bright child and on the whole I enjoyed school, despite being a magnet for trouble. I was a fighter. Another girl and I were known as the toughest fighters in the school, we would take on all-comers in the playground. It didn't matter to us whether they were boys or girls or how big they were. I met up with her a few years ago, she lives in Australia now, and we reminisced about our fighting days. We couldn't remember why we were so aggressive; in my case perhaps it was because I was thin and wiry, or maybe it was just a means to assert ourselves. There was one boy in particular, Robin James. He was a neighbour and probably my closest friend but we would fight. Full-on physical dust-ups. His mother used to come to our house and complain to my mother about the damage I had done to her little boy. He was mortified.

Despite this he was always coming round to call for me to go out and play which infuriated my mother, because he always seemed to arrive when I was practising the piano. I loathed and detested the piano, did not have a single iota of talent, but my mother was determined that I should learn. It became one of many battles between us, but on this she had to admit defeat and I soon ditched the lessons. So I was free to go out and play with Robin and it never took us long to get in trouble. One of our favourite tricks was to find some string and hold it across the road in the pitch dark of the blackout, so that anyone cycling along would get knocked off.

Remarkably, I was never caned at school although I probably deserved to be, but I regularly had to stand in the corner with my back to the class. Caning was the punishment of last resort; the mainstream punishment was being kept behind to 'write lines'. Endless, meaningless, copying out of some text or other. I don't think the punishment had much effect on me although I do have quite nice handwriting now, perhaps a legacy of those hours. At the end of the day when I didn't arrive home, my father would walk down to a neighbour, Tommy Lowe, who was a French teacher at our school, and ask where I was. The answer was always the same, writing lines.

One of the problems was that in those war years there was a shortage of teachers and schools had to take whatever they could get. Many were 'uncertificated' and had no idea how to control a class, and of course, children can sniff out any weakness in an instant. We weren't bad kids, just a handful who loved playing practical jokes. For example, we would get in trouble for firing water pistols in class. You can guess who the ringleader was. Talking out of turn was another crime I was regularly guilty of as well as looking around when I was supposed to be napping with my head on the desk.

Not all the punishment was deserved though and like all children I would rage at any perceived injustice and conveniently forget those times I had got away with things. The teachers' main weapon was that of humiliation. To my eternal regret I cannot sing; tone deaf. Anyway, this teacher would come in to school and take us for singing lessons. One day she stopped the class and asked who was singing out of tune. The boy next to me ratted: 'Ann Lewis,' he said. The teacher came over and hit me with her pointer. Another day it was sewing class. I wasn't any good at that either – the 'ladylike' talents seemed to pass me by. One day, aged about six years, we were making tray cloths and our teacher walked up to inspect my work. Then in a loud voice she said: 'Ann Lewis, your stitches are like dogs' teeth,' causing the whole class to collapse in laughter.

I must have been a trial to my mother. She had been privately educated at boarding school and then trained as a domestic science teacher at Berridge House, Hampstead, in London. My father was a metallurgist, the Chief Chemist at the Halkyn mines, and had travelled widely. He had graduated from Aberystwyth University and then studied for his MSc at the University of Idaho, USA, before working in British Columbia for fifteen years. He would tell me tales of how he had lived in a log cabin in the Rockies, travelling on horseback to prospect for gold. We had a black bearskin rug with its head on in our front room at home and the story was that Daddy had shot the bear. Later on I found it appalling, but as a youngster I was captivated by his exciting stories. He returned to Wales to marry my mother, but as a result of his travels he had lots of friends overseas and he received letters from all over the world. I was fascinated by the stamps and built up an impressive collection. To this day one of the greatest tragedies in my life is that I took the book to school and someone pinched it. I had been so proud of that collection.

Another childhood tragedy was the death of my first cat. My mother had help in the house, Miss Jane Jones, who lived in a little cottage up on the mountain top and rode around on a pony. She made a big impression on me and passed on her love of animals. It was she who gave me my first cat, Tim. I adored that tiny black and white cat but, when I was about eight, I was standing waiting for the school bus – such advances having then reached Pentre Halkyn – with the cat in my arms. It jumped out right in front of a coal lorry. It was horrible for a little girl, seeing my cat being knocked down and then running over and seeing all this yellow stuff oozing out. Tim was dead and I was devastated but received no sympathy from the other children, who scoffed that I was wearing black tights in mourning.

I have subsequently loved cats all my life. Alfie was a stray ginger tom. He was with Owen and me for years and then a couple of years ago he brought home Barney, a beautiful Bengal cat. I tried to find out who owned her without any success and, as she and Alfie seemed to get on OK, so I allowed her to settle in. Before long my niece Bethan realised that Barney was a 'she' and expecting kittens. The whole family live with me now and I love nothing more than watching the dynamics of their group, it's a great stress reliever.

My childhood was relatively unaffected by the war because I was only two years old when it broke out and eight when it finished and I remember very little about it. Of course there was rationing, but between living in the countryside next to a farm and a good friend of the family running the village shop, and my mother's brilliance as a cook, able to conjure up tasty meals from very little with the aid of Mrs Beeton's cookbook, we did quite well. I was affected by my father's absence though. He was asked to go and teach science at Rhyl Grammar School for a period. He did not like teaching and, although he was a patient man, we had strong words over my home-work. I was totally useless at mathematics, just could not get it, and we would both become frustrated at my inability to take it in. After the teaching stint he went to the munitions factory at Rhydymwyn and was also head of the local Observer Corps. He and his colleagues would go out on to the top of the mountain to spot planes. We had a special pack of plane-spotting cards at home to help identify our own from the enemy's. Once a bomb fell on Halkyn Mountain, probably ditched on the way back from a raid on Liverpool, and we had the brass nose on the mantelpiece at home. Otherwise we were largely sheltered from the realities of war, although there was a time when I was in the bath when I heard my mother shout: 'Liverpool's burning! Liverpool's burning!' From the front windows you could see the River Mersey looking as though it was ablaze. I would have been about five years old.

Both my parents were from Aberdyfi, on the west coast of Wales near Machynlleth. It was, and is, a lovely seaside village and I spent a lot of time there. Both my grandfathers had died before I was born but I remember my grandmothers well and spent a lot of time with them particularly around the time my younger sister was born. One was very much the entrepreneur, taking over her husband's chandlery business. The store sold everything imaginable and was a treasure trove for a young child. I loved playing with the loose nails, letting them run through my fingers and, of course, I was always indulged by the shop's staff. My grandmother's housekeeper had a son the same age as me and I was allowed to play with his trains. Always the tomboy I preferred his books too, and developed an affection for W. E. John's *Biggles* rather than the girls' equivalent, *Worrals*.

They were idyllic days and left me with a lifelong love for the village. I kept my mother's house there and there is nowhere I prefer to escape to. Sometimes, after harrowing trips out to Iraq and other war-torn countries, Owen and I would take off for Aberdyfi knowing that its unchanging charm and the friendships of families who had known mine for generations would put everything into perspective. It was the sort of village that became a magnet for all sorts of interesting people. There was a well-known romantic author, Berta Ruck, who lived a few doors from my grandmother. Her husband, Oliver Onions, also an author, lived next door. I would watch in fascinated horror as she emerged in long green robes with her hair in plaits to swim in the sea. In winter! She must have been mad; you would rarely catch me in the water in summer.

My other grandmother was the widow of the Presbyterian minister who I remember as a softly spoken old lady. She had suffered a disabling stroke so I only remember the times when I sat on her bed.

I do recall being told off for knitting a purple silk purse on a Sunday. She told me to put it away in case the minister saw me. One of my favourite things in Aberdyfi, one which endeared me to my grandmother and belies the wild child I was at home, was regularly singing hymns with a group of local evangelists on the sands.

The Welsh language and Chapel were major influences in my early life. The fact we were a Welsh-speaking family set us apart in our village, situated in largely anglicised Flintshire. My parents wanted my sister and me to be raised as Welsh speakers and consequently they spoke Welsh to us. They felt that we would learn English quickly enough when we started school and although at first I would play in Welsh alongside the other children playing in English it never seemed to matter. The only time I was conscious of the difference was on a Sunday when we walked in one direction to a Welsh chapel in Pentre Halkyn, while the other kids would be walking in the opposite direction to the church in Halkyn. My father felt particularly strongly about the survival of the Welsh language. Politically, I think he was a traditional Welsh Liberal but we never once discussed politics. By the time I was sufficiently interested he had died. Like most Welsh chapel-going children we were taught to recite – '*adrodd*' – be it biblical passages or poetry, so that I grew up quite confident of speaking in public. It would stand me in good stead in later life.

In the years immediately after the war things were difficult for many people in Britain and we were no exception. My father, who had been moved around during the war, was now out of work and it hit us hard. Even though I was only ten years old I was conscious that we had to be careful about money. My father was desperately looking for work and I would go through the newspaper job adverts in the *News Chronicle*, our daily paper. My young mind would obviously have little understanding of what was and what was not appropriate, I just wanted to help. It must have been heartbreaking for my father. I sat my eleven-plus exams about this time and had been promised a new bike if I passed. But, when I did pass, I only got a second-hand one. I remember the bitter disappointment, exacerbated by Mary Pritchard, whose fireman father bought her a brand-new bike. It was difficult for all of us and I often remember that time when I am trying to help families in my constituency where the main breadwinner has lost their job. It is a horribly destructive thing to happen and affects the whole family.

I do remember though that although things were tough my father was not prepared to compromise his principles. He was offered a

well-paid skilled job at Capenhurst in Cheshire, an early uranium en-
richment plant, but would not take it because, by then, he was very
much against atomic weapons and felt that, morally, he could not work
there. Ironically, years later it became known that Rhydymwyn, where
he had worked during the war, had played a part in the development
of the atom bomb. Had my father been aware of that work? It was
a vast complex and the work would have been secretive so it is quite
possible he had no knowledge of it. What he could not have failed to
be aware of was the plant's production of mustard gas but his work
during the Second World War, just like his service in the First World
War, was never a topic of conversation.

Eventually my father found work as a metallurgist again but it was
in Cheshire and he travelled there during the week, coming home
at weekends. This lasted a while and then he decided to move the
whole family. I was fourteen years old and really did not want to go. By
then I was settled into Holywell Grammar School having passed the
iniquitous eleven-plus. It was an educational system that was brutal,
unfair and divisive and affected a child's whole future based on an
exam taken at ten years of age. I passed the exam and undoubtedly
enjoyed a quality of education and life chances that I would have been
otherwise denied. Although I was a beneficiary of a grammar school,
I am a passionate opponent of the system that condemns the majority
of children to a second-rate education. I view Theresa May's plans to
reintroduce them with nothing short of horror. The insidious nature
of that system was brought home when my younger sister, Gwyneth,
failed her eleven-plus. We were to have a dramatically different education. She managed to buck the trend in passing O levels and went
on to become a highly qualified nursing sister, but many of our friends
were not so fortunate.

Meanwhile I had done well in the exam, but it haunted me afterwards as my school reports would frequently note 'did not live up to her
earlier expectation' rather too often. I was happy at school though and

had lots of friends – not all of whom my mother approved of – and all was well until I became very ill. I was diagnosed with pneumonitis, an unspecified lung disease, and was confined to bed for months. Friends were not allowed to visit in case they made me laugh. I missed a lot of formal schooling but on the other hand became a passionate reader. I read everything I could get my hands on, highbrow and rubbish, but I felt very isolated. When I did return to school the other children were told to be careful with me because I was 'delicate'. Can you imagine the indignity of it for a former champion fighter! I took little notice and can't remember missing out on anything the other children did.

I think my mother saw the move to Chester as an opportunity to get some more discipline into my life. In the country I had had a great deal of freedom but now I was to be sent to an independent all-girls' school, the Queen's School, Chester, and it was a total culture shock. It was quite a posh school and took a bit of getting used to. We had to wear a felt school hat in winter, a panama hat in summer, stand up when teachers entered the room, and were absolutely forbidden to eat ice cream in the street. To this day I get a thrill of joyful rebellion licking my ice cream in public!

My wild streak refused to be tamed and I started playing truant fairly regularly. On one occasion I went AWOL for a whole week. I am sure others who truant from school end up doing some exciting, rebellious things; I went to sit in the courthouse for the Chester Assizes. The minister at our Welsh-speaking chapel in Chester had suggested law as a possible career and Emlyn Hooson, the youngest barrister on the Chester and North Wales circuit, was a glamorous local celebrity. I had read of an upcoming trial in which he was appearing. It involved cock fighting and I was intrigued as to how the 'sport' had become established in posh Cheshire. Every day I would set off for school on my bike and then, after crossing the bridge over the Dee, would stuff my school hat into the basket and head for the law courts. I did that for a whole week before being caught. My headmistress telephoned my mother to ask whether I was getting better. My parents were both furious with me, particularly my mother.

During my formative years my father was away a lot and my mother left with two young children, one of them particularly headstrong. She was very much the disciplinarian and always looking for something to whack me with. In my mid-teens I was a member of a Welsh youth club in Chester, 'Yr Aelwyd'. I loved going there, especially when we were rehearsing for plays, but I was never very good at keeping an eye on the time, so it was quite usual for me to be cycling back through the city after dark with no lights on my bike. My mother's answer was to lock me out of the house to teach me a lesson. I became an expert at climbing in through the pantry window. On a few occasions I even slept in the garage.

We did have a difficult relationship, not least because she had firm views on what was and was not acceptable, but also because she had high expectations of both her daughters. With hindsight, I have a great deal of sympathy for her; I was the original difficult child. My sister Gwyneth on the other hand was much more obedient. Perhaps it was that, and the five-year age gap between us, that ensured my sister and I were poles apart and never became close. As we grew up we established a better relationship. I adore my niece and nephew, we are great buddies, but Gwyneth has never approved of my politics and there are many subjects we avoid even now. My father was more laid-back. I remember when he sold our house in Pentre Halkyn my mother was furious because she felt he could have got a better price. He was adamant that it was a fair price. He was always principled.

I wasn't all that bad. I may have been strong-willed and argument-ative but I was polite and, on the whole, did reasonably well at school. I threw myself into the drama club and played tennis quite well; there was even talk of Junior Wimbledon, although I do not think I was ever that good. Academically I could certainly have worked harder and I loved to challenge authority. I remember the headmistress at the Queen's School, Miss McLean, looking at me quite askance when I said I wanted to take an O level in Welsh. I suspect I only asked because I knew that it made things difficult for the school, which was in England after all. In the end they supplied the invigilator who was the Rev. Herbert Evans, Minister of St John Street Welsh Chapel. I knew him well and he had a great influence on my life.

I came to enjoy studying Welsh and wanted to take it to the next level but knew that there was no way the Queen's School could accommodate me at A level. My father was supportive and contacted the Director of Education for neighbouring Flintshire, across the border in Wales. It was agreed that I should work part-time at Hope Primary School while also studying at Hawarden Grammar School. I quite enjoyed being a student teacher except for the fact I had to teach Welsh history, something I had never studied myself. Meanwhile I combined Welsh with English, which I also loved, and Bible Studies, which fascinated me and also provided a gateway to a summer school in Aberystwyth.

It really is difficult to explain the role that the chapel played in my life. I was a wild child in many ways, although strong-willed would probably be a more accurate description. But I always enjoyed going to chapel, it was part of my identity and a big part of our lives both intellectually and socially. There was a strong Welsh community in Chester, several chapels, and that was where we socialised as a family. Looking back, I can see that perhaps we should have socialised more widely and I understand this current emphasis on 'Britishness', but that was the way it was. As well as attending chapel I went to Sunday school, something that adults did as well as children. Funnily enough I was quite argumentative at Sunday school! Our teacher's wife often complained to my father, but there were always points that I disagreed with and if you can't argue in Sunday school where can you?

We were brought up with a real sense of duty. There would be lots of charity work, there was a sick-visiting rota, and of course the missionaries. They fascinated me and, although it is hard to believe now, as a teenager I quite fancied being a missionary, although I think it was the lure of travel as much as anything. We had several attached to our chapel. They were based in India, and they came back every now and again and talked about their work and the places they had visited. It all seemed so exotic and adventurous as well as being worthwhile, a potent cocktail for an impressionable teenager.

The choice of a future career now loomed. I had some Saturday jobs while I was in school. The first was at a large Chester department store, Quaintways. I remember my mother dropping me outside saying: 'Go inside and get a job – and don't come out without one,' and I duly reappeared having been appointed to serve on the biscuit counter. That's where I learnt to count, selling Chocolate Vienna biscuits by the pound! Years later I was talking to John Prescott, reminiscing about our times in Chester, and he revealed that both he and his wife Pauline had worked at Quaintways although our paths never crossed.

I also worked in a local orphanage on Saturdays for a while and became very engaged in the social ramifications, deciding I would become a social worker or hospital almoner. For some reason my school must have disapproved because they sent me to a hospital in Chester to work with encephalitis sufferers. These poor people had swelling of the brain and many had severe disfigurement and although I desperately wanted to help, I didn't know how to and found it deeply distressing. It does seem wrong that young people with no training or preparation should be sent into such a situation; wrong for them and for the patients. Anyway, that was the end of that career path.

My father tried to encourage me to be a journalist. His father had been one in his youth before entering the ministry and he felt I would be well suited. He even had a good friend from our chapel who was managing director of the *Chester Chronicle* and was prepared to offer me a traineeship. But children never listen to what their parents want them to do and I certainly wasn't that kind of teenager. So I said no, rather foolishly with hindsight.

By my late teens one of my great interests was theology, probably spurred on by a county competition with a place at a summer school in Aberystwyth as the prize. Ah, freedom. I was also lucky enough to go to an international summer school at Borth, on the Cardiganshire coast, through the Urdd, the Welsh youth movement. I would have been about seventeen when I went to Pantyfedwen and it was to prove to be one of the biggest influences in my life. Pantyfedwen brought young people together from all over the world and had stimulating lecturers like Ritchie Calder – journalist, socialist, academic and peace activist. He also worked for the United Nations and would bring in guest speakers to talk to us. It was the first time in my life that I became acutely conscious of things like famine and poverty. Listening to first-hand accounts from my contemporaries on post-war rebuilding in Germany and massive poverty in Africa was really inspirational. I felt as though the whole world was opening up in front of my eyes. It would be fair to say it fired my imagination and an interest in human rights that has never gone away.

Pantyfedwen was about much more than the lectures though, it was enormous fun. Imagine thirty or so people in their late teens, often away from home for the first time, living in a seafront hotel and you get the picture. We would have lectures in the morning and then our afternoons would be free. I know that everyone recalls their childhood summers as hot and sunny, but I swear the weather when I was at Pantyfedwen was just like that!

We spent lazy afternoons on the beach, talking, messing around and just enjoying ourselves. We had three idyllic weeks to explore the area. We would catch the train into Aberystwyth or up the coast to Aberdyfi. Many a holiday romance innocently blossomed there, in my case with a lovely Austrian boy called Werner. After supper we would climb up the hill behind Borth; someone would inevitably have a guitar and we taught each other songs from our countries as well as the occasional communal hymn singing.

I was lucky in a way that today's generation often are not. I was taught what was then called civics and modern politics at school which gave me an understanding of the political system. Then there was the amazing experience of Pantyfedwen. The building was eventually sold and the summer schools ended, which is such a shame. It was a precious time of such freedom. Freedom to think and explore concepts with people from other cultures without any academic pressure. I was privileged. Pantyfedwen had a profound effect on me and afterwards I went home, passed my A levels and moved on to Bangor University to study English, Welsh and Biblical Studies.

CHAPTER THREE

THE TIME OF OUR LIVES

The university library was full of students, heads bent over books. Outside it was lashing down with rain and you could see nothing through the old leaded windows let alone the pier and harbour beyond. It was bleak and miserable, a situation made much worse by the New Testament Greek text in front of me. I had been struggling with it for over two hours and it still made little sense to me. I could not help thinking I was in the wrong place or perhaps in the right place, but studying the wrong subject.

I loved Bangor, one of the smallest cities in Britain, on the North Wales coast. To the south were the dramatic Snowdonia mountains, Yr Wyddfa; to the north the island of Anglesey, Ynys Môn, across the Menai Straits. It was idyllic in the summer months, bleak but beautiful in winter. The university dominated the town and there was a sense of vibrancy in its narrow streets as students made their way in and out of the cafes and bookshops by day, the pubs by night.

Unfortunately, one of the subjects I had chosen was Biblical Studies. However, I had not banked on having to learn New Testament Greek and soon struggled. My tutors were frustrated with me as my work seesawed from the excellent, when I was engaged in the topic, to anything but. It would be fair to say that I loved everything about being a student, except for the lectures and work!

On my first day I arrived on the train from Chester and walked down the long, steep stairs from the station to meet the Freshers Welcome Committee. There were students everywhere, many fidgeting nervously, but there was an overriding sense of excitement in the air. Freshers were greeted by a giant red-haired chap called Wendell Edwards who pointed you in the direction of your accommodation. Then there was this extraordinarily sexist tradition where the girls had to walk through a corridor of male students so that they could pick out girls they liked the look of. Like the other girls, I received a few billets-doux as a result of this cattle market, inviting me to some hop or other.

I had hoped to get into one of the college houses, but they were oversubscribed and instead I was billeted with a lady called Mrs Savage Jones in Upper Bangor Road. Despite her name she was pleasant enough, but my room was furnished with children's furniture, including a child's bed. I do not think I had a comfortable night's sleep the whole time I was there.

Sleep was not high on my agenda though. I was living away from home for the first time and threw myself into everything the university had to offer. And there were plenty of distractions at hand. I joined the English dramatic society and the Welsh one. I joined the English debating society and then the Welsh one as well. Bangor at that time consisted of three distinct groups of students: the Welsh speakers, the English-speaking Welsh; and the rest. There was a great deal of competition, even suspicion, between the groups and very little overlap. One of my closest friends was Beti Jones from Llanberis, a lively, fun girl who was at the heart of the Welsh societies. Another great friend was Sophia Mortimer, the Bishop of Exeter's daughter, who was also part of the English drama and debating societies. Years later I became friendly with her brother because of our shared interest in the Kurds. Later, he became a senior advisor to Kofi Annan at the UN.

As a result of all this socialising, I got to know a lot of people very quickly and then started to get elected to things. I became involved in student politics and was elected Secretary of the Students Union where I increased my popularity by negotiating discounts for students at shops, cafes and services in the town! I was also instrumental in organising a sit-in to protest against the 1956 Russian invasion of Hungary. Politics fascinated me and had I stayed the course at Bangor I might well have become Vice-President of the Union. My interest wasn't limited to student politics either, and at this point I started exploring my Welsh nationalist loyalties. A friend of mine, Emrys Roberts, was heavily involved with Plaid at university and persuaded me to hitchhike down to Carmarthen with him to campaign in the 1957 by-election. It was a 130-mile trek along narrow roads and took forever, but for me it just seemed a great adventure. The by-election was memorable for being the first time in the UK that a parliamentary seat had been contested by two women, Plaid Cymru's Jennie Eirian Davies and Labour's Megan Lloyd George. Sadly, I was on the wrong side of history as Megan Lloyd George took the seat from the Liberals.

I became engrossed with the debating societies and was always up for arguing a case. I distinctly remember proposing a motion that 'All women should wear sacks'. Sack dresses were all the rage, but for some reason it was quite controversial! But I was a novice and there were some superb exponents of their craft including my close friends Michael Williams and Gwyn Watkins, who went on to the final of The Observer Mace debates. I learnt a lot from them.

Michael was involved with the drama group, and produced me in *The Birds* by Aristophanes. He also wrote a glowing review for the college newspaper, *Forecast*, of another production I had a role in, *Lady Windermere's Fan*. Meanwhile, thanks to the time I had spent with the Welsh drama society, I won a few parts with BBC radio.

Michael and Gwyn were among a group of older students who had done their National Service before coming to university and therefore had so much more in the way of life experience than the rest of us. I was always drawn to this group; they were so much more interesting. As students do, we explored all sorts of issues, often well into the night. There was a favourite pub we used to go to in Upper Bangor, and we would settle in for the night, nursing the same drink for hours, as we discussed politics, drama and life. It all felt so adult, challenging and life-changing.

Less grown-up was a stunt my friend Daphne and I played when the Duke of Edinburgh visited the university. As students we were not particularly impressed by the visit, not a republican sentiment just a feeling that the whole thing would be a bit of a bore. For some bizarre reason, possibly something to do with feminism but I have totally forgotten, Daphne and I decided to perform a Walter Raleigh act, spreading a cloak for him to walk on. The time came, the Bangor weather obliged by leaving giant puddles all over the terraces, and down went my cape. The Duke looked totally bemused if not a whiff suspicious. 'I wouldn't dare,' he said, stepping around the obstacle. The newspapers loved it though, and pictures appeared everywhere generating weird letters, including one from Australia proposing marriage. I think it must indicate some early nose for making news.

Another distraction from my studies was my first great romance, Dr Ian Wilson, who I met through the drama group where he was doing lighting or props. I had noticed him immediately because he was older, sophisticated, cultured – and extraordinarily good-looking. It was not long before we got together. He was a fascinating man and through him I met other stimulating people, who also expanded my horizons. This included culinary ones: a friend from the north-west frontier province of Pakistan cooked the most wonderful spinach curries in just one saucepan, giving me a lifelong love of spicy food.

Ian was different from the other people I knew. For a start he was a scientist doing a PhD in the area of cancer research. It was serious, fascinating work and I admired his dedication, going with him at weekends to check on his mice in the labs. Despite being a scientist he was also very creative and carved wood skilfully.

We were very different people nevertheless. Our backgrounds, his urban English, mine rural Welsh, could not have been more different. Yet we fell in love and, to the consternation of our families, became engaged.

But despite the passion of idealistic youth, the differences between us made the relationship tempestuous. He simply could not understand why I was so wedded to the Welsh language and tradition. I suppose he saw it as parochial. He never came to grips with my 'Welshness' and I would become really annoyed at his insensitivity.

One fateful day we were having yet another blazing row, this time on a train, and I threw my engagement ring out of the window. That was the end of our relationship.

Inevitably, academic matters came to a head. Bangor employed a system which required you to pass end of year exams to return and, at the end of my first year, I only just squeaked through and was placed on probation. I suppose the mature thing to do would have been to make up for lost time and settle down to serious academic work when I returned. If I ever had such good intentions they soon disappeared. Life continued to be stimulating, my social life was buzzing, and dreary Welsh grammar and Greek texts failed to gain my attention. At the end of the year I duly failed my exams and over the summer I received a letter saying that my place at the university was being withdrawn. I would not be returning to complete my degree.

I had been expecting something to happen but had hoped a solution could be found, maybe a transfer to another course. Because I was so prominent on campus my forced departure created a bit of a stir among the student community and Michael Williams wrote a supportive article in the student newspaper, *Forecast*. I tried appealing against the decision, pointing out that I had worked hard to get to Bangor and had made a significant contribution to university life; I felt I deserved a second chance. But the authorities were implacable and that was that. My friends told me I would be OK, that I would find a way to be successful in life, but at the time I just felt angry, distressed and unanchored.

I was back in Chester with my tail between my legs. Naturally, my parents were bitterly disappointed. My father worried about my future, my mother worried about what she would tell people in chapel. They blamed all my friends for distracting me, whereas in reality it wasn't them, it was me. Now I had to be practical and find a job, something to tide me over and get me out of the house while I came up with a better plan.

I was taken on by a market research group and was sent out on the streets of Chester to ask people their views on anything from current affairs and the privatisation of the steel industry to toothpaste brands. It was hardly demanding work, but it did at least make use of my interest in talking to people. The only problem was that I would get so engaged in conversation with them rather than just asking the questions on my clipboard and I would soon be lagging behind my daily quota. At times I felt like a social worker. On the whole I quite enjoyed it except for when the weather got bad. Cold, wet and miserable, my colleagues and I would often make for the nearest cafe, order ourselves a hot drink and fill in the forms ourselves. I have always taken market research results with a pinch of salt ever since!

This was obviously no long-term career path, but the problem was that I did not know what long-term career path to pursue. In a reversal of roles, now it was my father who would comb the newspaper job advertisements on my behalf. One day he saw one for a BBC trainee studio manager in the Welsh newspaper, *Y Faner*, and encouraged me to apply. The post was in Cardiff, which sounded exciting. I had no idea what a studio manager did but it seemed as though it could be interesting and the BBC was a good organisation to join. There was a lot of competition for the job, but the then Head of Programmes, Aneirin Talfan Davies, obviously saw something in me, because he offered me the job.

The job of studio manager was a classic entry point into the BBC; Joan Bakewell started her broadcasting life in the same role. But first I had to go on a course to London to be trained. A main job was to make sound effects and I soon mastered simulating slamming car doors, rustling leaves and tinkling teacups. More difficult was differentiating between musical instruments, a step too far for the tone deaf. I loved it all and the glamour, excitement and buzz suited me down to the ground; this was show business! I was rubbing shoulders with household names such as Jack de Manio on the *Today* programme, the cast of the radio soap *Mrs Dale's Diary*, and Wilfred and Mabel Pickles on the quiz programme *Have a Go*. Not that they would have noticed me, studio managers were way down in the pecking order. As an avid listener of *Children's Hour*, the Toytown Train and Larry the Lamb were all favourites. I became a whiz at rubbing sandpaper with one hand and a roller skate on tin with the other. That was one of the sound effects I became skilled at!

The hours were long, as we worked shifts around the clock, and they put us up in a hostel in central London with other BBC employees, which was great fun. At the same time the Reithian public service ethos was embedded into our souls and we were always very aware of the BBC's reputation and status. So much so that when I found myself in the same lift as the then Director General, the austere Sir Ian Jacob, I found myself speechless.

After a few months I was judged to be safe to be let loose on the airwaves and chose to return to Cardiff, where I put my expertise with sound effects into practice. The job involved cueing the sound effects from gramophone records, the old 78 discs. You had to have a steady hand. Having previously marked up the groove you had to do jump cuts live on air, turning down the pot and lifting the stylus and dropping it down in the right place. If you made a mistake everyone knew. It was an important life lesson – how to keep your hands steady, regardless of how you felt inside. This ability to hide my emotions under a calm exterior has served me well ever since.

When I first arrived in Cardiff I was offered a place to live by the parents of a university friend in the suburb of Rhiwbina. It was very kind of them, but they were Christian Scientists; they expected me to keep to a strict curfew and did not allow radio or newspapers in the house. I did not stay long.

I had made friends quickly and moved into a shared house in Penylan with some girls who worked at the BBC and others who wanted to. We had freedom and were earning our own salaries and had a great time. Inevitably, most of our socialising was around the BBC and the Overseas Club which was next door to the old BBC building in Park Place. Everybody wandered in there at the end of the day to compare notes and gossip and there were lots of showbiz characters around. I remember Ednyfed Hudson Davies, later MP for Caerphilly but then a lecturer with a reputation as something of a womaniser. He would sit in the corner with his dog, Gelert, and when he saw a woman he fancied he sent the dog over.

It was in the Overseas Club that Julian Williams, a fellow studio manager, and I planned our practical jokes, a common cause that led to a lifelong friendship. Our poor boss, Mr Wyn Rowlands, was the usual target; he was a lovely man but also a perfect stooge. Typical of our pranks was Julian telephoning him to say that I was ill and Julian would be the only one working on that day's programme. Then we would play the sound effects of a car crashing into a telephone box. To be fair to him his concern was all for us, rather than being left high and dry on his programme. 'Are you alright, Mr Julian, are you alright?' he would call anxiously, before we eventually came clean.

It was while sitting in the TV production gallery, cueing a record, that I first set eyes on my future husband, Owen Roberts. He walked past and smiled at me, I think I mumbled hello or something, but I couldn't fail to notice this tall, good-looking young man.

Apart from our BBC circle of friends, my flatmates and I had a wider network of people we knew from home or had been at university with, so most weekends one of us would know someone who was having a party. It was at one of these parties that I was eventually introduced to Owen by my friend Manon, an old friend from Bangor who was now Owen's personal assistant.

Owen had recently joined the Welsh independent television channel TWW as a graduate trainee. Originally from a well-known Anglesey farming family, he was a graduate of Jesus College, Oxford. He was sophisticated, cultured and irreverent, with a huge passion for life. We hit it off immediately.

We shared a love of Wales and the Welsh language and both had strong views about inequalities in society. Owen had been a member of the Labour Party at Oxford and was also an active member of the Welsh Dafydd ap Gwilym Society. He influenced my political thinking a great deal and through his contacts we were regularly socialising with other young Welsh people who wanted to change society.

It was the early 1960s and things were changing, although the legendary permissive '60s would not arrive for another five years or more. There was a new mood in politics exemplified by President John F. Kennedy and for broadcasting in general, and broadcasting in Wales in particular; these were exciting times. Television was still in its infancy and commercial television even more so. The BBC, used to having things all its own way, suddenly had a competitor and the battle for ratings was on, with current affairs to the forefront.

In 1963 Owen and I were married. I was in my twenties and lead-ing the interesting, exciting and stimulating life I had always dreamt of. I knew that I did not want to remain a studio manager; I had a thirst to present or produce. The Head of Children's Programmes in Cardiff, Evelyn Williams, had given me an opportunity to present a children's programme. It was far from the cutting-edge news and cur-rent affairs that I hankered for but, like politics, once you got the taste there was no turning back. Almost every other studio manager was looking to break out as well, which made things difficult; there simply weren't enough opportunities and I was impatient. Owen had quickly established himself as a successful current affairs editor and we were financially secure, so he encouraged me to break loose and become a freelance reporter.

Having until now gone into work and done what was assigned to me, now I was on my own and having to think of ideas all the time. I was disciplined about it, I set up one of our rooms as an office and as soon as Owen left I would set to work. Thinking of the ideas for articles was only half the battle, I then had to sell them to someone. Havard Gregory, who ran Cardiff's BBC World Service operation, commissioned my packages sometimes; I also found an outlet with *Wales Today*, the early evening news magazine programme. But for all my love of television and radio reporting, I found myself drawn to print.

Initially at least I found print a more difficult taskmaster but I quickly came to appreciate the nuances and subtleties of the written word. It was not easy, and I had fewer print contacts, so the only way was to be thick-skinned and hit the telephone, constantly bombarding news and feature editors with ideas. I phoned every newspaper in Fleet Street to ask whether they would like me to write for them. When the National Eisteddfod came to Swansea in 1964, I knew few of the nationals would be covering it, but thought there was an interesting story in there. Only *The Guardian* showed any glimmer of interest and after I phoned them every day for a week they eventually gave me a chance. After that I started having articles accepted by them more and more regularly and in the end I wrote on Welsh issues for them for ten years. When I speak to young journalists now I sympathise that it is not easy to get started but tell them to persevere. If you do, the doors do open eventually, you just have to get a foot in the door.

By the time I started receiving by-lines in *The Guardian* I chose to become known as Ann Clwyd. I had been born Ann Clwyd Lewis and was now Ann Clwyd Roberts, but the long name seemed cumbersome and had the appearance of a double-barrelled name, which was highly unfashionable in the '60s. So Ann Clwyd it was, although selection committees would insist on calling me Mrs Ann Clwyd Roberts for a while to come.

For Owen and me, it was the time of our lives. TWW had disappeared to be replaced by HTV Wales, with Owen at its helm as Head of News in Wales. Among the founders of HTV were Richard Burton and Elizabeth Taylor and on one memorable occasion Burton brought her to Cardiff to celebrate her birthday. I don't think Cardiff had ever seen anything like it. Photographers were out in force, scrambling to get pictures of Elizabeth wearing her birthday present, a $307,000 Krupp diamond ring. Owen and I were among the partygoers – glamorous did not begin to describe it!

We lived in a flat at the Old Rectory in Wenvoe, on the outskirts of Cardiff. Our landlords and neighbours were Richard Atkinson, professor of archaeology at Cardiff University, and his wife Hester. She was one of those amazing gregarious people, full of energy and enthusiasm and a real mover and shaker. It was not long before she took me under her wing and got me involved in one of her pet causes, the mental health charity now known as MIND. The local branch was one of the first to open a charity shop – a Nearly New Shop as we called it – in Cardiff. I appeared in the *South Wales Echo* selling George Thomas MP a waistcoat. She was also a vociferous campaigner against the death penalty and got me to join in her protests against that as well.

At some point, probably in Bangor, I had metamorphosed from tomboy to a fashion-conscious young woman. Now I embraced the beehive hair, mini-skirts and kinky boots of the time wholeheartedly. It felt fresh, new and radical. This interest in fashion and my love of new experiences was to lead me in an interesting direction.

I have always had a streak of impulsiveness so it was no surprise to Owen when I went out shopping and came home with a shop. The Pontcanna area of Cardiff was one of my favourite haunts. It had a village atmosphere and quirky independent shops and was populated with media types from the nearby TWW studios. Unlike London, the shopping experience in Cardiff is more than a trading exchange, it is almost a social occasion invariably involving a chat. Which is how I fell into conversation with the owner of a small antique shop who told me all about his dream to move abroad to live in the sun. It sounded wonderful so I asked him what was stopping him. 'Finding someone to take on this place,' he said, jerking his thumb towards the shop. Further chat revealed that the rent was incredibly low so I said, there and then, that I would take it on. I hope his new life lived up to the dream.

Both my grandmother and great-grandmother had been shopkeepers, and while I had no intention of giving up my main career as a journalist, I was excited at the prospect of creating and running my own business. My plan was to open a fashion boutique, selling modern, stylish clothes for the young professional. Boutiques were the flavour of the moment, independent and idiosyncratic, reflecting the personality of their owners. What fashionable woman would not be tempted by the opportunity?

I was interested in fashion and the creative arts and keen to explore my own creative side and although I had no experience whatsoever of the fashion or retail industries that did not stop me. It was the 1960s and anything was possible.

What knowledge I did have of the fashion industry, other than my own bulging wardrobe, came from a radio series I had recently completed on emerging Welsh designers. The Welsh fashion industry, if you could call it that, was slowly developing but it was very much a cottage industry. Creative types, tempted by the beautiful landscape and cheap property, were electing to move to the Welsh countryside to pursue the 'good life'. Here they established kitchen-table concerns, producing beautiful things. What they lacked was marketing skill and outlets for their work.

I travelled many a country lane and rutted farm track trying to track these people down. Occasionally it was frustrating, especially when I had driven for hours only to find a locked door with a notice 'gone fishing' posted on it. But there were also gems. An unknown designer called Laura Ashley had opened a workshop in the remote mid-Wales village of Carno producing wonderful fabrics. When I first visited her I literally had to step over the hens in the farmyard to get to the out-building from which she worked. Her cotton-drill smocks, aprons and oven gloves in bold stripes were selling like hot cakes and I snapped up her smocks for the boutique. A decade later I visited her again. Al-though still in Carno she and her husband Bernard now had a thriving business. The pared-down look had gone and her trademark floral prints were causing a stir in Paris and across the world.

I dipped into our savings and, with the help of friends like Lena and Noel Williams, converted the old antique shop into a modern, desirable fashion boutique. Julian, a BBC set designer, helped with the styling and other friends and family joined Owen and me in wielding paintbrushes. Finally, I was ready for business and hung the fuchsia-coloured sign outside. I called the boutique An-An, a play on my name with reference to the Russian panda, which had been brought to London to mate with Chi-Chi and was featuring heavily in the news.

I was still intending to pursue my journalistic career, so a reliable assistant was next on the shopping list. Luckily my seventeen-year-old cousin Eleanor (Elli) from Denbigh had left school without any idea of what to do next. She was a bright, bubbly and attractive girl and I snapped her up. The customers loved her and she also doubled up as a model for the fashion shows we put on. Elli was not the only member of the family to contribute; her mother, Auntie Mary, brought down the family's two red setter dogs to feature on the catwalk when we participated in a televised show for charity.

Although I wanted to feature clothes by Welsh designers I had no intention of doing so exclusively. Totally inexperienced, Elli and I set about stocking the shop. I had a clear idea of the look I was searching for – the sort of clothes I wore myself – and after some research we set off on a buying trip to London. We had enormous fun on those trips; boarding the train in Cardiff in our most fashionable clothes and heading for the West End showrooms. They were invariably run by East End barrow boys and nothing like a Parisian atelier. We would browse through row after row of clothes, labels such as Ossie Clark, Jean Varon and Avantgarde, choosing things that caught our eye. Of course we had no real idea of what we were doing, what quantities to order and in what sizes, but we took a guess and got on with it. I suppose you could say we learnt through experience, often costly, but we had great end-of-season sales!

I also continued to search for Welsh products with mixed success. The Cardiff College of Art and Design proved fertile ground and its inspirational head of fashion, June Tiley, introduced me to her students. We ended up stocking much of their work; they were unique pieces and flew off the shelves. A particular favourite was a hat-maker from the Rhondda called Pearl Bailey who made truly exquisite pieces. As soon as some of her stock arrived the word would get out and there would be a queue in front of the door.

Less successfully I tried to stock Welsh flannel products, but had not realised that unlike Scotland's soft, tactile products, Welsh flannel had originated as a working man's fabric and was extremely itchy. In those days the mills were not very professionally run either, the opening hours were often erratic and delivery schedules unreliable to say the least. If I saw something I liked in the mill I would put in an order but, months later, I would still be chasing them on the phone for delivery.

The journalist in me was always on the lookout for good promotional angles. Through my contacts An-An took part in countless charity fashion shows which spread the word, but that was not enough for me. With an eye for a good story I snapped up the opportunity to become Wales' first stockist of paper clothes! We launched the range at a charity fashion show given for MENCAP and, modelled by Elli, they attracted a lot of attention. The range consisted of everything from trouser suits to long, formal evening dresses and they epitomised the concept of disposable fashion. Cheap and cheerful, they enabled women to keep up to date with the latest trends at budget prices – funnily enough they never really took off! They gained us a lot of column inches though.

The shop was a narrow two-storey building on Pontcanna's King's Road. The name had seemed like a good omen but we quickly realised this quiet side-street was not conducive to a lot of custom. I had yet to learn about retail concepts such as 'footfall'. One class of people who did regularly find us were the shoplifters. With the shop spread over two floors and only one assistant I suppose we were an easy touch. A gang once took a lot of stock and we had to call the police in, go to court and so on. It was an unpleasant experience.

Much as I enjoyed the buying trips and opening the packages, I soon discovered that working in the shop was not for me. I did my stints on Saturdays but can't say I enjoyed them much. People were quick to take advantage of small shopkeepers, running up credit and taking clothes on approval only to return them obviously worn. Elli was a particular target with people coming in when she was alone, claiming life-long friendship with me, and asking for discounts. She soon got wise to them.

I was very dependent on Elli so when she decided to leave it was the beginning of the end for the shop. Given our location, trade could be very slow, especially on weekdays, and once the initial novelty wore off I think it became a bit of a bore for Elli. She still didn't know what she wanted to do so I sent her to see a newly launched careers guidance service which I had recently written about. As a result, she decided to train as an orthoptist and although I was delighted for her it left me debating what to do next with An-An. I persuaded my friend Beryl Richards, who had a great flair for fashion, to return to the workplace after having five children and join me. It worked for a while, and worked wonders for Beryl's confidence, but things did not improve.

It had been a fun period in my life, but not a particularly lucrative one, in fact the shop probably ended up losing money. I do look back on it fondly, and even now I occasionally bump into some of my old regulars and enjoy reminiscing about our mini-skirts and kinky boots!

CHAPTER FOUR

EUROPE

In addition to working as a journalist and running a shop I had been chasing my dream of becoming an MP, networking furiously and putting my name forward to constituency selection committees. The nominations were not forthcoming so after eight years I opted for an alternative route into politics. I turned my back on Westminster, for the time being at least, to seek out a meaningful role in Europe. When I took the decision I had not anticipated being at the wrong end of a gun barrel.

The first time I was an innocent bystander, well fairly innocent anyway. Egypt's President Anwar Sadat was to address European MPs and his security team were somewhat over-zealous in refusing anyone entry into Parliament, including the MEPs. '*Je suis Tindemans,*' thundered the former Belgian Prime Minister. '*Laissez-passer.*' It was to no avail. I stood up to the guy barring my way, arguing my democratic right, when he physically blocked my way. The Halkyn prize-fighter responded; I saw red and pushed him, resulting in guns and rifles being levelled at me and my colleagues. Common sense eventually prevailed and we were allowed on our way. The press hailed my belligerence and the incident created something of a storm. Colleagues protested that if we were to behave like a fascist state when heads of state visited perhaps we ought not to invite them.

The second time was at a meeting of the Council of Ministers in Strasbourg. I had taken a delegation of angry steelworkers from Llanelli into the building and we decided to lobby the ministers directly while they discussed European steel production. We arrived, unannounced, outside their door and the delegation burst into a rendition of the Llanelli rugby anthem – 'Sosban Fach'. No one knew what was happening and all hell broke loose. The intimidating French police, dressed in black and armed, arrived to bar our way. They stood there looking menacing. We, being Welsh, carried on singing and kept walking. There were a few scuffles, but eventually we were persuaded to walk away. We had made our point.

I had arrived in Brussels in 1979 a seasoned party activist and opposed to British membership of what was then known as the Common Market. On an earlier facility trip for journalists I had stared aghast at what appeared to be the popular sport – popping champagne corks into squares in the ceiling of the Commission offices. I was also vehemently opposed to the Common Agricultural Policy, which seemed to be making the lives of ordinary people a misery by driving up the price of food while subsidising the farmers, leaving us with butter and sugar mountains galore. On top of that the parliament rotated between Brussels, Strasbourg and Luxembourg for a week at a time; a roadshow of papers in tin trunks being carted back and forth and members, advisers, secretaries and translators chalking up hotel and travel bills to the taxpayer. Many officials lived tax-free in Luxembourg.

I was there to represent the people of Mid and West Wales, whose politics, demographics and beliefs could not have been more different. It was an enormous constituency – only Winnie Ewing's Highlands and Islands constituency was bigger – and represented about a third of the land mass of Wales. To the north and west it was largely Welsh-speaking and rural. Although I had elected to back the consumer position on food prices, my arguments with the local farmers were largely good-natured and I had a lot of sympathy for the hill farmers and those on marginal land who were struggling to make a living. To the south the constituency became more urban and industrialised, taking in Llanelli and Swansea. This area would become a battleground in the industrial issue of the day, the restructuring of the steel industry. Then, right down in the south-west was beautiful Pembrokeshire where tourism was of vital importance to the local economy.

The European parliamentary entry of 1979 were the first to be democratically elected, so none of us quite knew what to expect. The confusion was somewhat exacerbated when Madame Louise Weiss, Doyen d'Age (the senior member), addressed us and urged us to 'have babies for Europe'.

I was part of the Socialist group, the largest political group in the parliament. Our seventeen-strong UK contingent was led by the legendary Barbara Castle. She had been one of the most influential ministers in the Wilson government, the longest-serving woman MP, and I never really understood why she had opted to come to Europe. Her only aim was to reform the Common Agricultural Policy. She was virulently anti-European and would frequently get up the nose of our socialist colleagues, but she was a formidable operator and working alongside her was an education in itself. She could be totally charming and was not averse to flirting with male colleagues to get her own way. She could also turn quickly if things went against her and become quite vituperative.

Being a small group, and not yet skilled at integrating with our international colleagues, we tended to stick together; mainly go out and eat in the evenings. Barbara had expensive tastes and was always on the search for lobster. She was also quite fond of her drink and would get quite pissed, so much so that if we had people over visiting us, we would have to cover up for her. She would often get tired and emotional and if one of our group pulled her leg she would not see the funny side. On one memorable night, after someone had said something fairly innocuous, she flung her fur coat on the bar floor and stormed off saying we would all be sorry later. Perhaps it was ungracious of me to recall this incident when she retired, but I was getting fed up of the hagiography. She later complained bitterly, saying she had never owned a fur coat. It must have been fake!

Anyway she was quite the operator, great at getting other people to run around working for her. Poor Joyce Quin, now Baroness Quin, was forever representing her on one committee or another, doing all the donkey work, while Barbara took all the glory. The men, in particular, were cannon fodder, but I was feisty, had been around too long, and had my own style of operating. A clash was inevitable.

When the big beasts of politics came to visit the parliament we would take it in turns to speak in reply. On one of Norman Tebbit's visits that duty fell to me. Barbara was not happy and wanted to do it herself but I stood my ground and the group backed me. She did not take defeat graciously and when I stood up to speak she just walked out. It cannot have been easy for her, though; after being a major star at Westminster she was now leading a group of seventeen insignificants. Also, during this period, her husband Ted died. He was a lovely man, a great networker who could smooth situations out, and I think she depended on him a great deal.

It was a claustrophobic existence. Moving from hotel room to hotel room, socialising with the same circle of colleagues, and away from home every weekday for three weeks every month. There were a few advantages to living out of a suitcase, of course. Your cooking and cleaning were taken care of and often the hotel would have a swimming pool in the basement, which I sometimes tried to take advantage of. On one occasion, while minding my own business swimming around alone in the pool, a naked man ran in and hurled himself into the water. It was not an edifying sight. It was Lord Harmar-Nicholls, an elderly fellow British MEP but not, I hasten to add, one of ours.

When he clocked who I was he was mortified and, shouting, 'Sorry, I thought you were a fellow,' made his excuses and left rapidly. It was a story I dined out on for quite a while.

When I was at home I had this enormous, geographically dispersed, mainly rural constituency that took forever to get from one end to another. I do not think I have ever been so exhausted. After the rich food of Strasbourg all I wanted when I got home was a boiled egg and some brown bread. Despite all this I loved the job.

No sooner had I arrived at the European Parliament than another major contraction of the steel industry threatened; this time South Wales would be in the thick of it. The nationalised British steel industry had been struggling for decades. Having been starved of investment it was now out-of-date, unproductive and over-manned and by 1980 it was losing over a billion pounds a year. The Thatcher government appointed Ian MacGregor to sort it out and we all knew where that was going to lead. Sure enough, closures and mass redundancies were announced; 15,000 jobs to go in South Wales alone. It was not just the scale of closures it was the speed with which they were going to be implemented. The government had applied an arbitrary March deadline for break-even; the axe would fall in three or four months.

The prospects for the communities of Llanwern, Port Talbot and Llanelli were horrendous then, as they are now. These were steel towns, where for every job in steel-making at least another three were dependent on the works. The result of the redundancies would be deprivation on a scale not witnessed since the Great Depression of the '30s. It was a lunatic act of wanton destruction. My colleagues in the Labour Party, the Welsh TUC, Plaid Cymru, Welsh Liberals all called for a re-think. Even the Welsh CBI – the bosses union – asked for a delay. But the government was not budging.

Looking back now it is hard to understand the intransigence of the government and its total disregard for the human consequences of its policies. Thankfully, even the Conservative Party has moved on a bit from those inhumane days. At the time the Secretary of State for Industry, Keith Joseph, wrote to Thatcher: 'The government's attitude [to the restructure of the steel industry] will be regarded as a critical test of our determination to curb inflation and public expenditure and to make nationalised industries stand on their own two feet.' Thatcher's government had been in power little over a year; this was to be the first test of its anti-nationalisation, anti-union credo.

That there was a need to restructure the industry was in little doubt. Even in France and in West Germany – where there had been significant investment to modernise the steel industries – there was overcapacity. But I watched in awe as thousands of French steelworkers lost their jobs in four years without a single one of them being forced on to the dole. Every redundant man was offered early retirement, on almost full pay, or a job in another industry with retraining and special arrangements for relocation. The Germans absorbed something like 5,000 redundancies in the Ruhr without a single steelworker finding himself out of work. In South Wales we were facing rundown at suicidal speed and whole communities facing a future on the scrapheap of unemployment.

Along with my colleagues Allan Rogers and Win Griffiths I made numerous speeches in the European Parliament, pleading for help for my constituents which their own government would not give them. At our request the EEC Commissioner for Industry, Viscount Davignon, offered to arbitrate between the steelworker's union and British Steel in an attempt to slow down the redundancies.

The Employment and Social Affairs Commissioner, Ivor Richard (now Lord Richard), openly criticised the British government for its lack of social policy to deal with such enormous changes. Ivor would become an important ally. He had also tried for the Labour nomination for my Euro constituency but bore no ill will and I always found him very approachable and helpful. We worked together quite a lot as I sat on the Social Affairs and Employment Committee of the

European Parliament, where my colleagues found it extremely difficult
to understand Britain's attitude.

There was money available in the EEC's social budget to cushion the
effects of restructuring heavy industry; special allowances that allowed
men to stay in their jobs for a period while they retrained, or alternative
employment moved into the area. But it required match-funding from
national governments, and whereas France and Germany made good
use of it, the British government turned it down. To add insult to injury,
the Chancellor of the Exchequer vetoed a budget that would have
seen the Common Agricultural Policy cut in order to tackle the social
consequences of unemployment and restructuring of the coal and steel
industries. The millions of pounds that had been set aside to help the
steel communities in Britain were depleted. The Thatcher government
argued that it wanted fair play for Britain from Europe, but at the first
opportunity it voted against it. It was madness.

The madness manifested itself in other ways. Duport steelworks in
Llanelli had been an independent steelmaker before being bought by
British Steel and was a modern and efficient plant. By 1981 it faced
closure as part of BSC's restructuring. Imagine the workers' sense of
injustice when they found out that their plans to save the works were
doomed – because BSC had inserted a clause into the agreement that
the plant could not be sold to another steelmaker. Donald Evans, the
union leader there, called me. He was a good man and he and his
colleagues had been working night and day to try to secure a future
for the plant but now they were at the end of their tether. He told
me about the pernicious clause and I exploded. I felt it was immoral
and probably illegal and told Donald I would find a way of fighting
it. The European Commission on Steel and Coal was supportive
and advised that such a clause was in contravention of EEC free-
competition policy. At my request, they wrote to British Steel and the
British government asking MacGregor to remove the clause. I chased
it up but British Steel claimed not to have received any communication

from the EEC. I checked. The letter had been sent but I asked for it to be sent again. Again British Steel denied seeing it. It was descending into a farce.

Meanwhile the people employed at the works were getting ever more desperate. With the plant scheduled to close in a fortnight, with the loss of 1,000 jobs, the town was in despair and its whole economic future threatened.

We were getting nowhere at home. The UK Minister for Industry, Norman Tebbit, was unsympathetic and brushed us off. He said there was nothing that could be done to save the plant. But a glimmer of hope existed; the European Commission had put forward a proposal involving work-share and reduced working hours. Ivor Richard promised to do what he could to get the Industry Ministers to adopt the plan but they failed even to convene a meeting. Direct action was called for so I invited a delegation to Brussels to put their case directly to ministers.

The Council of Ministers, representatives of the member countries, was very secretive and did not meet in public so confronting them was far from easy. I discussed my plan with a few sympathetic associates and plotted it carefully. I found out when they were next due to meet and where in the building the meeting would take place. My pass would get us into the corridor outside the room; if we moved quickly we might succeed. On the day I met the steelworkers in a local bar and shared the plan with them; they were up for it. I told them to follow me, that if we were challenged to ignore it and push on. We never made it into the actual meeting, security guards and police made sure of that, but we got very close and there was quite a rough scuffle in the corridor. The ministers could not have failed to be aware of our presence as 'Sosban Fach' rang out. Although the delegation went home with nothing, Donald said that at least they knew they had done all they could. Duport in Llanelli closed a month later and unemployment in the town shot up to 18.9 per cent.

Back in 1975 I had voted against EEC membership in the referendum and joined in the choruses of 'Bye-bye Common Market, So long EEC.' I had fought my election as an anti-Europe candidate, all in favour of British withdrawal from the community. I had even been told that in a constituency with a significant agricultural vote I had no hope of winning. I had railed against the wine lakes and butter mountains and had been in good company: Michael Foot, the Welsh TUC, and Uncle Tom Cobley had been singing from the same hymn sheet. But two years in, having seen how much better they handled the social cost of industrial reorganisation elsewhere in Europe, my views were changing.

It now seemed to me that remaining in Europe was in the best interests of the British people. I knew I was setting myself up in direct opposition to official Labour policy, but I felt that I should be honest with myself and with my constituents. I visited all the individual constituency parties which I represented and explained my views. It would be fair to say they were somewhat put out that I had actually changed my mind but also that I found myself at odds with party policy. Several intense discussions ensued. I actually enjoyed the process, forcing myself to articulate my thoughts and put them over. While I did not receive their backing for my views I do think in the most part I won their grudging respect for my stance; we agreed to differ and I got on with my work.

An exception was John Marek, secretary of the Cardiganshire constituency. He was incensed at my change of mind and never invited me to a constituency event again. Elsewhere I accepted as many speaking engagements as I was able to, taking the proverbial bull by the horns, and making my views known. Funnily enough one of my allies was Roger Williams, who later joined the Liberal Democrats and became MP for Brecon & Radnor. When he arrived in the House of Commons I used to take great enjoyment from teasing him about being one of my former supporters. 'And I'd do it again,' he would retort, 'if only you switch parties!'

I actually faced less opposition than I had expected; I think the farming community felt I had, in its view, come to my senses. The industrial part of the constituency had been part of the debate on steel and could see that we had more support in Europe than in London. All that remained was to try and change Labour Party policy! I came across quite a lot of hostility as a result of my change of heart. Fellow MEP Janey Buchan did not speak to me for years afterwards and blamed my views for Labour's loss of Glasgow Hillhead in a by-election.

I tried to explain to colleagues in Britain that socialism did not stop at our borders; in fact the whole history of the movement was one of internationalism. Working day-to-day with colleagues from other countries had made me realise we did not have all the answers and that we had more to gain than lose by being part of the European Community. For example, when car manufacturing giant Ford planned to move production from my constituency to the Netherlands I contacted one of my Dutch colleagues. We jointly arranged a meeting between representatives of the two plants and the Welsh workers were supported by their Dutch colleagues, even though they stood to gain thousands of jobs. International solidarity; isn't this what we had dreamt of?

Above all I was convinced by Europe's attitude to social policy, which was more enlightened and humane than anything seen at Westminster during the Tory years. Again times have changed and now much more emphasis is put on social cost when mass redundancies or closures hit a region. In 2016 the steel industry in Wales faced another, possibly terminal, blow, and once again Port Talbot looked into the abyss. This time there was more consideration for the workers affected, and more planning to try and alleviate the impact.

Having said that, in a remarkable demonstration of hypocrisy, the Tory government was quite happy to prioritise the trade relationship with China ahead of protecting steelmaking in the UK: it blocked attempts to regulate cheap Chinese steel being dumped in Europe and then had the effrontery to imply part of the problem was the European Commission's inability to act quickly.

All of which illustrates that there was, and still is, much that was wrong with Europe's institutions. But it took the Labour Party generations to win reform at Westminster; compared to that, Europe seems to be making progress.

As an MEP I attended a meeting when Tony Benn came out to address the European Socialist Group. I didn't disagree with him on much, but Europe was one of those issues on which we never saw eye to eye. He argued that socialism could not work in Europe; it had to be rooted in a nation state. The challenges came thick and fast. The Germans wanted to know why British socialists were not prepared to work with colleagues from other countries on shared objectives such as full employment and peace. The Italians took a more emotional approach – was Benn accusing them of not being real socialists? It is fascinating that thirty-five years later, the next time Britain would hold a referendum on membership, it would be Tony's son Hilary who would take one of the lead roles in the Remain campaign. Hilary may have had differing views to his father, on this as well as on foreign policy, but they share the same core principles and are among the most decent and honourable men I have met in politics.

But back in 1982, although there were socialist governments in France, Germany, Denmark, Italy, Ireland and the Netherlands, who did not find EEC membership incompatible with their aims, the British Labour Party remained committed to withdrawal. During my time as an MEP, Michael Foot and Eric Heffer came out with the same message and got a similar response, and when Neil Kinnock won the party leadership in 1983 I had to virtually drag him out to Strasbourg; he just didn't want to know. Today it is the Conservative Party which is divided on Europe and I am glad to say the Labour Party has moved full circle and, with a few exceptions, is now a fully participating member of the European socialist movement.

I do become despondent when I witness the level of debate on Europe in Britain and I think our media, broadcast and print, have much to answer for. The general public, not just here but elsewhere in Europe, are woefully uneducated about the work of the European Union, as it is now called, which goes part of the way to explaining the low turnout at elections. Where there are inefficiencies, undemocratic practices and abuses of power, they need to be addressed. Where there is good work and progress there must be recognition. We have to move away from a debate dominated by misshapen bananas and jingoistic rhetoric and start addressing the real issues that face people across the continent.

Personally, as an MEP, I found working day-to-day in pursuit of policies I believed in was a salutary and stimulating experience. Once I got over the seemingly unpronounceable names of other MEPs – and I particularly recall struggling with Ludwig Fellermaier and Heidemarie Wieczorek-Zeul – I began to appreciate what we could accomplish together. The prevailing wisdom at Westminster at the time was that Britain was superior to other European countries in almost every aspect of public life. I soon learnt differently.

One of the greatest eye-openers was when I was appointed Rapporteur for the International Year of Disabled Persons. I worked closely with colleagues on researching the issues facing disabled people over a six-month period and was deeply disappointed, not to say embarrassed, when I was forced to conclude that Britain was by far the worst country in which to live as a disabled person.

I listened to hundreds of personal stories from people across Europe and overwhelmingly they told me that they did not want to receive charity, but the dignity of being able to work for a fair wage. They were angry at being palmed off by free passes to museums and wanted practical action. I was heartbroken to see the hopelessness of people imprisoned in antiquated institutions or the walls of their own homes because of a lack of suitable housing and access to public spaces.

What was needed was a fair minimum wage; protection from public expenditure cuts; access to education, transport and buildings; and employment quotas. I believed we should aim for the common standards across Europe, taking the best from each country, and reward innovative design that made opportunities accessible to everyone.

I had tried to keep my report's recommendations realistic, not wishing to raise expectations only to shatter them again. I was delighted when they were overwhelmingly accepted by the European Parliament – I even had strong support from Conservative MEPs – but it would be up to individual countries to implement the recommendations. Over the years I continued to champion the rights of disabled people and was delighted when, under the New Labour government, the battle of British disabled people to have the same protection as their European colleagues was finally acknowledged.

One of the most rewarding things about being an MEP was the friendships with people from other countries with shared aspirations. I was lucky to enjoy many a long dinner and discussion with the Italian MEP Pietro Lezzi and the German Lilo Seibel-Emmerling. Freed from living under a Westminster microscope, an MEP has the time and distance to formulate ideas and discuss them openly with colleagues with different experiences and perspectives. As a result, dare I suggest that the MEP is often a more rounded politician.

CHAPTER FIVE

PEACE ACTIVIST

For me, my term in Europe coincided with my growing involvement with the peace movement. Pacifism was a strong tradition in Welsh chapel circles. Two of my uncles died in the First World War and my father fought at Ypres, but it was never something he talked about. My time at Pantyfedwen reinforced my belief in unilateralism and by the 1980s I was certainly sympathetic to the aims of CND, the Campaign for Nuclear Disarmament. By the '80s the resurgence of the Cold War changed everything and tens of thousands of British people joined CND in protest at the American siting of their inter-continental missiles on British soil and our own commissioning of Trident missiles. My support of CND was shared with many other Labour members, especially our then leader Michael Foot. It was very much a movement of the time, not only in the UK but across Europe. I certainly enjoyed going on peace marches with Greek and Italian friends.

I even went to America on a peace tour, where we met politicians at Capitol Hill in Washington and then went on to New York. We stayed at Quaker House and I spoke at a rally at the biggest Methodist church in the city. I felt quite at home there, not only because of my background, but because as we walked in we were faced with a statue of Christ which turned out to be the mould used for Epstein's *Christ in Majesty* at Llandaff Cathedral in Cardiff, near my home. Our delegation was headed by actress Julie Christie, a prominent campaigner against nuclear weapons. She struck me as modest and shy but highly principled. The media loved her because she was extraordinarily beautiful. On our trip, she wore no make-up at all and was only concerned with getting our message across.

There was a lot of rubbish written in the Tory press at the time, claiming CND was an agent of communists. There were members who were communists for sure but they also came in other hues, many of them politically unaffiliated. There were a lot of ordinary women who felt their views were ignored by the political classes and who were concerned about the nuclear threat and its effect on their children and grandchildren.

They wanted answers to questions, such as why we needed enough nuclear weapons in Europe to destroy the continent thirty times over. And why we needed enough weapons to kill everyone in Russia twenty times over. The nuclear arms race was out of control and for the price of two Trident submarines we could provide primary schools and teacher training for half the population of the Third World. Which was the greater indicator of future world peace, many of us asked?

Anyway, in September 1981, I helped organise a women's rally in Cardiff before a group of women and children set off on a peace march to protest about the siting of Cruise missiles at an American Air Force base in Berkshire. I was the only elected politician to make a speech that day and I looked out over a large crowd as I spoke of lethal weapons like Cruise, escalating a hostile situation until the world was blown up. Speeches made, we linked hands, began singing, and set off in the general direction of Newport. After a token mile or so I dropped out and went home but many continued with their peace march until they reached the gates of the Air Force base. It was Greenham Common.

Thirty-six Welsh women made the 120-mile walk. When they reached the base they chained themselves to the perimeter fence and the Greenham Common Peace Camp was born. It would stay there for two decades. Lots of other camps were subsequently established there, reflecting the rainbow coalition that was CND. There were women-only camps, a new-age camp and camps with religious affiliations; Red Gate, for example, was known as the camp for artists.

The Greenham protestors were largely, but not exclusively, women and it was this as much as anything that shocked the sensibilities of Middle England. Many of the women were wives and mothers, not previously politically active, who simply left home to protest about something they felt extraordinarily passionate about. I admired them: people like Eunice Stallard from Swansea and Helen John from Llanwrtyd Wells, who went to prison for refusing to pay a fine. They were principled women fighting for all our futures, but to believe some of the tabloid press they were a group of flaky women, abandoning their children to pursue a drug-fuelled lesbian fantasy.

I visited on a number of occasions to show my support and on one occasion joined them in linking hands to encircle the perimeter fence. I was always conscious of the good humour and camaraderie but also of a quiet, steely determination to see the job through. We all follow our paths in our own way and theirs was no trivial commitment, especially the permanent residents living in cold, muddy fields with virtually no sanitation. On one visit I met a diplomat from the Russian embassy, who gave me a lift back to London; I expect that in those Cold War days, that made me suspect ever after!

In 1982 the Royal National Eisteddfod of Wales, a festival of music and poetry, was held on my patch in Swansea and I was honoured to be President of the day. I took the opportunity to make a plea for peace and nuclear disarmament, risking the wrath of the *eisteddfodwyr* (eisteddfod-goers) by using the occasion for political purposes. But my message was well received; one woman coming up to me afterwards said, in Welsh of course, that she spent sleepless nights worrying about someone pushing the nuclear button by mistake. 'One false move and that's it,' she said. 'It's the future of my grandchildren I worry about, I've had my life.' Others told me they felt helpless, that there was nothing they could do. But I pointed out that in Germany, for example, a new political party opposing nuclear weapons had forced Chancellor Helmut Schmidt to reconsider his policy. I believed then, and continue to believe, that ordinary people have power but often forget they have it. Public opinion definitely matters.

We were fortunate that we lived in a democratic country where we are allowed to have opinions, and expect them to count for something. The Turkish Peace Association was in a very different place. A number of their members, many formerly pillars of the establishment – lawyers, MPs and writers among them – had been put on trial by the military junta in 1982 simply for their views. They faced eighteen years in jail.

It was the usual thing. A friend of mine in London was approached by a Turk who was a relative of one of those on trial. Would I help? I looked into the issue, was incensed at what was happening and raised the issue in the European Parliament. I also wrote a pamphlet with another MEP, Roland Boyes, highlighting the issue and arguing for their release. As a result, Amnesty International contacted me and asked me if I would go to the trials as an observer.

Following the emptying of my handbag and a comprehensive search, I found myself in a barred and Spartan courtroom, a converted gymnasium in the Metris prison, Istanbul. Facing me were three military judges and a golden death mask of Ataturk. Here twenty-nine members of the Turkish Peace Association were reaching the end of a two-year ordeal. They sat on wooden benches, surrounded by armed guards. Defendants from outside Istanbul had had to travel for hours and hours to the trial by bus and return each evening. It was all very shocking. All the charges against them related to the period before the military junta even took power, and consisted of little more than impassioned campaigning against the siting of nuclear weapons at NATO bases in Turkey.

The TPA leadership read like a list of the great and the good and the main defendant was Mehmet Dikerdem, a 67-year-old former ambassador. Like the other prisoners, the previous year he had been incarcerated in a dungeon for ten months despite suffering from cancer. Alongside him sat Orhan Apaydin, one of the most prominent lawyers in the country and President of the Turkish Bar Association. The trial itself was a farce. Although the prisoners were allowed defence lawyers, they were not allowed to speak. They had been told that any speeches made prior to the military coup in 1980 could not be used against them, but they were. This was only the tip of the iceberg; it was believed there were numerous more people in prison on political charges.

After witnessing a few days of the ongoing trials I returned to Wales primed for action. I made a speech in Swansea attacking the cruelty and injustices of the regime and called for sanctions against it. I was particularly incensed at the attitude of the British government, which carried on as though nothing had happened. Thatcher had recently entertained Turkey's Foreign Minister as an honoured guest.

After returning from Europe and taking my seat at Westminster I heard that the Turkish Prime Minister, Turgut Özal, was coming to address a meeting of Tory MPs. It was too good an opportunity to miss so I gatecrashed the meeting and listened to what he had to say. When he had finished I put up my hand to ask a question but the Tory chairman would not call me. I was so furious that I strode across the room to the Prime Minister and cornered him; he was such a small man, even I towered over him. 'Don't think that what you heard here is what most people in this country think, because it's not.' He looked at me in astonishment, but understood perfectly well what I had said. So I continued, 'In any civilised country those people wouldn't be on trial.' I was so angry. He replied, 'Well, what do you want me to do?' I told him. 'Give them an amnesty.'

The next day he had a meeting scheduled with Labour leader, Neil Kinnock. I got to Neil first, briefed him, and asked him to give Ozal a hard time. He obviously did. Two weeks later those people were all out of jail. The Dikerdem family and others, like the impresario Ali Taygun, subsequently became friends of mine.

A couple of years ago I went on an inter-parliamentary human rights committee visit to Turkey with a Swiss MP. We wanted to visit political prisoners and had been told by the Speaker of the Turkish parliament that we could have access to some Kurdish MPs who were in jail. Then, a week before we got there, they released them all with the exception of a Turkish general. Apparently he had clashed swords with President Erdoğan; it had become a personal thing and he had been sentenced to thirty years in prison and had already served two of them. So we went anyway and asked to see him only to be told that he did not want to see us. I did not believe that for a minute and demanded to know who he had said it to. They said they did not know so I asked them to check. And on it went for a couple of days before they let us visit. We spent about an hour and a half with him and took his details; he looked very gaunt and ill and he feared he had cancer. Happily, a few weeks after our visit he was released and his daughter sent me a message saying her father was extremely grateful and looked forward to taking me for dinner on the Bosphorus the next time I visited Istanbul.

Although the European Parliament gave me the first platform to pursue human rights issues, one of the most rewarding issues I was involved in was securing recognition for minority languages. In 1981 the European Parliament drafted proposals to encourage people to learn and speak regional languages within Europe, languages like Catalan, Breton and Welsh. John Hume, of the SDLP, was instrumental in bringing in the debate, as was Ivor Richard, the Social

Affairs Commissioner. Ivor spoke passionately in favour of teaching through the medium of regional languages. '*Cenedl heb iaith, cenedl heb galon,*' he said, which translates as 'a nation without language, a nation without a heart'. It was a moving moment as speakers had been given permission, for that day only, to speak in unofficial languages as long as we translated our words.

I too took the opportunity to speak in Welsh, pointing out that historically thousands of Welsh people had been denied the opportunity to learn and speak their own language. Dozens of people had been to prison because of their passionate commitment to keeping the Welsh language alive, a commitment I share. Although just under a quarter of people in Wales speak Welsh, for those of us who do it is enormously important in terms of culture and identity, and many who do not speak it tell me that they wish they did and value it anyway. I was fortunate; many Welsh speakers of my parents' generation – and even my own – chose not to pass the language on to their children, under a misplaced sense they were somehow 'modernising' and improving their children's prospects. I think they got it wrong.

The EEC's pilot projects for multilingual development were agreed and with it came £56,000 for the Welsh language. It was not an amount that would change the endangered status of Welsh overnight, but it was a breakthrough, and gave the impetus for recognising and saving regional languages a massive endorsement. In Wales, the movement to educate through the medium of Welsh has grown rapidly and is the preferred choice for many parents who do not speak the language themselves. Even youngsters who are not educated in Welsh now learn enough of the language to bolster their sense of identity and understanding of their heritage. Even if it is just enough to say hello and goodbye, ask for the toilet (a particular favourite of Welsh teachers for some reason) and sing with gusto at rugby matches. None of which can be a bad thing.

There has been considerable change in Europe since the 1980s.

The European Union has expanded to twenty-eight member states, sadly to go back to twenty-seven with our exit. When I became MEP in 1979, it was only nine, and three of us, the UK, Denmark and Eire, had only been members for six years. It expanded again in the 1980s to incorporate Greece, Spain and Portugal. I was lucky to be selected to chair the Portuguese pre-accession committee. It was a country I always had a great deal of affection for, having spent my honeymoon there. Now I was able to indulge my love of fresh sardines on regular trips there, although more than one posh restaurant turned up their noses at such 'peasant food'! When the European parliamentary delegations visited, the host country was always anxious to impress and put on its best face. On one trip our delegation was taken on a tour down the river Douro. At one of the port-wine lodges we hit a stumbling block, women were not allowed, but special arrangements had been made for Margaret Thatcher and were now made for me. I was honoured to be presented with the Silver Medal by the Wine Growers' Association and later the Portuguese Prime Minister, Mário Soares, hosted a dinner in my honour. He presented me with a medal and then two people came up to the top table with a wooden boat – a model of the boats that used to carry barrels of port wine up the Douro. They had booked two seats on Portuguese airlines to bring the boat back to the UK.

One of our delegation was Stanley Johnson, father of future London mayor and MP Boris. Stanley was a very interesting man who had worked for the European Commission as an environmentalist and was now a fellow MEP. He was always supportive of the UK's European membership and, in my opinion, he always spoke a great deal more sense than his son, Boris. He was also a novelist and would be forever scribbling away in his notebook, even in the darkness of the port-wine lodges.

Although I enjoyed being an MEP immensely, Westminster was still a draw. By the end of my time in Europe I had been elected to the National Executive of the Labour Party, but was still treated as a traitor when I visited the House of Commons. I felt an outsider once again and wanted to be on the inside. In 1984 I finally became an MP, but I am convinced I was a better one for having served a term in Europe, because it broadened my horizons and I became more internationalist in my outlook. Back in Britain I was to find a lot of the body politic still inward-looking.

CHAPTER SIX

GANG OF THREE

I had finally made it. Fourteen years in the trying, but I finally walked through the St Stephen's entrance at Westminster as a Member of Parliament.

I took in the atmosphere, the history of this mother of parliaments, and smiled to myself. It was impossible not to feel history weighing on my shoulders. Taking in the awesome grandeur of Central Lobby I felt a shiver going down my spine.

Keir Hardie, my predecessor, the first leader of the Labour Party, had stood here. And, like him, I hadn't arrived to make up the numbers. I was here to make a difference

At first everything was overwhelming. Despite having experience as an MEP, the traditions and protocols of Westminster were all new to me, like being at a new school. The first thing was to be formally introduced as a new member. Watched by my relatives in the Strangers' Gallery and accompanied by two supporters, I was led into the Chamber. There, accompanied by cheers from other members, I was walked to the front where I took the Oath of Allegiance in both English and Welsh. The Speaker had a few words and shook my hand. Then my party leader, Neil Kinnock, shook my hand too.

Neil was MP for the neighbouring constituency of Islwyn and

looked genuinely pleased to see me. I think he was anticipating a sympathetic supporter. 'About time too', he beamed. I was relieved. During my election campaign there had been a bit of a to-do with the party hierarchy over my eve of poll rally. I had wanted Tony Benn to speak, but was told by Labour headquarters that he wasn't available. It was the middle of the miners' strike for goodness' sake, it was the perfect platform for me and for him. I appealed to him directly; he told me he hadn't even been asked and that he would be delighted to come. Come the night, they were hanging from the rafters at Penrhiwceiber Working Men's Club, we couldn't squeeze another body in and my soon-to-be constituents cheered themselves hoarse.

With the ceremonial over, I turned to find somewhere to sit on the opposition benches. I made for the back, I'm naturally more comfortable there, and found somewhere to squeeze in. I think I sat next to Alice Mahon, near her at any rate, and I've pretty well sat there ever since with the exception of a few stints on the front bench. The Speakers like people to settle in one place, it makes it easier for them to remember names, and anyway the company was congenial and it suited me. After listening to that afternoon's debates for a decent period, I made for the dining room for afternoon tea with my family.

Anyway, the day after my induction business began in earnest. Ray Powell was now in the Whips' Office of all places and responsible for allocating office space. This was no doubt why I found myself with a desk in a corridor. Clare Short sat in the desk in front of me, behind me was Jeremy Corbyn, who frequently brought his dog with him. I never did work out how they had crossed Ray, but it was well known that he saw this role as a means of exerting power over people; favouring ones he liked and making life difficult for those he didn't. He was not a fan of Ken Livingstone, the former GLC leader. When Ken entered Parliament three years later he was not allocated a desk at all and had to work out of a telephone booth because Ray did not like him.

It was far cry from my Strasbourg office with its en-suite shower room, a day bed and stunning views overlooking the river. I unpacked, put up a couple of photographs and a pot plant on my desk and surveyed my new home. It would have to do. I think I was in that corridor for about three years.

The corridor did have its historic connections; King Charles I's death warrant had been signed near where my desk now sat. It was little consolation. We had to share our corridor with Tory MPs, giving us no privacy at all. At the time the miners' strike was at its peak and I was regularly making and taking calls from Kim Howells, then a researcher with the South Wales NUM, to update myself on what was happening. In those days there were no mobile phones so I had to get used to muttering into the telephone handset while covering it with my hand.

One Monday morning I returned to my 'office' to find water pouring through the ceiling from the lavatories above; all my books, papers and personal things were ruined. I had to put newspapers down on the floor to try and absorb the worst of the water, but our workspace remained damp and smelly. The Whips' Office did nothing and ignored my pleas and those of my colleagues. 'Never mind King Charles, there'll be some more death warrants signed if someone doesn't do anything about this,' raged Corbyn. I took matters into my own hands. I borrowed a pair of wellington boots from fellow MP Brian Sedgemore, an umbrella from someone else and called in the *Evening Standard* for a photocall. Within minutes of the early edition hitting the streets someone turned up to begin the clean-up operation.

Being elected in a by-election makes you special. When you arrive everyone tends to know who you are, there's none of the anonymity of a group intake. Then again, I wasn't new to the political scene; I had been an MEP for the past five years and a member of the Labour Party Executive for the best part of a year. But now I was a Westminster insider, even Dennis Skinner acknowledged me in the tea room. I had finally arrived.

Several Welsh colleagues popped along to wish me well. As a Euro MP I had worked closely with the two Swansea MPs Alan Williams and Donald Anderson, as well as Llanelli's Denzil Davies, and it was good to see their friendly faces. Some of the others were just plain begrudging and unpleasant. They were the old guard of the Welsh Labour Party who resented having a woman MP among their number, especially one who tended to attract attention.

Having been a Euro MP for five years I was used to working in a modern parliament building which accommodated its women members. One of the first things to strike me at Westminster was the lack of women MPs. I had not been in an overwhelmingly male environment before, either in the European Parliament or in my days as a journalist. It took some time to get used to. There were only twenty-three of us in total, and Virginia Bottomley and I had been sworn in on the same day. Parliament just wasn't geared for women. There was a lack of women's toilets, although when Barbara Castle arrived after the war things had been considerably worse. She succeeded in getting one extra ladies' loo and it became known as 'Barbara's Castle'.

My first stand for women was on the subject of a hairdresser. It was ridiculous that there was a barber but no one to deal with women's hair. When I mentioned it I received a dismissive reply that the barber did women's hair as well. When I went along it was to find a traditional barber's shop, equipped with cut-throat razors and ivory brushes. My hair was washed and then he started drying it by holding a hairdryer to the side of my head. I asked if he would blow-dry it and he looked perplexed. I explained that women's hair was normally styled as it dried by wrapping it around a brush. He looked at me as though I was mad. It took a while but we eventually managed to get a unisex hairdresser on site, which I think was an enormous relief to all of us.

My other gripe was the food in the dining rooms and tea rooms. It was, and to an extent still is, reminiscent of school dinners. Breakfast was particularly difficult if you didn't want a 'full English' or porridge.

I consider it one of my great triumphs that I got grapefruit on to the breakfast menu!

Come the election I was pretty organised and I had found somewhere to live. I was not being arrogant, it was just that in South Wales the challenge was getting nominated. Safe seats aren't called that for nothing and defending a 13,000 Labour majority meant that defeat was unthinkable. Had I failed, I would deservedly have served the rest of my life in the political wilderness.

I think I said as much at my selection interview, made it clear that I didn't just want to defend the majority but increase it. The people of the Cynon Valley had enough stacked against them without an MP who was simply going through the motions.

So on election night, watching my pile of votes mount at Aberdare Town Hall, I managed to stifle my very real excitement with a quiet pledge to myself. My constituents deserved to be well represented; they needed someone to fight their corner and I was a fighter. I was totally exhausted, physically and emotionally, when I got home that night, but how proud to hear Owen call me 'Ann Clwyd MP'.

Settling into Westminster wasn't as difficult as it had been in Europe, but nevertheless I was the new girl. Everyone else was assigned to committees, had their own groups, and – just like joining a new school mid-year – I would have to bide my time.

It isn't done to get to your feet in the House too early; that smacks of precociousness, so I contented myself with listening to debates, lobbying on behalf of my constituents and feeling my way with a few written questions. But I couldn't hide in the shadows for ever and outside the doors of Westminster one of the biggest political battles of the time was raging. The miners' strike, and my constituency, was on the front line.

On 7 June I attracted the Speaker's attention and rose to speak. I followed the convention and paid tribute to my predecessor and painted a picture of the constituency. Then I let rip. I spent a lot of time on that speech, getting the tone just right: indignation on behalf of the miners, controlled anger with the government. It went down well with the party and at home.

People accuse Westminster of existing in its own bubble and to an extent they have a point. While Parliament is sitting I would spend the morning in my office, the afternoon in the Chamber or in Committee and then, in my early days, the evenings in the dining room or tea rooms waiting to vote in late-night divisions. Then, often in the early hours, I would crawl back to the flat to sleep. Having said that, at weekends and in the recesses I was quickly back to reality. My constituents had real problems and my friends had real lives, so I don't think I was ever isolated.

There was a lot more hanging around in the House then, and late-night sittings, even all-night sittings, were quite commonplace. When I was on the Gas Privatisation Bill I remember seeing the sun come up over the Thames one morning. Filled with flu, I thought I must have been an absolute idiot to come to this place. In recent years things have improved and Parliament now has more sensible business-like hours. It has changed the atmosphere of the place though. Now that business ends at 7 p.m. on Tuesdays and Wednesdays people tend to vanish into thin air and I think that there are far more lonely people among out-of-town MPs. There used to be a lot of hanging around between divisions and you would have time to talk with other members, to share views and develop your thinking. You soon got to know who would provide sensible advice, who made good sounding boards and who were a waste of time!

A year or so into the job I found a card from the Whips' Office in my internal mail. I had been assigned to a Private Bill relating to Felixstowe Docks, which held little interest to me or my constituents. As was the custom, there was no discussion; it was a *fait accompli*. Soon afterwards I was also assigned to a committee on the Gas Privatisation Bill and quickly realised that I could not be in two places at the same time. I sensed that I had been set up to fail by the Whips' Office but nevertheless took the issue up with them. 'Run from one to another' was the advice I received from Ray Powell. It was absurd.

From a constituency point of view, the Gas Bill held much more relevance but in parliamentary terms a Private Bill took precedence. A Private Bill was an archaic system whereby a committee acted as executive and judiciary on an application to provide exemption from, or an extension to, the applicant's legal powers for a specific issue. Applicants were usually local authorities, or other public bodies, but the procedure was also open to private companies, such as the Felixstowe Docks & Harbour Board which was seeking to extend its operations; in effect trying to gain planning approval through the back door.

For the committee examining the evidence it was a tortuous process and more than one member described it to me as a 'living death'. Large legal teams were assembled at great cost and, of course, were incentivised to drag proceedings out as long as possible. Given that anyone with an interest in the issue was excluded it was little wonder then that no one in their right mind would want to sit on one.

As I scuttled between the two committees my less-than-stellar attendance at the Felixstowe committee was causing a problem. The Whips' Office was on my case. It was a virtual four-line whip and a refusal to attend, I was quickly informed, could lead to a fine or worse. I dug around and found out that back in the nineteenth century an Irish MP had refused to sit on a Private Bill on the grounds that it did not have anything to do with Ireland. He was imprisoned by the sergeant-at-arms. I don't think the current sergeant would have appreciated having to drag me out of the House, but I was angry at having been setup and frustrated at being held hostage by such an outmoded practice.

One afternoon in a tea room, a colleague introduced me to Dale Campbell-Savours, an intelligent but independent-minded Labour MP for Workington. I unloaded my frustration and he was delighted;

there was nothing he enjoyed more than stirring things up. He was a walking encyclopaedia when it came to parliamentary procedure and, having given my problem some thought, he came up with a brainwave. 'You're sponsored by the Transport and General Workers Union,' he said. 'Claim a conflict of interest.'

Well that did the trick but also sparked a heated debate in the House. Willie Hamilton MP, another maverick, had also advised me to challenge the status quo and now claimed me as his soulmate: 'a rebellious and stubborn character, a lady of my own heart'. All very well for him and Dale to egg me on, but it was me who was facing prison! Anyway, in response to my withdrawal the whips had assigned another poor soul to the committee, Terry Lewis, but he was not allowed to vote on any issue on which evidence had already been presented. After fourteen days of sitting this was farcical and he refused to attend as well.

The Felixstowe Bill, with implications of shady shenanigans given that the applicant was a major donor to Conservative Party funds, eventually ran its course. The issue of attendance at Private Bill Committees did not. This was grist to the mill for Dale and another colleague, Brian Sedgemore, who loved nothing more than campaigning against the status quo. An inquiry into the procedure was ordered in 1987 and when it reported the following year it noted that it was considered unacceptable to try and enforce the attendance of Members. I felt exonerated, even triumphant; I had succeeded where many others, including nineteenth-century Prime Minister, Benjamin Disraeli, had not!

I had enjoyed myself hugely and found political soulmates in Dale and Brian. We had made a good team and now embarked on a lifelong collaboration and friendship. They became my closest colleagues; the people I would go to when I needed to bounce ideas off someone. Brian was the intellectual in the group, a ferociously intelligent man but, as I constantly pointed out to him, not the most collegiate! Dale was the master strategist, loved nothing more than dissecting a problem and coming up with a plan of action which, as I often told him, meant putting me in the front line. My role? They would accuse me of being the idealistic dreamer in the group but I was also the doer; the one that got things done.

Over the years we became a unit, a gang of three. That's not to say we agreed on everything, a key part of the relationship was ferocious political debate. There were many summers when we would drive across Europe to Dale's home in Volterra, Italy, for a holiday, just the three of us. They were a great opportunity to re-charge our political and ideological batteries, gossip and plot. The only downside being Dale's unreasonable insistence on doing the whole trip in one go.

We were friends as well as political colleagues and we would often repair to my family home in Aberdyfi, where we did the same things. Owen would enjoy our debates, which could often become quite heated, and was not averse to stirring things himself! During 'term time', Brian, Dale and I would be in and out of our respective offices and dine together in the Commons' dining rooms, hatching more plots.

Something the three of us had in common was a disinclination to take anything at face value; we always wanted to see things for ourselves. When London had a growing homeless problem in the 1980s the government tried to sweep it under the carpet. Sitting in the dining room one night I suddenly said, 'Come on, get your coats,' and we headed off for the Embankment. For the next fortnight we made many sorties to the underbelly of London: the large station terminuses where runaways arrived; the vents outside tube stations where hot air provided some respite against the cold; and the doorways of major thoroughfares where the dispossessed huddled in rags and newspapers.

We would often be out into the early hours of the morning hearing the heartbreaking stories of those poor souls who had fallen out of step with society. Many had alcohol and drug problems, some of them mental health problems and I would have loved to drag Thatcher, she of the 'No such thing as society', down to see for herself how people existed in the latter years of the twentieth century in one of the world's most affluent cities.

It was hard to maintain a distance in the face of such hopelessness but the three of us were experienced and knew quite well that we could not help them individually but could possibly help then collectively by challenging the way society worked. We could campaign for more shelters, lobby ministries to address the underlying issues, try to make a difference. But on one occasion, even we were moved to take direct action. One evening we came across a young teenage girl on the streets; she was vulnerable and clearly terrified. Terrified, it emerged, of being raped. Initially suspicious and hostile, she did eventually talk to us and we gathered she had run away from home in Brighton. We tried to persuade her to return to her parents. We bought her a rail ticket home and in the meantime put her up overnight and fed her. A few weeks later I tried to follow up using the Brighton address she had given us, but it did not exist. I never knew what became of her.

The three of us also shared an interest in overseas aid. Mine had been aroused at Brussels, Brian had developed his interest as a journalist at Granada Television and Dale had travelled extensively and lived overseas. All three of us also shared well-developed antennae when it came to propaganda. In the lead-up to the Hong Kong handover we were highly sceptical of the simplistic portrayal of China as a backward, barbarian country. It felt overdone and we decided that we wanted to see things on the ground for ourselves.

On arrival at Hong Kong we set off to learn something of the refugee problem which appeared to be overwhelming the colony. In scenes now tragically replayed in the Mediterranean, the Vietnamese had been arriving in large numbers, usually in perilous craft that earned them the nickname Vietnamese boat people. Initial sympathy had started to run out as the numbers became ever greater. By the time we visited, refugees were being held by the Hong Kong police in holding camps. We visited one. It was horrendous, with people held in what amounted to cages – albeit massive ones – set on concrete floors. These rural peasants were now living in an environment that had not a single blade of grass and they were desperate. When we arrived they clamoured for our attention, hoping we had arrived to free them. All we could offer was to bring attention to the conditions they were being kept in when we got back.

Before returning we decided to take a look at China. The governor's office in Hong Kong was horrified. Undeterred we set off on a cata-maran for Macau and joined a regular tour to cross the border into China. We didn't have a visa, hadn't planned a visit, and just wanted to be tourists for a few days.

As we reached the border with China our bus halted. A young of-ficial boarded the bus and, after seeing our passports, demanded that the three of us disembark. Our passports were examined again and Brian's withheld. It was not that long since the Tiananmen Square demonstrations had ended in the mass shooting of protestors. Foreign media were considered hostile and we were thrown out. We returned to Macau for the weekend where we spent our time trying to pick up bargains in the shops selling Chinese carvings.

Once back in the UK we complained to the Chinese ambassador, who was very apologetic and said that if we funded our own air fares he would arrange for us to travel around China to see the country for ourselves. The following recess we took him up on his offer, Dale having negotiated a great deal with Chinese Airlines. On arrival in Beijing our hosts unveiled an itinerary for us; a tour of the major tourist spots including the recently opened Terracotta Army exhibi-tion. Hang on a minute, I told them, what we wanted was to see how ordinary Chinese people lived. We wanted to visit schools, hospitals, housing developments. This threw them into a panic and they went away to consider our proposal.

Meanwhile we introduced ourselves to the British embassy in Beijing. They were not too happy to see us. They warned us that everywhere we went we would be spied on, with hidden cameras and eavesdropping equipment. There were cameras on every street, they said, primed to monitor the comings and goings of foreigners. They added that they could not guarantee our safety if we moved outside the tourist areas.

The Chinese government agreed to our alternative itinerary and, with our minders in tow, we set off. Clearly our hosts were primed to steer us clear of trouble zones but they ensured our safety and, of course, acted as interpreters. Although some of our requests raised eyebrows they accommodated our wishes. One day Brian pointed to the surveillance cameras on the street and asked why there were so many. We were told that they had been installed to monitor traffic during the forthcoming Asian Games. 'OK', I said, 'can we see the control room?' We were taken to this building where an enormous wall was covered in screens, hundreds of them. Each showed a street corner or junction. As we were gazing at these a man walked down the stairs and approached us with hand held out. 'It's nice to have visitors,' he said in a broad Brummie accent. 'We've never had any before.' Apparently, he was out there working for an Overseas Aid project!

In 1995 I was invited to one of my periodic appearances on BBC's *Question Time*. Also taking part would be Dafydd Wigley of Plaid Cymru and Peter Lilley of the Conservatives. I knew Dafydd well and looked forward to debating issues with him. Lilley was a different kettle of fish. An economist, former Financial Secretary to the Treasury and now Secretary of State for Trade and Industry, he was a formidable opponent on economic issues. Dale, who described my knowledge of economics as being roughly on a par with his former budgie, was terrified I would make a complete idiot of myself. It was agreed he and Brian would coach me. For hours they took me through the current economic issues, anticipating Lilley's line of attack and equipping me with a defence. They also gave me the ammunition to counter-attack. By the end I was exhausted but prepared. The show went well and I think Lilley wasn't the only person to be astounded by my grasp of the economic debate!

Dale and Brian continued to be my closest colleagues and we all supported each other. However, a series of serious health diagnoses meant Dale, reluctantly, had to resign from the front bench and then give up his seat. In 2001 he moved to 'the other place' and took his seat in the House of Lords, Brian and I watching from the gallery. We continued to meet regularly for dinner but two years later my relationship with Brian fractured over Iraq. Brian was extremely opposed to the invasion and, following my speech on the eve of the vote, shouted 'murderer' at me across a crowded Members' Dining Room. I was stunned. Other friends who opposed the war accepted my position; we agreed to disagree. Brian could not and he did not speak to me for about six months. Eventually we were reconciled but things were never the same. Sadly, Brian died in 2015 and Dale and I attended the funeral together wrapped up in memories of our 'glory days'.

Dale continued to be a steadfast friend. Other friends note that we bicker incessantly and we do enjoy winding each other up. He takes great delight in pointing out any flaws in my arguments; I figure if they pass the Dale test then I am on safe ground. I wind him up as well, especially about his title – Baron Campbell-Savours – a fine name for a socialist firebrand, and the House of Lords. When something dramatic is happening in the Commons it is never much of a wait before Dale appears in my office in search of intelligence. He is a party animal through and through. He has a sharp sense of humour that not everyone appreciates, and an even sharper mind, but he can be exceptionally kind and has proved a major strength and support when the going has become tough.

CHAPTER SEVEN

CYNON VALLEY

There were two things you needed to be selected as a candidate in South Wales back in the 1980s; the hide of a rhinoceros and, above all, a lot of luck.

My first stroke of luck was a wonderful man called Bill Parfitt who was an active member in the Cynon Valley Labour Party. Bill was also an official with the National Union of Mineworkers and he had supported me in my unsuccessful attempt at securing a nomination for the constituency some ten or so years earlier. The NUM had been long-time supporters not only of me but of increasing the number of women in politics. So when the sitting MP, Ioan Evans, died suddenly in 1984, Bill was on the phone. I called round to see him and he pushed a yellow nomination form across the table. 'I've been waiting for you,' he said.

Bill's gruff and tough exterior hid a heart of gold. He was an 'old school' miner who had worked in the pits for years and was partial to what they called 'underground language'! He didn't suffer fools gladly, told it as it was and commanded a great deal of respect locally. Above all, he cared about people and injustices and was a pragmatist rather than an ideologue. Bill and I had a few run-ins in our time. He would take it upon himself to let me know when he thought I was veering off-course. He never pulled any punches either. Although I always listened to Bill, I did not always take his advice, preferring to plough my own furrow and take the consequences. He sort of respected that. 'Be it on your own head then!' he would warn.

You knew where you were with Bill, which is more than can be said for some of the members of the constituency party. The Cynon Valley party was, and is, fiercely independent. It has a great radical tradition dating back to Keir Hardie. It was a dominant force in the local community and its membership answered to no man or woman. Like many South Wales constituencies, it was riven by factions. There were individuals and groups harbouring deep resentments against each other, sometimes dating back so long they had probably forgotten what it was all about. The wider membership tends not to get involved in the committee meetings, finding it all too boring, so control of the local party is in the hands of a small, inner clique.

There were very few women members and a tradition of deals made over pints in smoke-filled rooms. A few of the active members were modernisers like Bill, but they were very much in the minority. Bill enlisted the help of two dynamic members from the Cwmbach ward, Margaret Evans and Beth Day. They were great women, practical and loyal, and over the years we would become firm friends. Margaret used to come down and stay with us in Aberdyfi in the summer and we would take my old boat out. Labelled an ocean-going yacht in the press, in reality it was little more than an old tub. I later shared a small yacht with friends but by then I was so busy I hardly ever had time to spend on it. Anyway 'the tub' was seaworthy enough for Margaret and me to perform a couple of rescues of holidaymakers in trouble.

Bill asked Margaret and Beth to take me around the ward to introduce me and within an hour I was knocking on doors. Things were not too bad; most people were friendly and polite even though I could tell a few of them wouldn't consider voting for me.

I encountered a great deal of resistance within some factions of the local party. They all wanted their preferred candidate to win and their minds were closed to anyone else. In my case things were made worse because I was a woman, an outsider, and a North Walian. I am not sure which was considered worse. By now I had been through the selection process a few times and learnt not to show any reaction; I certainly was not going to be bullied. So no matter how many times I was given a rough ride I stuck to my guns, smiled sweetly, and carried on. Often Margaret would ask me why I put myself through it. The simple answer was that I had no choice – not if I was ever going to become an MP. Anyway, in a way I enjoyed the cut and thrust!

My second stroke of luck was the other candidates seeking the nomination. One of the largest and most vociferous factions was supporting Julian Evans, the son of the previous incumbent, who wanted to inherit his father's seat. He was nominated by the Hirwaun ward but dropped out of the race early; I do not think he even made the shortlist. His supporters were furious and out to exact revenge on those they felt had betrayed them.

Six of us made the shortlist. Caerwyn Roderick had lost his seat in Brecon and Radnor; he was from Hirwaun, but did not get their support as they had come out for Ioan's son. Alun Williams was the local candidate, a trade union official also from Hirwaun and also not nominated by them! Reg Race was another former MP, NUPE-sponsored, who had lost his seat and was looking to return to Parliament. But, as a Londoner with no connection to Wales, he had no hope in hell. And Brian Davies was on the list at the behest of Labour HQ who were desperate to get a seat for him. He had tried for several unsuccessfully. He was to the right of the party which was never going to play well in the Cynon Valley. He did eventually get a seat and is now in the House of Lords. Gwilym Roberts was the sixth.

The die was cast. On the night of the nomination the six of us made our way to the Community Hall in Trecynon. It was a horrible wet night and the place was freezing but there was a huge turnout of delegates. Each of us made our speeches, outlining what we would bring to the constituency, and sat back down. I sat down with my supporters and tried to calculate which way the vote was going to go. Normally I would have counted on NUM delegates but the strike was on; most of them could not afford their subs so were not eligible to vote. Margaret and Beth were downbeat. They had been virtually ostracised by parts of the party for championing me and were afraid it was all going to be for nothing. One man walked up to Margaret on the way into the meeting and put a huge cross through my picture on the leaflet. 'That's what I think of her,' he said.

The way these things happen is the votes are counted and then whoever comes last drops out, and their votes are reassigned. The first to go was Gwilym Roberts then Caerwyn Roderick and he was followed by Reg Race. That left three of us in the running and I believed Alun Williams was my most dangerous opponent. I never quite understood why he went out next, it must have had something to do with the factional fighting.

Anyway, it was to be my lucky night. The Abercynon ward which had supported Alun switched their votes to me. They did not want me but they wanted Brian Davies even less. Such is the contrariness of politics.

The next few weeks passed in a blur. Cynon Valley was a safe seat but I was determined to show that I could improve on the previous majority. I soon found out that some people in my own constituency party who had supported other candidates for the nomination blamed me for their demise and were in no mood to put it behind them. They made no pretence of their feelings and some of them never did canvass for me in any campaign. So much for solidarity!

The by-election took place in the middle of the miners' strike, which made it easier to canvass because everyone was at home during the day, sitting outside in the spring weather. Whatever hostility was coming from parts of the constituency party it was not replicated by the larger membership of the people on the streets. People were welcoming, keen to talk. I had a track record of campaigning for the steelworkers in Europe and for compensation for mineworkers suffering respiratory diseases. I also had the novelty value of being a woman!

My soon-to-be constituents lived in one of the most deprived areas of Britain. They felt letdown and ignored by successive governments, had little or no interest in the machinations of the local Labour Party, they just wanted someone to go and fight on their behalf. A month later I was sent to Westminster with an increased majority and nearly 60 per cent of the votes cast.

On the home front there was much to do. I had a clear idea of what made a good constituency MP. I wanted to be a modern MP. The party was used to an MP with a wife who looked after the constituency in her husband's absence. In this the Cynon Valley was no different to the other South Wales constituencies.

I believed that people had a right to expect their MP to work on their behalf. It should not come down to knowing someone in the local party who could 'have a word' for you, it should not entail going round to the MP's home, cap in hand, to ask for a favour. And I believed when a constituent needed your attention they needed it then, not in a week's time.

I set up a constituency office in Aberdare and appointed Jean Fitzgerald to run it. Previous MPs had only functioned through the support of their stay-at-home wives; now I had Jean as my constituency assistant. She stayed with me through my whole parliamentary career, through thick and thin, and when we both lost our husbands we got each other through it. We have become friends as well as colleagues and Jean does not hesitate to give as good as she gets. As I recalled at a party to celebrate twenty-five years representing the Cynon Valley, Jean always had a choice of two greetings for me: 'Hello lovely' was one and 'p**s off if you know what is good for you' the other!

Jean is a great front person; her natural empathy though is both her

strength and her weakness. I hate to think of the times she has driven
me mad by wanting to mother everyone, often helping people out by
digging into her own pocket! She is the first point of call for constituents. People call Jean or go and see her and then she will be straight on
the phone to me to work out a plan of action to get the problem sorted.
We were in constant phone contact – to the occasional despair of both
our husbands – but the system worked well. When people contact their
MP it is usually a matter of last resort and this way we were able to re-
spond quickly. Today it hardly sounds revolutionary, most MPs I know
have constituency offices, but back in mid-1980s Cynon Valley, it was
viewed with great suspicion and not everyone approved.

I suspected any innovation I introduced would be greeted with suspicion by some members of the local party, so I adopted a pragmatic
approach – I ignored them. There were some modernisers, like Bill,
but even he and I had a falling-out over surgeries.

As a Euro MP I had not held regular surgeries – given the area
covered by my constituency it simply was not practical. I felt that the
office not only replaced the need for surgeries but was actually a better
system because the constituent got immediate attention. But it was
an issue too far for the local party and Bill backed them. After several
heated conversations I realised I would have to compromise. I agreed
to run regular surgeries but that I would review it as and when the constituency office found its feet. In the end, I kept occasional surgeries
because some people felt more comfortable approaching me that way.
Today things have changed and emails, phone calls and visits to the
office tend to substitute.

There was another subject on which I was not prepared to compromise and which has continued to be a thorny issue throughout my
years as MP – I chose not to live in the constituency. I bought a flat in
Aberdare but my main home was in Cardiff where Owen worked for
the BBC. In my opinion living in Cardiff made not the slightest difference to my efficiency as an MP. Cardiff was only twenty minutes away,

near enough for me to come up for meetings, constituency events and to run surgeries.

❧

The Cynon Valley is a beautiful valley with steeply wooded sides and fast-flowing rivers. The villages have a beauty of their own too, such as the terraced housing of Penrhiwceiber clinging to the valley sides in total symmetry. It has a proud history. For a start it was a cradle of socialism as the parliamentary seat of Britain's first Labour MP, Keir Hardie, although the only thing that marked it was one back street which was named, and incorrectly spelt, Heol Kier Hardie. When the Labour Party celebrated its centenary in 2006 the Cynon Valley Constituency Labour Party members raised £5,000 to commission a bronze replica of his bust at Westminster for Aberdare. Knowing how well regarded he was in India, where he had caused a sensation campaigning for independence, I contacted the Indian High Commission and they offered to provide granite from Mumbai for the plinth, leaving Aberdare with a lasting tribute to its most famous MP.

I also started the annual Keir Hardie memorial lecture which has drawn in many illustrious socialists since its inception in 1985. In 2016 the speaker was Labour leader Jeremy Corbyn, and more than 1,000 people packed into the Leisure Centre in Aberdare to hear him talk about workers' rights, proving that political debate is alive and kicking in the valleys.

In the nineteenth century Aberdare was one of the most influential centres for literary and musical culture in Wales. Its publishing output, in English and Welsh, was prodigious and there were choirs and brass bands in every village. How many other towns have a statue dedicated to a choir leader? Aberdare erected one to its favourite son, Caradog, who, as well as being a talented violinist with the Aberdare Philharmonic, became the leader of the town's highly successful choir. In 1872 he was invited to lead the South Wales Choral Union, made up of choirs from across the valleys, to compete in the Crystal Palace Challenge Cup – sweeping the board and doing the same the following year.

But as the coal industry declined in the latter twentieth century, so too did the formerly vibrant Cynon Valley. When I became MP in 1984, one in five people of working age were out of work, creating widespread poverty. Physically the valley was scarred by the legacy of heavy industry and coal mines, abandoned when they had ceased to be of value to their owners and with little or no consideration for the people living below the coal tips. Over half the houses had been built before the First World War and the number without baths was three times the national average. There was a larger than usual percentage of owner-occupied housing and people took great pride in their homes, many were like palaces inside. But they did not have the money, and the grants that would have brought their homes up to a standard considered a minimum requirement elsewhere in Britain had been cut.

That was the problem back in Thatcherite Britain; there were no votes for the Conservatives in industrial areas like South Wales, so they were largely ignored. Since most English MPs could not pronounce Cynon (cun-non) when they referred to my constituency, it sounded like 'sign-on' valley, earning a sharp reproof from me.

It was incomprehensible that the area lost its special development status, but I nevertheless used my past experience and contacts to identify every possible piece of available European funding. Local authorities, health boards, the police – every area of the public sector suffered from the Conservatives' public spending axe despite desperately needing investment. Ill-fated schemes such as the Valleys Initiative were ineffectual.

The most devastating condemnation of social policy in the '80s was the death rate in the valley, the largest contributor being respiratory disease. It was nearly 25 per cent higher than the rest of the country. The heartbreaking experience of watching a former miner panting for breath, clinging to his oxygen mask, became the norm at so many houses I visited. The compensation system was tortuous and inefficient and created additional burdens for those who suffered, such as having to travel an hour or more to an assessment centre. I campaigned for the establishment of an assessment centre in Mountain Ash Hospital and at least it made life a little easier for them.

Crime follows poverty like a dog with a bone and the Cynon Valley was no exception. As unemployment and deprivation grew, so inevitably did crime, in particular drug-related crime. It was hard to watch former tightly knit communities break down under the pressure and yet all those involved, the council, police and community groups, worked hard to try and halt the onslaught. Once Labour came into power in 1997 it became easier to get support. Several initiatives were launched as part of the Crime Reduction Programme and Home Secretary David Blunkett came to see the work being done in the Cynon Valley and speak about tackling crime. Yet there is no magic answer and the drugs problem, particularly among young people, continued to be an issue.

A case that illustrated the consequences began innocuously enough. I was sitting in my office in Westminster, waiting to go into the Chamber for a debate, when Jean called. She had received a letter from an elderly lady called Edna Phillips. Her home on the Penywaun estate had been burgled and she felt the police were not taking her seriously. Such letters had become quite common in the decade I had been an MP. Crime had doubled in the Cynon Valley and the police said they just did not have the resources to deal with it. The issue was that the Home Office classified the Valley as a 'rural area', although it suffered the same problems as inner cities in terms of deprivation, bad housing and high unemployment. I contacted the police's divisional commander, asking him to look into it, and I was able to report back to Mrs Phillips that an officer would visit her to discuss her complaint.

Six weeks after I received the original letter a shocked call came from Jean. The local news was reporting a brutal murder in Penywaun;

locals thought the victim was Edna Phillips. Mrs Phillips had been savagely attacked by two teenage girls, one her next-door neighbour. High on a cocktail of drink and drugs, they had throttled her with a dog chain and stabbed her eighty-six times. The news shocked the whole country and the local community was devastated. As details became clearer it emerged that Mrs Phillips had been tormented by her neighbours for years because she had complained about their loud music and drunkenness. It seemed that everyone had known about her problem but she had been too proud to ask for help.

Although it was too late for Mrs Phillips I called for an emergency debate in Parliament on the way vulnerable, elderly people were not protected in society. Although Mrs Phillips' case was uniquely horrific, there are many, many more elderly people trapped in their homes, their lives made a misery by the anti-social behaviour of neighbours. Frequently other members of the community are aware of the problem. People are reluctant to report incidents to the authorities and when they do quite often nothing is done. Something that is causing massive personal stress to them is seen as a minor misdemeanour.

We have to get better at dealing with these issues as a society and the first step, in my opinion, is to increase the number of community police officers. What is seen as a statistic at a remote police station becomes a real person to the 'bobby on the beat' and therefore there is a greater chance of intervention before things get out of hand. I have consistently fought for increased police resources in the Cynon Valley and continue to do so.

My relationship with the police during my time as MP has been mixed. I have come across many dedicated officers who work hard to improve the lives of the people in the community and I have worked alongside the police and other agencies on many initiatives that have benefitted the people of the Cynon Valley. I have a good working relationship with the present Chief Constable, Peter Vaughan.

However, I have also had cause to complain about the heavy-handed way in which the police have sometimes behaved in the past. I do think things have improved enormously over the past thirty years and would like to think that some of the behaviour we saw on the picket lines during the miners' strike would not be tolerated by today's police force. The miners' strike left many scars, few deeper than a communal loss of trust in the police. Time and again I have constituents coming to me with complaints about heavy-handedness and insensitivity and I have to say that I have been able to understand their feelings better since my own brush with the law.

In 1997 I was stopped by a police car for what the police claimed was a failure to stop at a red light in Cardiff. When the police approached my car they did so as if I was a major criminal. It was quite frightening. I am actually a cautious driver and knew perfectly well that I had not jumped the light, but they were not having any of it and prosecuted me. I had to resort to my own detective work and put together a dossier of photographs which proved that the police couldn't even have seen the light from where they had parked. The magistrates dismissed the case instantly stating that, to put it kindly, the police had made a mistake. There was no further case for me to answer, but it is behaviour like this which causes people to lose trust.

Dealing with the police on behalf of constituents is only one type of issue that an MP faces regularly. We should have had a hotline to the local benefits office, so frequently did we contact them to clear up some issue or other. The housing department at the local council was not far behind. I was lucky in that my friend Margaret was Chairman of the Housing Committee in my early years as an MP and we worked well together. One young couple came to me because they had sunk all their savings into buying a home only to find out that, after buying it, it was not fit for habitation and condemned by the council. Margaret always had a knack of seeing the big picture and appreciated both the human cost to the family, but also the practical problem of removing one house in a row of terraced houses. A housing grant was found and the family were delighted. They did the house up beautifully and, over twenty years later, both Margaret and my office still receive Christmas cards from them.

Cutting through bureaucracy is a key service. Individuals struggle to get through the red tape to get something done, but a call to the relevant department from an MP usually has a very different result. Often it is just common sense. There was a well-known rugby star living locally, Dale McIntosh, originally from New Zealand. He contacted me because his grandfather had died and he could not fly out to for the funeral because he had surrendered his New Zealand passport six months earlier when applying for British citizenship. Dale was a Maori and he was desperate to get home for the week-long traditional funeral. He had been trying, with increasing desperation, for days to resolve the matter, even travelling up to London in person, and by now four days of the week-long funeral had passed. As his MP I was able to call the department and get common sense to prevail. He flew out, sadly too late for the Maori ceremonial passing of his grandfather's spirit, but he arrived just in time for the actual burial.

Such stories are legion for all MPs but not all of them have happy endings. Often when someone approaches their MP they are already at their wits' end, desperate for help.

On one memorable occasion a man came to see me. His eyes filled with tears as he relayed the fact that his wife had left him for another man. I pointed out that there was not much I could do about it and he became quite angry. I had to ask him to leave in the end – just as well I never pursued a career as a social worker! He harboured a grudge against me ever after, sending accusatory letters. I never did understand what he actually thought I could do.

I have been MP for this proud valley for over thirty years and I like to think that, on the whole, things have improved. There is still far too much poverty but it is undoubtedly a better place to live. The provision of education has improved enormously. People have far more access to education than they have ever had. Employment remains our greatest challenge but at least the jobs we do have are not killing people. The rail link down to Cardiff has been restored, giving people access to more employment opportunities. With time it is hoped the redevelopment of the Phurnacite site will also generate a considerable number of local jobs.

The Cynon Valley has also benefitted from European funding which has provided roads and infrastructure as well as a great deal of environmental cleaning-up. In fact, the greatest change I have seen is probably environmental; our rivers are clean again and the slag heaps have disappeared. I recently travelled up with a GP friend from London, granted the sun was shining, but she said it felt as though she was in Switzerland! How green is my valley now?

The people in the valley remain its greatest asset; warm, optimistic and friendly, they are also hardworking – given a chance – tell it as it is, and have a great sense of humour. As a North Walian I am always amused by the variety of nicknames: one well-known party member in Aberdare is called 'Dai Flat Cap'.

Whenever I felt dragged down by the constant battle to get resources or the internecine machinations of the General Committee of my local party, it was the ordinary people, the salt of the earth, my constituents, who kept me going.

I had only been in Parliament a little more than six months when the selection process for the next general election began. Labour had a policy of mandatory re-selection which meant that if anyone else gained a nomination you had to go through the whole process again, unless you could get an overwhelming majority on the first vote. Because one man in my constituency had been nominated by one delegate, I had to go through it all again.

I was in despair. I had only just got my feet under the table and there was so much to do, but now I would have to put the time into canvassing in the constituency all over again. It had been a close call last time and I was far from confident of being re-selected. Despite crashing out last time, Reg Race was having another stab at the seat and Alun Williams had not given up on his ambitions. The people who had supported me previously once again stood up to be counted. I think many of those who had not now felt embarrassed, and felt the whole situation brought the local party into a bad light. I worked hard to canvass the delegates, pointing out the work I had been doing on the constituency's behalf, and in the end it passed smoothly enough.

A few years later things were not as straightforward, and when it came to the selection meeting night at Blaengwawr School I remember Margaret and Beth suggesting we sit near the door, so we could beat a hasty getaway if things went pear-shaped. This time it was a Cardiff solicitor, Chris Short, who triggered the process. The main complaint was that my interest in human rights and role on the Foreign Affairs Committee meant I was not working for the constituency's interest. It was a nonsensical accusation, one does not preclude the other, but it is one that everyone who sits on the Overseas Aid or International Development Committees is routinely accused of.

In the end I managed to secure the nominations I needed to avoid a second ballot and the matter was put to bed. But there was a strange postscript. Chris Short, who had triggered the re-selection, wrote to me to apologise, shortly before being jailed for stealing from his clients' accounts.

The final re-selection drama was partly of my own making. Towards the end of the 2010–2015 coalition government I had been feeling pretty low and lacking in energy. I had been through a traumatic time with Owen's death, followed by a severe bout of pneumonia, a recurring illness which went back to my childhood. It left me feeling totally drained, so when the selection cycle kicked in I decided that it was time to step down and announced that I would do so at the general election. With hindsight it was a rash announcement; ideally I should have waited until I was recovered before making such a momentous decision, but the selection timetable was such that I had no choice.

What happened afterwards became a farce. Labour HQ specified that the constituency should have an all-woman shortlist. At that point the local party threw its toys out of the pram and the constituency secretary announced that the local party was going on strike and would have nothing to do with the selection.

Of course, in the months this had been brewing up I had made a full recovery and was feeling reinvigorated. I had lots of things I still wanted to do, not least my work on the NHS, so I reconsidered and constituency friends persuaded me to stand for another term. The process had yet to kick off, so it seemed like a perfect solution that would get everyone off the hook.

Normally what happens in the case of re-selection of a sitting MP is that there is a trigger ballot and if over half the membership wants you to stay that is the end of it. However, the party's National Executive would not accept that I was a sitting MP because I had announced my retirement. It caused a furore within the party and I received widespread support from other MPs. Still, the NEC would not budge. I think two women had applied for the nomination so friends advised me to formally apply to cover myself and in the meantime Jean and other supporters began the work of canvassing party members. Through their hard work I soon had over 107 members signed up. It was undoubtedly the wisest course of action – I was so angry by then I had even given a passing thought to standing as an independent candidate; S. O. Davies had done so in Merthyr when he was deselected and he won! Fortunately, it did not come to that and on 7 May 2015 I was re-elected MP for the Cynon Valley. It was the first time that Owen had not been at my side.

CHAPTER EIGHT

COAL

I was trapped thousands of feet underground, cold and hungry and very, very tired. But each time I curled up into a ball on the hard, dusty floor of the coal mine to try and get some sleep representatives of British Coal would spot me through the fire doors and wake me up. It was illegal to sleep underground, they said. It was not illegal to eat and drink but they refused us that as well. 'Thank God for Jean,' I thought, not for the first time in my political life! My long-standing constituency secretary had once worked at Tower Colliery and, practical as ever, she had stuffed my pockets with Mars bars before I set off on my protest. I don't even like Mars bars but they soon became the proverbial manna from heaven. I was determined to hold out and force British Coal into negotiation, but there was a limit to how long I could physically manage. How ironic was that? Years championing the case of miners whose health had been wrecked working underground and now I was counting the hours underground. I think it was only anger that kept me going, anger at British Coal's stance and anger at the decades of injustices suffered by miners at this and other pits.

Tower Colliery was the last deep mine in the Cynon Valley and, despite its rich seams, had been earmarked for closure by British Coal.

As the local MP I felt it my responsibility to do all I could for the people who worked there and the community which depended on it. As the debate raged, the local NUM lodge suggested that, as a final effort, I might want to go underground to meet the men and stage a 'sit-in'. We travelled light on the journey; there would be food and blankets waiting for us at the bottom and it was important to move quickly before British Coal got wind of our plans. But we didn't move quickly enough; they were able to cut us off before we could reach the other miners, which was why I was now on my second day underground with no food, no warmth and no sleep.

The Tower Colliery sit-in took place in 1994, but, even when I was elected MP for the Cynon Valley in 1984, it didn't take a prophet to work out that issues concerning the coal industry would play a large part in my professional life. I arrived at Westminster during one of the bitterest industrial disputes the UK had ever seen and my maiden speech highlighted not only the suffering of the striking miners and . their families but the ongoing suffering of those whose health had been ruined pulling coal out of the ground. But my association with the mining communities went back much further. My grandfather's family had first-hand knowledge of the difficult working conditions and exploitation endemic in the slate quarries of North Wales, where working conditions were treacherous and industrial diseases such as silicosis widespread.

Working as a young BBC broadcast journalist in Cardiff, I had been one of the first reporters on the scene of the Aberfan disaster in October 1966, one of the greatest examples of corporate negligence that's ever been seen in this country. Back in those days it was common practice to dump mining debris on huge tips; I had grown up having picnics on the lead mining tips on Halkyn Mountain in Flintshire. The South Wales valleys were dotted with much larger coal tips, and they too were part of the landscape, children regularly playing on and around them. In Aberfan, though, there were concerns about the size of the tips right above the village and school but the National Coal Board had largely ignored fears raised by the local authority.

On the morning of 21 October 1966, everything changed. When I arrived I wasn't actually sure what had happened. I heard that there had been an accident as I was driving towards Cardiff, so I turned around and headed to Aberfan. I could see that part of the tip had fallen away and there was a big crowd of people walking around. It turned out later that we were walking on the disaster scene. It took ages to comprehend that underneath all of that was a primary school. The atmosphere was both electric and sombre; men worked in silence trying to get beneath the rubble. I remember the feeling of shock as the scale of what was happening became clear but I had a job to do, to report what was happening. At first I worked on my own, putting together an early report, and then reinforcements arrived from Cardiff and we worked as a team.

The children's parents had, of course, been first on the scene, frantically trying to move earth with bare hands. Then the police arrived, and soon miners from Merthyr Vale Colliery. As news spread hundreds of miners, health workers and ordinary people arrived to try and help. It was total mayhem. I remember the noise of the heavy diggers brought on to the site to try and help move the debris, and also the eerie silence when they stopped to enable the rescuers to listen for any noise. After a while everyone realised that no one else was coming out alive. I stayed for hours, rooted to the spot at times, hoping against hope for some good news, my instinct being to bear witness, to tell the world about this unimaginable tragedy to hit a small mining community.

Over the next few days it would become a media feeding frenzy and there was plenty of criticism of intrusive reporting by some of the national newspapers. But, on that first day, I can only recall reporters like me standing with tears in their eyes, as we realised there was not going to be good news, as the exercise moved from a rescue to the recovery of the bodies of 116 primary school children and five teachers. I was only involved on that first day but over the ensuing weeks, months and years I followed closely the inquests, inquiries and protracted compensation battles which highlighted the 'callous indifference' (that's how the official Tribunal Report described it) of the National Coal Board.

In the summer of 1973 I met John Emlyn Evans; he was sixty-five years old but looked nearer eighty. His wife told me she was often mistaken for his daughter. John suffered from pneumoconiosis, a respiratory disease also known as Miners' Lung. His eyes were drawn back into his skull, his shoulders curved and his skin had the colour and feel of a taut and empty sausage skin. Once he'd had a 44-inch chest, blond hair and, said his wife, 'sang like a nightingale'. The day I met him he sat in his armchair at his Bridgend home with a bottle of oxygen at his side. He hadn't been able to sing for years. Talking was an effort and his wife had to do most of it. She told me that they hadn't shared a bed for years, he rarely slept more than three hours a night, the rest of the time he was coughing and spitting, and it was too disruptive. But she didn't sleep well anyway, if she couldn't hear him coughing and wheezing she would creep out of bed to check he was still alive.

John now qualified for a 100 per cent disability benefit but when pneumoconiosis had been first diagnosed, almost twenty years previously, it had only qualified him for 10 per cent benefit. He had carried on working underground to support his family, a decision that had undoubtedly contributed to his current position. At the time the Industrial Injuries Council was recommending downgrading pneumoconiosis as a disease, threatening benefits to anyone less than 50 per cent disabled. Meanwhile miners with breathing problems not caused by pneumoconiosis, such as chronic bronchitis and emphysema, received no benefit as these conditions were not classed as industrial diseases. Seeing first-hand the suffering of John and his many counterparts across South Wales brought home to me the human price the men paid for hauling coal out of the ground. I wrote a substantial feature on the subject for *The Guardian*, which attracted the attention of the NUM who reprinted it as part of their campaign. For me, it was the beginning of a long relationship with the union.

The first time I went underground was in 1974, again writing a piece for *The Guardian*. I can still remember how nervous I was, having to crawl to the coal face, wriggling through tight, constrained spaces. My photographer had enough and flatly refused to wriggle any further until I said 'I'm going anyway!' When the piece appeared dozens of readers wrote in, the gist being that the then Prime Minister Ted Heath and his Tory friends ought to go underground too and see the conditions for themselves.

When I fought the 1984 by-election for Cynon Valley we were still campaigning for a broadening of the category to include emphysema and chronic bronchitis incurred while working in dusty industries. The rate of respiratory disease in the Cynon Valley was some 25 per cent higher than England and Wales as a whole and it was a heartbreaking experience to see a miner gasping for breath, even while using an oxygen mask, yet not getting a penny in compensation. It was not just wrong, it was cruel and unjust. Despite years of campaigning on this issue I was unprepared for the scale of suffering I encountered when canvassing; it seemed that at every other house there was either a former miner with an oxygen tank or a bereaved widow.

What angered me then, and angers me now, is that vulnerable people are forced to fight the system. Surely 'the system' is there to support those who need it, it should not resond only to those who shout the loudest or begrudge every penny spent. Common sense and common decency should make campaigning unnecessary.

Coal was the lifeblood of the Cynon Valley. Like most of south

Wales its communities had grown up to service the mining of precious anthracite coal that had powered an empire and its industries. And not just mining, but the engineering workshops, craftsmen and hundreds of shops, pubs and small businesses that indirectly depended on the miner's pay packet. At the industry's peak, in the 1920s, over 20,000 men had worked in the Cynon Valley mines; at places such as Tower, Ynysybwl and Penrhiwceiber, as well as others in neighbouring valleys. By the time I became the Labour Party candidate for the constituency in 1984 the writing was on the wall.

The Cynon Valley by-election took place in the middle of what would become the final miners' strike. Prime Minister Margaret Thatcher was determined to break the trade union movement in general and the powerful NUM in particular. If the cost was a criminal waste of natural resources, the end of a way of life for communities across the British coalfields, and – with little or no planning – the dumping of thousands of men on to the scrap heap, well so be it.

From the 1960s onwards, successive Conservative governments massacred the coal industry for predominantly ideological reasons. Churchill set the tone in November 1910 when he sent in troops to break up the riots in Tonypandy with the command to 'drive the rats back down their holes'. It was an aggressive and provocative act which ensured he was viewed with ill-feeling in South Wales for the rest of his life. The miners epitomised class struggle in Britain, from the General Strike in 1926 to the defeat of the Heath government in 1974, and the governing party in 1984 was in no mood to forgive and forget.

On St David's Day, 1 March 1984, it was announced that twenty coal mines would close with the loss of 20,000 jobs. South Wales was the only producer of anthracite in a Britain which was short of this premium coal by a million tonnes a year. Yet, the NCB planned to close the anthracite mines. The Margam steelworks at Port Talbot is situated next to the largest untapped reserve of prime coking coal in western Europe. Yet coking coal pits were scheduled for closure and investment in a new mine at Margam refused in favour of the import of a million tonnes a year of foreign coking coal into Port Talbot alone. The government should have been investing in coal not closing mines.

It is easy with hindsight to say that many people recognised this as a fight to the death. NUM leader Arthur Scargill's abrasive and combative style might not have been to everyone's taste, and it certainly did not help smooth a path to conciliation with the Coal Board's equally confrontational Ian MacGregor, with whom I had had previous dealings concerning the steel industry. Scargill believed the twenty closures were only the tip of the iceberg, claiming they were part of a bigger plan to close over seventy pits. This statement was vehemently denied at the time by Ian MacGregor, but Cabinet papers released in 2014 eventually revealed that MacGregor actually wanted to close seventy-five.

Scargill visited the Cynon Valley several times during the strike and was greeted as a hero. I walked alongside him on a march and shared a platform with him and South Wales leader Emlyn Williams at a packed rally in Aberdare. He was a good old-fashioned rabble rouser, somewhat egotistical but, then again, most fighters are. However, even had the NUM been led by Mother Teresa herself, the Coal Board and Thatcher were going to kill it off. MacGregor had been hired to do a job and I think many of his lieutenants were uncomfortable with his position. Certainly in Wales, Phil Weekes, who had risen through the ranks to the top job, was perceived as having 'gone native' in his empathy for ordinary miners. Relations with his boss were rumoured to be icy.

It was a long and bitter strike that saw the miners, their families and their communities suffer. History is never far away in Wales and the mining community was only too aware of the fact their predecessors were starved back to work in 1926. Time and time again my constituents told me that they would not let it happen again. The striking families were supported by friends and relatives, they cashed in insurance policies, raised second mortgages on their homes, sold their cars and determined to fight on but they were struggling. The hardship on the faces of the children was particularly hard to see.

I was so angry that the Tories had no idea how people were being affected that I brought Robert Key, MP for Salisbury and previously PPS to Ted Heath, to Aberdare to see what was happening. He was horrified; he told me that people 'looked different'. Of course they did, they were pale and drawn and dispirited. I remember him saying the Conservative Party was never about bringing suffering and despair like this to people but I'm not sure all his colleagues would have empathised. Over time, the Tory party has tried to lose its image as the 'nasty party', but old habits die hard and thirty-two years later another Conservative government was unapologetic in making drastic cuts to disability payments.

A hallmark of the 1984–85 strike was the role of women. If the government and the largely hostile media had expected the miners' wives to urge their men back to work they were mistaken. Women's committees were very much part of the struggle whether it was fundraising, food distribution or standing shoulder to shoulder on the picket line. Ann Scargill epitomised this new-found voice by staging an underground sit-in with her women's group. It is ironic that, as with Greenham Common, women were on the front line of opposition to Britain's first female Prime Minister.

The women in my constituency decided that if everyone could have one hot meal a day the men couldn't be starved back to work and established no fewer than thirteen strike-feeding committees. They established support groups where they could meet regularly to share their experiences, have a bit of a cry but also a lot of laughs, read out letters of support and the poems that many wrote. Out of the hardship came a great deal of creativity and also a realisation of what they were capable of. Many women from the area credit the empowerment that came in the 1984–85 strike to their later achievements.

As the strike wore on, I think many outside the trade union movement became embarrassed at how the miners were being treated; food parcels came in from all parts of the country. Traditional supporters within the Labour movement did their bit and constituency parties in non-mining areas 'twinned' with mining constituencies to support them. The results weren't always what we expected. The Cynon Valley CLP was twinned with the Islington CLP, and a group of them, led by their backbench MP Jeremy Corbyn, moved into Aberdare for the day and provided the struggling community with a much-needed fillip involving clowns, fire eaters, Turkish kebabs and all-day entertainment. It is an event still remembered with affection.

As a newly elected MP it was an exhilarating and busy time. I was in London most of the week, but was also involved in meetings that organised soup kitchens and the distribution of food and clothes, as well as joining the picket lines. The sense of community was strong. Only one miner went to work in the Cynon Valley, a man called Paul Watson from outside the valley, who was driven to the Phurnacite smokeless fuel plant in Abercwmboi every day by his wife. Every time the car went past huge numbers would come out shouting 'scab', leading to an equally large police presence.

Throughout the strike there were allegations about police intimidation, a matter I raised several times in Parliament after witnessing it first-hand in my constituency. I saw women pinned to the wall, men herded into groups and frogmarched backwards through the street to humiliate them. Just being in the vicinity of a picket line was dangerous. I was threatened with arrest simply for standing on a pavement with local councillor Margaret Evans. Nearby, a man was pulled off a wall by the police and dragged along the floor, causing facial injuries. His wife, who went to help him, was kicked in the stomach. The intimidation was not only physical, it was often psychological. I witnessed them baiting the protestors, waving the wodges of money they were earning while the strikers were starving. This was Britain in the 1980s and the behaviour of the police then drove a wedge between themselves and the communities they were policing, a breakdown in trust which would have implications for decades to come.

The same happened in other mining communities up and down the country and I believe Home Secretary Amber Rudd's 2016 decision to reject an independent inquiry into events at Orgreave was wrong. She told MPs that there were no deaths and no miscarriage of justice, but there is plenty of evidence that the police on the picket lines, to put it kindly, 'mislaid the rule book' in their attempt to break the miners' strike. The opinion among my MP friends is that she has failed to put right a wrong, shared by former mining communities across the UK. The police have not been held to account for their actions. At Orgreave, nearly a hundred men were left without jobs and faced serious charges of riot until their trial collapsed after the police evidence was found to be unreliable.

After a year with no wages, March 1985 saw a delegate conference of the NUM vote to abandon the strike and call for an organised return to work. Throughout South Wales, indeed throughout all the mining areas, miners marched back to work behind their brass bands with heads high and banners aloft. It was a sign of defiance. I walked alongside the Tower miners who were cheered as heroes all the way along the emotionally charged route up the Cynon Valley to Hirwaun. When we reached the pithead there were hundreds of people. It was like something out of a film set. Recalling the scene later I wondered what happened to all those extravagantly embroidered banners; they were living history and I felt they ought to be collected together for posterity.

In South Wales the NUM tried to get those sacked during the strike reinstated, but the Coal Board held the upper hand and was in no mood to be conciliatory. As far as the Thatcher government – who memorably described the miners as 'the enemy within' – and the Coal Board were concerned, this was only the beginning of the end. A widespread programme of pit closures followed and within a decade the British coal industry was privatised.

When Margaret Thatcher came to power in 1979, some 27,000 men worked in the South Wales coalfield. By the end of the miners' strike in 1985 it had been halved. By March 2005, the now privatised coal industry employed fewer than 7,000 people, only 4,000 of them at the eight remaining collieries.

I have no doubt whatsoever that the South Wales mining industry was deliberately punished in the aftermath of the strike by starving it of any investment. We were told that the coalfield would not receive any capital investment until its losses were wiped out. However, it was a 'catch-22' situation because without investment it was condemned to outdated units, inferior machinery and an undermanned workforce. It was ideological nonsense.

In its heyday there were thirty-nine pits in the Cynon Valley employing around 27,000 men; by the time I became MP in 1984 the number had fallen to three and eventually only Tower Colliery remained – the last deep pit in South Wales.

From 1992 onwards we fought to save Tower. Debates, rallies, delegations, petitions – you name it, we did it. Should the mine close there was little prospect of other jobs; unemployment in the Cynon Valley was running at 30 per cent and would rise to nearly 40 per cent if Tower closed. Two years later, just before Easter, I marched with the miners to the Department of Trade and Industry in London with another petition and we called on Michael Heseltine to come and face us. Not normally publicity-shy, he hid inside while his civil servants gave us the thumbs up at the windows. Days later, lodge officials were told the pit was earmarked for closure. I could not believe it had actually happened. Tower had been profitable to the tune of £28 million over the past three years and only months earlier John Redwood, the Secretary of State for Wales, had congratulated the miners for improved productivity. British Coal, as the privatised organisation was now called, claimed geological problems and, when that was refuted, market forces.

I was in constant touch with the local NUM lodge. Late one night I was in the House of Commons when my phone rang. It was Lodge Secretary Tyrone O'Sullivan, asking whether I was prepared to stage an underground 'sit-in'. Very early the next morning, Thursday 14 April, I drove down to Aberdare not knowing whether or not the protest would take place, but when I arrived I was told it was action time. Retired miner Glyn Roberts would accompany me underground. Our aim was to force the issue into the national media.

On the mountain top, in the dark above Hirwaun, I put on my safety kit and, as dawn broke, I pretended to pose for a photograph. As soon as the man on duty turned his back, Glyn and I disappeared into the pit, passing two bemused miners before plunging into the darkness below the Rhigos Mountain. It was like being sucked into a wind tunnel at high speed and, struggling to keep my balance, I slithered and stumbled to the bottom. Half an hour later we saw lights; the manager had sent pit deputies to intercept us and tell us we were trespassing. We tried to move on but were physically restrained, the air doors held fast against us. We were trapped in the cold section of the pit, unable to meet up with the other miners. Glyn and I sat on a trunk containing first-aid equipment and a blanket which the deputies later snatched from us. They were particularly unpleasant, taking it in shifts to make it as uncomfortable as possible for us, refusing us food, drink or blankets and ensuring we got no sleep. We dubbed them 'the guards'. The hours ticked by. To try and get warm we curled up on the floor near the vents, but they were blowing dust around. It cannot have been good for our lungs. It was a hard, long night.

In the meantime, the Labour Party had issued a pre-arranged press release on my behalf. I said I intended to remain underground until Neil Clarke, the Chairman of British Coal, put the colliery into the modified review procedure and, while the review was taking place, honoured its obligation to the miners. I was fed up with Clarke who had, within the space of a week, said the pit was closing the next day, would go into review procedure, and that it would remain open with the miners taking a wage cut. I felt he was playing a game with people's lives and needed to understand he had a fight on his hands.

The next morning we were able to speak to Tyrone on the pit phone and he told us to come up. The lodge had voted against closure by twice the majority of the previous week and British Coal said it would 'lift the axe'. Two hours later Glyn and I got into the cage and flew up to the surface. We were out, slightly disorientated, and facing the press. It was at this stage that I realised I was wearing the manager's safety helmet as we faced the cameras for what would become an iconic photograph. Everyone was clamouring for a comment, but I was guarded, I kept thinking that it had been too easy. In response to the question: 'Have you won?' I replied, 'I'll wait and see!'

Sure enough, the following Monday British Coal reneged on Friday's promise. It produced a list of every man in the pit, with a draconian pay cut, half their salary, noted next to their names. The men were told that alternatively they could take a redundancy package with a deadline of 6 p.m. the following day. Just before I walked into Employment Questions in the House of Commons, I was told the men had voted for closure. I was devastated. The dishonest manoeuvrings of the government and British Coal had killed the last pit in South Wales. Tyron said that when he signed the papers on behalf of the NUM he felt emotionally drained. He said he felt a similar level of despair as when, as an eighteen-year-old, he had heard the news of his father's death in an underground roof fall at Tower.

But that was not to be the last chapter in the Tower story, the men were not done yet. Within ten days of the pit closing they had put together an audacious bid to buy the pit as a workers' co-operative. Over 200 men contributed £8,000 each to own a share of the mine. When it reopened they were also able to take on trainees and contractors.

When the news broke, Michael Heseltine sent one of his ministers to the tea room of the House of Commons to give me a message: I was asked to tell the miners to 'throw in the towel'. I told him to tell them himself. To his credit, John Redwood pledged his support to the buy-out and the rest, as they say, became history. It continued as one of the largest employers in the Cynon Valley for a further fourteen years. Having mined the northern coal seams, the colliery officially closed in January 2008. Planning permission was then won for open-cast mining on the surface workings and Tower still continues to play an important role in the community.

The Tower miners took a brave and important stand. They showed that British Coal's assertion that the pit was being closed because it was uneconomic was patently untrue. They showed that they and their colleagues were hardworking responsible men, whose motivation was the dignity of work for themselves and the next generation. When the seams were finally exhausted, the whole community celebrated with one last march behind the famous banner. The men invited me to cut a red ribbon to mark the occasion and there were so many people present I had to use a loudhailer to make myself heard. I had marched with them at the end of the strike, I marched with them when Tower reopened, and I was proud to be on that last march too. For me, their attitude was summed up by their concern about what happened to the site in the future; they wanted to leave a legacy, jobs and houses.

I always think of Tower as an inspirational story, so perhaps I was less surprised than most when it was turned into an opera by the eminent Welsh composer Alun Hoddinott, featuring one of Tyrone's memorable sayings: 'We were ordinary men; we wanted jobs so we bought a pit.' I was at the opening night in Swansea, a roaring success – luckily my part was played by a professional singer – I am tone deaf! The production moved on to tour Wales funded by the Arts Council of Wales. The company was approached to stage the production in London, as well as a European Tour, but funding was not forthcoming.

Tower also opened a visitor centre, telling the story of coal in the valley and the fight to preserve the colliery. The original ambitious project was scaled down and eventually forced to close. It was a great shame on a number of levels, not least because it had been earmarked as a suitable home for a project I felt passionate about.

My memories of the beautiful union banners held aloft on the march back to Tower remained with me and I determined to do something about it. When I was made shadow Heritage Secretary in 1992 I seized my chance and launched a campaign.

There were, literally, thousands of banners all over the country. Some stored in museums, others in cupboards, garages and even garden sheds. Some were tenderly cared for, others sadly neglected. In the past, no march or rally would have taken place without them. They were part of the history of the Labour movement but also works of art. One of the most beautiful ones was that of the Penarth coal trimmers, which had been painted by the Cardiff artist W. E. Britton. As news of my intended campaign began to circulate in the trade union movement, offers of help came in. The Iron and Steel Trades Confederation lent me their 1920 silk and watercolour banner, used in the General Strike, as a backdrop for the campaign launch.

Labour Leader John Smith thought it an excellent idea and agreed to join the embryonic Trades Union Banner Board which also included Jack Jones, former General Secretary of the Transport and General Workers' Union, and a number of prominent trade union leaders. We appealed for news of surviving banners to enable us to catalogue them and their location and also to help with conservation and restoration. The letters poured in from trade unionists from all over Britain, supporting the concept and also furnishing us with details and photographs of local banners.

I felt that what was really needed was a home where the banners could be restored and exhibited and where better than the Cynon Valley! At the time Cynon Valley Borough Council, as it then was,

was pursuing plans to create a major museum development in Aberdare and the Chief Executive, Tony Roberts, was keen to include the banners. He commissioned a report from Coopers & Lybrand to investigate costing and funding.

John Prescott formally launched the idea of a National Centre for the Preservation of Trade Union Banners in the Cynon Valley at the Labour Party Conference in 1995. A detailed study was commissioned from the National Museum of Labour History, grants applied for and a potential home identified. The former stables at Aberaman Colliery met most of our criteria and we began negotiation with British Coal, supported by Elfed Morgan, leader of the local council.

Then we were approached by the Tower Colliery Trust, which was working with the National Trust to establish a visitor centre, and the Trade Union Banner Board agreed that it would be the ideal home for our centre. It was not to be, however. The Tower Visitor Centre didn't materialise in the way it was envisaged, as local authority reorganisation merged Cynon Valley into Rhondda Cynon Taff and I moved on from the National Heritage brief. I think everyone involved was still supportive but there was no one left to drive the project.

Another major employer in the Cynon Valley, but a far less inspiring tale than Tower, was the Phurnacite plant at Abercwmboi. I think most MPs have issues that cause them to tear their hair out in frustration and for me this was definitely one of them. When I arrived as MP in 1984, the Phurnacite plant had the dubious distinction of being the biggest industrial polluter in Britain and was therefore one of the main issues in my postbag. Now, over thirty years later I am still fighting to bring an end to this sad chapter in the Cynon Valley's industrial history. Progress drags on, tortuous and snail-like. I do not give up on issues and do not get worn down. I am certainly not going to let go of this until we lay all the ghosts to rest. Perhaps its redevelopment will be my personal legacy to the constituency.

The plant in Abercwmboi near Aberdare dates back to 1942 and produced smokeless fuel in the form of briquettes for over fifty years. It had seven chimneys belching out different-coloured smoke and was located cheek by jowl with the houses of Abercwmboi and Cwmbach. The women used to tell me they couldn't hang washing out to dry because it just turned black with soot. Even growth of nearby trees was stunted. The people working there used to tell of horrific working practices that made it seem as though little had improved since the Victorians. They were often made to work up to their waists in sludge which, after the plant was closed, we learnt contained cadmium, and other toxic chemicals. But mostly it was the emissions. I was outraged that people in the Cynon Valley were suffering pollution on that scale, if it had been in England it would have been shut down years ago.

The issue was complex. The plant provided 800 jobs in an area with chronic unemployment. They were dirty and dangerous jobs, men standing waist high in sludge, inhaling toxic fumes, but they were jobs and they were well-paid jobs. Anywhere else, a community would have rebelled against it. In the Cynon Valley it seemed there was no choice. The local economy was so dependent on the plant. There was no other work and it was not just the families of its workers who were dependent but local pubs, shops and even the local collieries which provided coal to the plant. When the Phurnacite plant had made considerable profits in the 1960s and early 70s there had been an opportunity to modernise the plant by switching to a different product. That would have reduced pollution by 90 per cent and enabled it to compete with foreign producers. But no, the Coal Board syphoned the profits off elsewhere and by the 1980s the outmoded plant was in financial trouble.

Emerging environmental and medical research was indicating that there was a high cost to pay for such polluting industries and incidences of cancer and respiratory diseases appeared to be considerably higher in Abercwmboi than elsewhere. I managed to get a consultant in communicable diseases, Dr Arun Mukherjee, to investigate the claims, but he could not find any evidence. Undeterred, it became exactly the sort of issue that made my blood boil. If this was not exploitation, what was? Taking it on wasn't popular though, I think about half my local Labour Party were employed there. I chose to campaign through environmental groups and managed to get Friends of the Earth involved, but attempts to clean up its act were too little, too late, and in 1990 it was closed down by the Factory Inspectorate, leaving a derelict site on which sat around 100,000 tonnes of highly toxic material.

The dumps contained a poisonous mix of mercury, asbestos, phenols, ammonia, hydrocarbons and gas mixed up with tar. In summer, it bubbled out of the ground. We all thought that the owners, British Coal, would take care of the site until it was reclaimed but my constituents showed me skulls of animals and carcasses of birds, hedgehogs, even sheep, that were stuck in the soft, sticky tar. There were no warning signs or fences to keep children and animals away. Children being children, they frequently played on the site, subsequently falling ill with sores, ulcers and blisters. I was not overly surprised that British Coal did not behave better, but I was outraged they were allowed to get away with it. Was there not a principle that the polluter must pay?

It was poignant that the people who had suffered when the plant was operational were now suffering from the toxic waste on their doorstep. A local action committee was set up and I started lobbying the Welsh Office, repeatedly raising questions in the House of Commons. Again the 'system' was working against the people it was designed to protect. I was horrified to discover there was not even a register of contaminated land in the constituency, and the pressure group had to demand an environmental impact assessment, something that should have taken place as a matter of course.

Then the Welsh Development Agency and Coal Products Limited came up with a plan. They intended to encapsulate the waste and bury it underground. They said they did not need to take it away. We were sceptical. I asked to see a similar project elsewhere. They had to admit there wasn't one, it was all very experimental. I asked about the lifespan of encapsulated waste, it was something very short, about twenty years. It was no long-term solution and the community deserved better. It took fifteen years but eventually, in 2005, more than a decade after the plant's closure, a £12.4 million clean-up operation finally took place, one of the biggest reclamation schemes seen in Wales.

The full scale of damage caused by the profiteering operation of British Coal can't only be measured in environmental terms. Its real tragedy was the effect on the people who worked in it and lived next to it. Needless to say the fight for compensation for those whose health was damaged was long, drawn-out and bitterly contested. Workers in coking plants did not fall within the parameters of the British Coal Respiratory Disease Litigation, so claims had to be pursued as personal injury claims under common law.

It was a long fight but finally in 2012, at the seventh attempt, British Coal was finally called to account. Four ex-workers won significant compensation in a test case, brought by the unions, at the High Court in London. A judge ruled that the plant had left the men with lung cancer and respiratory disease after British Coal had failed to provide necessary protection. That gave hope to the other ex-workers who had lodged complaints, although the judge had ruled that not all cancers could be included as they were a disease of the general population.

The wheels of justice grind exceedingly slowly. It was July 2015 before the High Court gave leave for a group action by the remaining petitioners. Sadly, some of the claimants are unlikely to live long enough to see a penny of their compensation.

With the land eventually cleared there was a mood for optimism. The local authority, Rhondda Cynon Taff, earmarked the site for development of a school, housing, retail and recreational facilities in its local development plan. Large parcels of flat land on the valley floor are rare and it seemed an exciting opportunity give the whole valley a boost and create welcome employment opportunities. But, as ever, it became a long drawn-out saga that is still ongoing.

Initially, the land itself was subject to dispute between Coal Products Limited and the Welsh Development Agency, subsequently the Welsh Assembly government. I had numerous meetings with both parties, each time leaving with promises of action. It's now nearly five years since I went to see Wales First Minister, Carwyn Jones, pointing out the major contribution this would make to local employment. He told me to leave it with him; he would have it sorted out by the end of the year. That was five years ago. Councillor Andrew Morgan, the leader of RCT, and I are forever on the case with ministers at Cardiff Bay and Coal Products, but although each time it seems as though the finishing line is in sight, nothing actually happens. To call it frustrating is a massive understatement and local residents are understandably angry with the delay. It is such an important scheme that I find the procrastination unforgiveable.

Unfortunately, frustration is often the order of the day for an MP and something I have had to learn to live with. But I never give up. A major part of my role has been to champion people's claims for compensation – they probably run into thousands – by chasing the relevant government department, local authority or corporation.

Bureaucracy can be exhausting and nothing annoys me more than thinking something has been accomplished only for institutional inertia to kick in. When Labour came to power in 1997, we finally won compensation for those miners who had had their health ruined by working conditions underground. The problem was that the process was taking forever and the men were becoming weaker. By 2002, the number of medical assessments was dropping off and the DTI was falling behind target. By now, though, I had a strong ally.

As vice-chair of the parliamentary Labour Party I had weekly meetings with Tony Blair and I would take the opportunity to put my concerns to him. I would go in with the latest numbers, updating him on the shortfall and demanding action. I was pushing at an open door because he was also MP for a mining constituency and I think he quite liked using me as an excuse to move things along. We both shared a fear that miners would die before they received what was owed to them and he wrote to the DTI, stressing the need to speed up the process and prioritise the oldest claimants and those that were most disabled. Funnily enough things then started happening. As they say, it's not what you know, but who you know!

CHAPTER NINE

LIFE ON THE BACKBENCHES

'I've got a message for your Chief Whip,' began a message on my constituency answerphone. 'Just let him come to Aberdare to try and deselect you and he'll be tarred and feathered and thrown in the river.'

When I rebelled against the party whip, only months into government, I knew what was in store, but I also believed that I had acted in the best interests of my constituents. I had enormous support in the Cynon Valley and there were plenty of other messages in the same vein, although not quite as colourful.

It had not been an easy decision. After eighteen years in opposition the Labour Party was finally able to concentrate on delivering a fairer, more compassionate society. We wouldn't have won the 1997 election, let alone the landslide, without party discipline. And yet within months I found myself voting against my own government.

It was very painful. We had only been in government a short time and here I was walking through a different lobby to the party leadership. As the new Secretary of State for Social Security, Harriet Harman had introduced a benefit cut that disproportionately penalised lone parents. It was sheer madness. My postbag was flooded with furious letters from constituents. They had voted Labour into power and now Labour was turning against them.

As soon I saw the proposals I was horrified and alarm bells rang. Other colleagues felt the same and we tried hard to reverse the policy. I was an elected official on the parliamentary Labour Party Executive and would meet the Prime Minister weekly to discuss what bothered our MPs. All six of us on the PLP executive, without exception, argued and pleaded for a rethink. We explained that a major revolt was very likely. We believed the Prime Minister was listening.

Harriet was clearly between a rock and a hard place. The Treasury was heaping on the pressure to cut budgets and the party was keen to demonstrate that the hand-out culture of the past was over and that, from now on, the focus lay on getting people off benefits and into work.

All very well, but in the Cynon Valley there were about 1,500 single parents and only 200 jobs available. What were they supposed to do?

I pointed out that this situation was mirrored in countless Labour constituencies and that it would be very difficult, if not impossible, for those of us to vote with the government. We asked for the benefit cuts to be postponed until the whole package of reforms was up and running, but the party leadership calculated that they could avoid an open revolt.

It was hard to stomach hearing a former Tory Prime Minister describe Labour policy as 'inhumane', but John Major was right. It was also hard to stomach the fact it was women, Harriet and her Women's Minister Joan Ruddock, who were leading a campaign whose main victims were other women. When Joan addressed a Labour Conference in Cardiff, she was jeered and booed.

The situation left a sour taste among women MPs, who felt compromised between their desire to protect vulnerable single parents and a natural inclination to support their party. A number of MPs, particularly the new intake, were pressurised into voting with the government and told me afterwards that they bitterly regretted voting against their conscience.

In the event, the party leadership miscalculated. Even though it had enough of a majority to win the vote, forty-seven Labour MPs voted against the government and a further hundred abstained. A minister and two private parliamentary secretaries resigned and Alice Mahon was sacked from her post as a ministerial aide.

Up until the last minute I had intended to abstain but the recycling of the shabby arguments about inheriting these cuts from the Tories – as though we had an obligation to carry out their dirty work – and the behaviour of the whips in closing down the debate prematurely made me see red. I believed we had been elected to improve the neglected welfare state, not give it another kicking. We had more money to play with than any government for years; we could afford the Millennium Dome, so why should the children most at risk of poverty be singled out. Some colleagues were actually crying. One said to me, 'I can't believe we've been put in this position – a new Labour government and they're asking us to do this.'

Once again I found myself in a group of rebels, hauled before the whips to explain my actions. But how could the party explain to the Cynon Valley, a Labour stronghold, that it intended to penalise the poorest people in society? People could not believe that their Labour government was actually doing this.

The day after the vote I was on the Penywaun estate, one of the most deprived housing estates in South Wales. I was there to launch a book of stories written by single mothers, *Dreams and Nightmares* by the Penywaun Young Mothers' Writing Workshop. Hayley, a 23-year-old single mother, typified the issue for me. She had a four-year-old son and lived on £81 a week. After electricity, coal, food and other necessities there was often nothing left and she had to borrow money from her parents. If she did have anything left over she would save it towards Christmas presents for her son, not wanting him to miss out any more than he had to. Already struggling to cope, she was faced with an even greater battle to survive. She had a job in a local shop until that closed. She told me she would like another one, but there simply was no work. The future for her and her son was bleak.

So there I was, less than a year into a Labour government and I had collected another black mark against my name. Any opportunity of ministerial advancement was now well and truly down the drain. Yet in many ways that didn't bother me. I was not alone; I believe only one of the forty-seven rebels were ever promoted again by Tony Blair or Gordon Brown. Others appreciated our stand though and each of us was sent a badge with '*47 Real Labour MPs*' stamped on it. I still have mine.

Some MPs are content to remain on the backbenches enjoying the relative freedom to speak out on issues close to their heart. I, like many others, wanted to be in the thick of the action and began to climb the greasy pole. I served on the opposition front bench for six years but by the time we were in government I was no longer there. Michael Stewart, government minister under Harold Wilson and latterly Baron Stewart of Fulham, stopped me in the corridor one day and said, 'It's an absolute disgrace that you haven't been made a shadow minister,' but that's the way it was. There is a lot to be said in favour of being a backbench MP. I enjoy the freedom it gives to speak on issues that interest me.

British politics has been enriched through the work of some excellent backbenchers over the years. People like Leo Abse, Gwyneth Dunwoody, Paul Flynn, Chris Mullin, Dale Campbell-Savours and John McDonnell. These are the people who were unafraid of speaking out in support of controversial positions; who were prepared to take on vested interests; who enriched the debate through their passion and persistence. In my early days in Parliament there were many more free-thinkers who could follow causes, pursue issues with a great deal of vigour and, on occasion, great wit. Today's intake is more career-oriented. They want rapid promotion and do not really enjoy the freedom and the experience that the backbenches offer.

Being a backbencher is not the living death that many imagine. For most of us it is an opportunity to get involved in causes we believe in, whether raising issues in the Chamber or shaping legislation through committee work. And our democracy would be much the poorer without these contributions because with the party leadership focused on their manifesto policies who else is going to take up the cudgels for people like 'J'?

'J' lived in the Cynon Valley. She was an attractive woman in her forties but like so many women she was not satisfied with the way she looked and as she got older had found herself losing her self-confidence. She wrote to me in desperation because after spending her savings on silicone breast enhancements the procedure had been botched and she had to have a double mastectomy. She was shattered and, as she saw it, her life was in ruins. But she was determined that the clinic would not do the same to other vulnerable women and asked me to intervene.

I was sympathetic so I said I would look into it. What I found out horrified me. Cosmetic surgery on the NHS was generally very safe and well regulated. The private industry on the other hand was growing ex-ponentially with little or no regulation. Any unscrupulous cowboy could open a clinic and as long as the patient's consent was given, anyone could operate regardless of whether they were qualified to do so.

One of the weapons available to the backbench MP is what is known as a Ten Minute Rule Bill where you make your case for a new bill on a subject in a speech lasting no more than ten minutes. They rarely get anywhere but they are a useful way to draw attention to an issue and attempt to pressurise the government into taking action. I introduced such a bill on the regulation of the cosmetic surgery industry in 1994 and it generated a great deal of media attention. Coverage in the *Daily Mail* and on the BBC's consumer programme *Watchdog* opened the

floodgates and my postbag was inundated with stories of real suffering. I was invited to campaign with consumer organisations such as
Which? and became aware of the sheer numbers of people, mostly
women, who had suffered botched cosmetic surgery.

My initial concern was with silicone implants. So many women
contacted me suspecting that the silicone had somehow leaked into
their bodies, making them ill. We set up a pressure group called SOS
– Survivors of Silicone – and I took various deputations to the Department of Health to try to persuade it to investigate. But our pleas fell
on deaf ears. I also brought a group of affected women to the House
of Commons to meet women MPs and speak about their experiences.
At the time we had a female Secretary of State for Health, Virginia
Bottomley, and I was keen for her to meet the women. I could not
believe it when she refused, giving no adequate explanation. I felt that
was a total disgrace.

One of the issues was that people did not even know how many
silicone implants had been carried out in this country. There was no
register or follow-up. I continued to lobby on the issue and when a
Labour government came into power in 1997 I was hopeful we could
make more headway. I had several meetings with a group of concerned doctors at the Department of Health and tossed ideas around.
The omens were good. An independent review body was ordered and,
following its recommendations, the department established a national
breast implant register. It was an important step forward.

Then in 2010 I received a massive shock. It had emerged that PIP, a
French supplier of silicone implants, had been using cheap, industrial-
grade silicone. As a consequence, women all over Europe had suffered
leaking and exploding breasts. As I watched the story unfold on the
news, I thought that at least in the UK we had the register and we
would be able to identify the women at risk. Not a bit of it. I found out
that the Labour government had discontinued the register, claiming

it was too expensive to maintain. A register, for goodness' sake! I was absolutely furious and made my views known in no uncertain terms.

Silicone was only the tip of the iceberg. The other aspect of cosmetic surgery which concerned me was laser eye surgery, offered almost exclusively by the private sector. I realised there were few if any regulations for the training of doctors who work in private clinics, and any doctor, regardless of experience, could offer treatment.

Eye surgeons in Harley Street and at Moorfields Eye Hospital contacted me to express their concern that there was nothing to prevent someone from setting up a business without a medical background. Although thousands of laser treatments on eyes were successful, a small but significant number resulted in permanent damage to eyesight and in one case a poor woman was left unable to shut her eyes. It was then left to the NHS to try and correct the botched surgery, putting the victims through several additional operations and at great cost to the public purse.

The lack of regulation was horrifying and the medical establishment felt impotent. Sir Norman Browse, a former President of the Royal College of Surgeons, agreed to give a joint press conference with me at the House of Commons. It is not often that the President of a Royal College emerges to give such a conference with a politician, but it reflected his concern that anyone could set up shop as a cosmetic surgeon. Unless they specifically claimed to be a doctor or surgeon, they were not even committing an offence. 'Animals,' he said, 'are better protected than humans.' Doctors could not operate on animals without a veterinary surgery qualification but a vet could perform cosmetic surgery on a member of the public quite legally.

A big problem was the over-exaggerated claims by the myriad advertisements in women's magazines. Advertising Standards Authority guidelines prohibited unrealistic claims or the use of misleading images, but browse through any of today's women's magazines and

you will see advertisements for treatments which tell you that the procedures are simple and risk- and pain-free.

A woman called Joyce contacted me and drew attention to a promotional leaflet she had been provided by a private clinic describing
liposculpture as a straightforward, minor operation. She went ahead
to have fat removed from her knees, thighs and hips and was awake
through most of the two-hour operation. The pain, she said, was
intense. She was discharged dressed in blood-stained bandages and
received none of the promised follow-up appointments. Today her legs
remain disfigured.

One of the more distressing letters was from a woman who had
received liposculpture in a Harley Street office. Her operation was
carried out under general anaesthetic by a GP with no attending
anaesthetist. It later emerged that the GP had no cosmetic surgery
qualification. She came round in agony while the operation was still in
progress, but the doctor insisted he had to carry on otherwise her legs
would be uneven. She said she screamed throughout.

Afterwards I kept up the pressure on the Department of Health
through written questions and the media, but they kept insisting the
numbers of complaints were low. It is hardly surprising since many
of the women were too embarrassed to complain. Some had not even
told their partners and one woman told me she had made up a story
about being in a car crash to prevent her family finding out what had
happened. Apart from the physical trauma many of these women also
suffer severe depression. One told me that she felt her life had been
shattered and that she had been left feeling suicidal.

In a debate in Westminster Hall in 2000, I took the unusual step
of using parliamentary privilege to name a man I considered a
cowboy practitioner. David Herbert was known as the 'flying doctor'
for the speed with which he carried out surgery. He performed about
thirty-five procedures a week spending, on average, forty minutes on
a face lift.

The BBC's *Watchdog* programme had, over the years, exposed some of the numerous complaints against him. Allegedly, one woman nearly died after a bowel infection following a tummy tuck; another was left with a gaping hole in her stomach. Several women had to have corrective surgery after David Herbert performed breast surgery on them and the list of allegations went on and on. I had raised the allegations with the General Medical Council and in the House of Commons but Herbert was still practising. With every other avenue closed I decided to 'name' him, I saw no other option. Herbert was finally struck off the medical register.

As I write I am still campaigning for better safeguards in this area. In 2012 I introduced another Ten Minute Rule Bill, supported by the Royal College of Surgeons, seeking to further tighten regulation in the cosmetic surgery industry. However, it is a very lucrative industry with highly paid lobbyists and much work remains to be done to tighten up loopholes. In 2015 I raised the issue again, against a background which had seen the number of private cosmetic surgery procedures rise to over 45,000 a year. 'Boob jobs' increased by over 300 per cent between 2002 and 2011. Men as well as women are now resorting to surgery in an effort to achieve some idealistic shape. Too old, too thin, too fat – never 'just right' appears to be the mantra. Unbelievably, there have even been two-for-one offers for general surgery.

The Royal College of Surgeons and the British Association of Aesthetic Plastic Surgeons have both criticised the government for failing to introduce greater regulation. The RCS has also called for the General Medical Council to be given powers to tell the public which surgeons are qualified to undertake plastic surgery.

Parliament continues to debate the issue and proposals to tighten regulations are being considered. In August 2016, Health Secretary Jeremy Hunt launched a consultation on measures which would 'name and shame' cosmetic surgery clinics that failed to provide good quality care. The proposals included online ratings for clinics that provide cosmetic procedures. However, the ratings will only apply to clinics and not to individual clinicians. I will continue to plug away at it and I expect I will still be trying until the day I finally leave the House.

Tenacity is a must for a backbencher. You can often feel as though you are getting nowhere, but for some of us that just spurs us on. Some issues, like the regulation of the cosmetic industry, continue for decades and after a while you find yourself inextricably associated with them. You get to know the people involved and feel a commitment to them.

That is what happened in the case of some young men in my constituency who, back in the 1990s, came to tell me about their experiences at the Bryn Estyn children's home in North Wales. I can see their faces now as they each came to my constituency office in Aberdare and told me such horrific stories of their childhood. They were considered to be 'naughty boys' or out of control and were taken from their families at a young age and placed in this so called 'care' home, hundreds of miles away. They were little more than children really. The abuse there was rife and they described it graphically. Some had tried to run away at one time or another, only to be taken back by the police. No one would listen to them, that was the cruellest thing. They were left feeling betrayed and defenceless. By the time they talked to me they were grown men, some of them fathers, but still their hands shook as they held their mugs of tea.

There were others from my constituency involved but were unable to speak about it, they were still too traumatised. The men that came to see me were still suffering. One of them later committed suicide. They all found it difficult to speak out. At first the words came haltingly, then more quickly until it all spewed out. They were angry, they trusted no one and did not know where to turn for help. They identified the police as the people who kept returning them to that hell. I was aware I had an enormous responsibility to them.

What they wanted did not appear to be much. After numerous complaints leading to suppressed investigations and inquiries, they finally wanted someone to get to the truth and a public acknowledgement of what had happened. They wanted the perpetrators. I asked them what compensation would be appropriate? But as one of them said to me, 'I don't want money, all I want is for someone to say sorry.' In a word, justice. By the end of that first meeting I felt worn out, wrung dry by the emotion of it all.

The whole sordid story of what became known as the North Wales child abuse scandal came to light in the 1980s through the courageous stand taken by whistle-blower Alison Taylor, a residential care worker. She said she had been disturbed by the incidents of abuse children in her home had described to her. She had reported them to her superiors, then the local authority and then the police. On each occasion no action was taken and she was sacked.

Alison did not give up. She went to the media and finally a series of investigations finally took place. What became known as the Cartrefle report was carried out in 1990 but was hampered by a lack of co-operation from the social services and not published on the advice of the council's insurers. Alison continued to build a dossier of allegations and submitted it to North Wales Police. After a lengthy investigation some 300 cases were referred to the Director of Public Prosecutions, but only seven people were prosecuted and convicted.

The court cases opened a Pandora's box. There were mounting accusations of a much wider network of abuse which had been covered up and allegations of collusion by members of the police. A new Director of Social Services at Clwyd County Council found evidence that previous allegations had either not been investigated properly or ignored and the council commissioned its own inquiry headed by John Jillings.

The inquiry was hampered from the outset. For a start the panel was refused access to police files and over 100 boxes of documents were withheld. A number of us smelt a rat when the council, on the advice of its insurers, would not allow the inquiry to place notices in the media seeking information. Like other concerned councillors and MPs, I placed my own notice in the local press and six young men contacted me. I took detailed witness statements from the four who felt able to talk in detail about their experiences, each harrowing interview taking a long time and leaving me emotionally drained. If I felt like that how on earth could they have been feeling?

All those young men had been damaged by their experiences. Their future relationships were affected, some got into trouble with the law. Of the many young men who gave evidence to Jillings, to the police, or subsequent inquiries, a shocking number later committed suicide, self-harmed or died in mysterious circumstances. Society failed and continues to fail these men.

The Jillings report was completed but not published, on the advice of the council's insurers and legal teams. Zurich Insurance, parent company to the insurers of the council and also North Wales Police, advised that the report might encourage people to seek legal redress. It warned that, if the council published the report, it would jeopardise its public indemnity cover, leaving individual members liable.

Malcolm King, chair of the social services committee, was furious and threatened to make his views public only to be personally vilified by the insurers who wrote to the Chief Executive: 'Draconian as it may seem, you may have to consider with the elected members whether they wish to remove him from office if he insists on having the freedom to speak.' The concept of democracy, of an elected member exercising his right to free speech, was clearly alien to them.

On the advice of the insurers only twelve official copies of the report were made and they were subsequently shredded, causing public uproar. I managed to get a look at a copy of the report and was stunned at the findings which pointed to rape, bestiality, violent assaults and what amounted to torture of these young people.

Such was the public backlash that the Welsh Secretary, William Hague, sought to establish a public inquiry into the investigations. I knew that an inquiry would make the whole issue sub judice, stifling any public debate for years, so I tried to get the allegations on record. In 1996 I tabled four Early Day Motions. To do that I had to block parliamentary business two nights running by keeping the debate running late into the night. At least it got some of the findings of the Jillings report into the public domain, but I got into considerable trouble with my party's whips. After my first attempt I was called in to see Donald Dewar, the Chief Whip, a dour and austere Scot. He went straight on the offensive, with no attempt to find out what my objection was at all, and told me I was making myself unpopular. Rather pompously, I replied that I had not entered Parliament to win a popularity contest. Had he been prepared to listen I could have explained that this was the only way I could get what had happened in North Wales on the record. I temporarily succeeded in blocking the order for two nights but eventually it was approved without a vote. It was rushed through.

The Waterhouse inquiry was, at the time, the biggest inquiry ever held into allegations of abuse in the British childcare system. More than 200 witnesses were called and the experience of reliving their abuse proved so traumatic that half of them subsequently had to receive psychiatric counselling. The final report named twenty-eight alleged perpetrators, but their names were redacted. I was furious and raised numerous questions in Parliament to no avail.

Then, in 2012, a copy of the Jillings report re-emerged. Everyone had thought that all the copies had been pulped but amazingly one had escaped the net. I immediately demanded that it should be published. The BBC sought to access it under the Freedom of Information Act. After a year of wrangling it was finally released but in a highly redacted form. The conclusions were hair-raising. Jillings reported that the panel had found abuse on a significant scale. 'The scale of what happened and how it was allowed was a disgrace and a stain on the history of child care in this country,' he said. The report severely criticised the North Wales Police.

I do not think we have yet drawn a line under what happened at Bryn Estyn and other homes in North Wales. The issue has now been going on for so long; there have been investigations and media exposés and yet many of the perpetrators still have not been punished. I feel outraged at the continuing injustice and suffering on the part of the victims.

One of the main issues that concerned me, and which I continue to pursue, is the role of the insurers and the vulnerability of local authorities. The insurers' representatives at the Waterhouse inquiry did accept that they may have gone too far and that at times their correspondence was 'intemperate'. Among the many recommendations of the Waterhouse report were those calling on the Law Commission to investigate the conflict of interest between the insurers and insured, and the need to focus on the local authority's vulnerability to defamation action. In 2004 the Law Commission concluded that the law of defamation should be amended to protect local authorities. As long as inquiries were conducted fairly and not motivated by malice, any reports should be privileged. Additionally, it was recommended that new powers be introduced to allow local authorities to set up statutory inquiries with the power to compel witnesses to attend and produce documents. All of which made sense. All of which were overdue. None of which have been delivered.

One of the good things to come out of Waterhouse was the appointment by the Welsh Assembly government of a Children's Commissioner for Wales and many people have contacted the commissioner to speak of abuse they received at Bryn Estyn and other care homes. Having spoken with survivors of abuse, I know that one of the worst things for them was not having anyone to listen to them. The abuses may be termed as 'historical abuses', but for those who suffered, the issues are very much alive and we need to support them.

A key issue in North Wales continues to be whether there was a paedophile ring at work. It makes me feel physically sick that people who have been known to the authorities for a considerable time have not been made to answer for their actions and may, of course, still be preying on innocent victims. I continue to fight for transparency, for the publishing of reports and for continued investigation because that is the right thing to do. But for me it is also personal; these atrocities were committed in and around Wrexham and Chester, the areas where I grew up.

It is many, many years since I left the area but I still have a profound attachment to it. I think that link with a childhood home is the same for most people, certainly those who have a happy childhood. You can never underestimate the effect childhood experiences have on the rest of your life. Another legacy of my childhood that I have pursued in political life is that of animal welfare. For me, there is something special about the bond between humans and animals. I certainly feel we have a responsibility to ensure they are not mistreated which is why, over the years, I have been active in animal welfare.

For example I have always been against blood sports, and was delighted to be able to vote for Michael Foster's bill outlawing hunting with dogs. I listened to the arguments of the Countryside Alliance and others but, for me, there is no place for such a barbaric practice in today's world any more than there is for cockfighting, badger baiting and so on. I just fail to understand how people get enjoyment from watching an animal suffer.

In this case reasonable argument won the day, but back on home turf I was incensed to hear about a gang of youngsters who cornered a fox cub outside a supermarket and killed it by battering its head against the wall and then stamping on it. Such behaviour can only be described as sick and disturbed and defies comprehension. Having found out who the ringleader was, I prepared to go round to his house and give him a piece of my mind. I had faced down some unpleasant people in the Middle East and was not about to be intimidated by some local yob. Luckily Jean managed to stop me as I am not sure I could have been responsible for my actions and I can envisage a headline along the lines of 'Vigilante MP' across the local newspaper. Rather wisely in retrospect, I let the police deal with it and the gang was successfully prosecuted.

On the backbenches I have been lucky enough to pursue my interest in animal welfare. I have regularly spoken out on the use of animals in experiments and supported Jim Fitzpatrick's motion to ban the use of wild animals in circuses.

After reading a report by the Farm Animal Welfare Council, calling for the phasing out of battery cages for hens, I decided to go and visit what I can only describe as a 'hen factory'. It was hellish. I cannot begin to describe the horrifying noise, smell and sense of claustrophobia that comes with so many birds packed into tiny confined spaces. These poor creatures were unable to stretch their wings, to peck or scratch or even make nests in which to lay their eggs. I raised the issue in Parliament several times, especially when the EU appeared to be backtracking on its commitment to prohibit the practice, and supported Eric Martlew's Early Day Motion to hold the EU to its original timetable.

In 2000 I was lucky in again winning a place in the Private Members' ballot. When this happens the floodgates open as every pressure group and lobbyist in the country tries to get you to adopt their cause. As the mail begins to arrive by the sackful you do start to wonder what you have gotten yourself into. There are some members who are so overwhelmed that they pass on the opportunity to present a Bill, but it really is too good an opportunity to miss. At worst you can use it to get publicity for your chosen cause, at best you get the government onside and your Bill can become law.

My staff and I sifted through hundreds if not thousands of requests and, having narrowed down the field to a manageable size, I chose to champion the extension of laws against female genital mutilation. I had sat on the Select Committee on International Development when it reported on women and development and had been horrified to hear what sort of abuse was taking place under the umbrella of female circumcision. I was shocked at the extent to which it was prevalent in elements of British society. Some of the evidence we took was unbearably poignant. Young and adolescent girls, often against their wishes, were held down and cut by unqualified women in unsanitary conditions.

It was particularly prevalent among some communities of African extraction, such as the Somalis in Cardiff. We heard there was a proliferation of illegal 'cutting parties', where very young girls were dressed up in party clothes and taken to someone's home with friends of the same age. Only when they got there would they be ushered in to a back room, one by one, and forcibly held down and mutilated.

Depending on the specific tradition of the community, the ritual would involve partial or total removal or other injury to the external female genitalia. The rationale varied from purification to family honour; aesthetic reasons to the protection of virginity; the enhancement of fertility; or to decrease sexual desire. Although it was practised by some Christian, Jewish and Muslim groups it is not a religious practice and leaders of all the main faiths had spoken out against it.

Nevertheless, our desire to curb the practice was seen as typical liberal Western interference in other people's cultures. Germaine Greer had supported the practice in her recently published book *The Whole Woman*. Her argument was taken apart by Liberal MP Dr Jenny Tonge in the International Development Select Committee, leading us to conclude that Germaine Greer's arguments were simplistic and offensive. 'They take no account of the purposes neither of female genital mutilation, nor of the lack of choice for those young girls on whom it is inflicted. Equating the forcible clitoridectomy of an eight-year-old girl with the voluntary body-piercing of an American teenager is absurd.'

Apart from the complications arising from the unsanitary conditions in which the procedure usually takes place, there are long-term consequences associated with pregnancy and childbirth. Women who have been mutilated in this way have a 30 per cent greater risk of having to undergo a caesarean section, a 70 per cent greater risk of haemorrhage shortly after childbirth and up to 55 per cent increased risk of stillbirth or early neonatal death.

The reason I chose to take up the cudgels was that although the practice had been illegal in Britain since 1985 there had been not a single prosecution. Additionally, the law only prohibited the practice in the UK. This allowed women to take their daughters overseas on a 'holiday' where the procedure would be carried out. My bill sought to widen the scope of the original Act to cover a wider range of acts of mutilation, but also to make it illegal for such a procedure to be performed outside the UK to any UK national. It would also increase the maximum penalty from five to fourteen years' imprisonment.

The problem with Private Members' Bills is that without government support they can wither on the vine. I was lucky that the then Home Secretary, David Blunkett, was very supportive. He took me to one side one day and said that he was supporting my stand and had instructed his department to help me in any way they could. I also got a lot of help from Amnesty who had been campaigning on the issue for a number of years.

It was hugely satisfying when my Female Genital Mutilation Bill became law in 2003. But as I said at the time: 'Although it's very nice to get a law through Parliament, if it isn't acted on it isn't worth the paper it's written on.' The law is only one weapon. We need teachers, doctors and police to stand up to this barbaric practice and be prepared to confront minority ethnic groups on the issue. It is a matter of considerable disappointment that there has only been one prosecution in the past two years and that failed on a technicality.

FGM was one of several issues concerning women that I have been involved with over my years in Parliament. As a woman yourself I think you are more aware that things are often stacked against other women and then want to do something to redress the situation.

When I look back on the issues I have been involved in during my parliamentary career it can seem like a pretty bleak catalogue. But then again, I see my role as that of championing the underdog and righting wrongs and there are not always a lot of laughs in that.

Having said that, there are lighter moments. During the Thatcher years I think many of us were bitterly disappointed that under Britain's first ever woman Prime Minister, the lot of ordinary women was getting worse, especially in the areas of sexual discrimination and equal pay. So when my name came up to ask the first question during Prime Ministers' Questions on International Women's Day I was keen to seize the moment. PMQs as they are known are probably the most visible part of parliamentary proceedings, intensely gladiatorial and widely watched – if I ever missed a session an eagle-eyed constituent would be sure to write in asking where I was!

On this occasion, though, I had just returned from a holiday in India with Owen and some friends. We had had a great time but, stuck in an old car with no air conditioning, had to drive around the dusty roads with the windows open. By the time I got back I had lost my voice completely. Not wishing to lose my PMQs slot I went to Bernard Weatherill, the Speaker, and asked if there was a precedent for asking a colleague to read out a question on your behalf. There was and Dawn Primarolo stepped in to help.

My question, as asked by Dawn, was straightforward.

Given the Prime Minister's new-found enthusiasm for having more women in public life and in the workforce generally, may I ask her how she expects that to come about while women's pay still lags as far behind men's as it did ten years ago and while the government refuse to fund state nurseries or give financial help to working mothers? Or does the Prime Minister's advice to women simply consist of telling them to follow her example and find themselves a wealthy husband?

It brought gasps from the Tory benches, hoots of laughter from my own, and a look capable of killing from the PM. Needless to say, the sketch writers and cartoonists had a field day.

CHAPTER TEN

REVOLVING DOORS

Satisfying though being an elected MP can be, I think most of us have harboured a desire to advance up the greasy pole. I was certainly no exception; I was chomping at the bit to change the world. Labour's old system of MPs electing members of the shadow Cabinet, sadly abandoned in 2011, gave me front bench opportunities. By the time Labour won the 1997 general election I had been sacked, again, following an 'unauthorised' visit to Kurdistan, so I focused on other issues, especially Iraq, and eventually the opportunity passed me by.

Do I regret it? Of course I do. It would have been so satisfying and rewarding to be developing an agenda rather than reacting to one. To implement the reforms I had kicked off. It was satisfying that such an important subject was finally in Labour hands, sad because it might have been me at the helm.

Regret is not a part of my make-up; I prefer to look forward rather than back. And I don't think I would have done anything very differently. I had my time on the front benches in a number of portfolios and enjoyed it enormously. In our parliamentary system the role of opposition is extremely important, holding the government to account, challenging and questioning. When that longed-for call comes and you are informed that you are joining the frontbench team initial elation is soon overtaken by the daunting prospect of mastering a brief. However much you think you know about a subject you soon find out that you have only scraped the surface. It takes years to master a brief and few ministers get that luxury. In my case I held seven different posts in eight years. No sooner was I settled in to one brief than I moved, having to be the 'new girl' all over again. It was a case of revolving doors, but I wouldn't have swapped it for the world.

My first role was hardly the most exciting; in fact it was a peculiar brief, combining two separate areas of policy. In 1987 Neil Kinnock made me frontbench spokesperson on education and women's affairs – a full three years after arriving in the Commons. To make it more peculiar I shared the brief with Jack Straw and Jo Richardson. I never did understand the rationale for the combined role.

I didn't even know much about education, English education that is, but my boss Jack Straw was very helpful and supportive. He even offered the services of his mother, a former teacher, to get me up to speed with the issues.

For the first time I had the luxury of a researcher to help me. Marjorie Thompson came highly recommended from Plaid Cymru MP Dafydd Elis-Thomas. She was clearly very bright – she went on to chair CND – and an able researcher but she was American and unfamiliar with the UK education system. Eventually it emerged that she was Dafydd's girlfriend. After his divorce they lived openly together but I did feel miffed that he had not been upfront with me at the outset. Years later Dafydd apologised for not coming clean.

I worked hard to get on top of the complex brief. I championed the provision of more nursery school places, campaigned for the inclusion of arts in schools and for the inclusion of the Welsh language as a foundation subject in the core curriculum in Wales. I also fought for better employment protection for part-timers and pregnant women.

I decided to tackle the continuing issue of the 'glass ceiling' which was preventing women's representation in senior roles. It was something I felt strongly about, not least because of the lack of women in Parliament at the time. I was outraged that only 5 per cent of the government's advisory bodies were chaired by women. When it also emerged that less than 10 per cent of nationalised industry board members were women, I swung into action. I knew there were know-ledgeable and capable women out there and began developing policies which we could implement when we got into power. I had hardly got going when I was sacked, returning to the backbenches.

The beauty of the system of shadow Cabinet elections was that a year later I was elected to the shadow Cabinet. This time I got a role which I truly loved, that of shadow Secretary of State for Overseas Development. I was lucky to have Dale as my deputy. His ill-health – which would soon curtail his career as an MP – prevented his taking the front-line role for which he would have been brilliantly suited. But his loss was my gain. He was particularly effective on the procedures of the House of Commons, leading Lynda Chalker, so often at the receiving end of his interventions, to describe him as my Rottweiler!

I had always been interested in human rights and overseas aid and my time in this role further cemented my conviction that this area would be a major part of my future career. It was during this time I made my first visit to Iraqi Kurdistan as well as to Cambodia and East Timor. What I saw in each of these countries made a lasting impres-sion and became such a major part of my political life that they de-serve their own chapters. As does the whole topic of 'arms for trade', one of the darkest chapters in British aid policy.

The House of Commons fosters a deliberately adversarial at-mosphere and there were certainly few punches pulled when Lynda Chalker and I faced each other over the years. During my time at Overseas Aid we crossed swords regularly, on the plight of the Kurds, on British arms sales to Indonesia and on the lack of British support to the victims of famine in Africa in 1991. Because of the Gulf War, famine in Africa was being largely overlooked, particularly by the

British government. Neil Kinnock and I had just started a 24-hour fast to highlight the issue, when Chalker announced that the promised £11 million aid package was to be postponed. Britain had gone from being the second most generous donor in the big seven nations to the second most miserly. Lynda Chalker also took a broad swipe at the European Community over what was, in her view, a lack of response. There was understandable uproar in Brussels and she was soon forced to climb down. As I pointed out in the House of Commons, the government had tried to deflect its own inadequacies with criticism of the EC.

We had another of our regular dust-ups over British beef supplies sent out to Russia. Dale and I had been out in Moscow on a fact-finding mission to see for ourselves the plight of ordinary Muscovites following the collapse of the Soviet Union in 1992. There were critical food shortages and Britain had been providing food aid. We were told that large quantities of our best beef had been sent out but we could not see any of it in the shops. We kept asking questions and eventually our 'minders' took us to an industrial estate on the outskirts of Moscow. The warehouses were enormous, several storeys high, and we had to use a lift to get us to the designated floor. There were rows upon rows of boxes of British beef in massive freezers, which we had been told had been there for over a month. No one could read the English labels. Meanwhile on the ground floor, French pork was being brought in and immediately shipped out to the shops. When I got back I raised the issue, criticising Chalker's department for inadequate monitoring and management of the project.

The lack of accountability was becoming something of a theme and Dale was growing concerned about some of the projects the department was funding in India. The government was investing millions in building the Rihand power station as part of the Aid for Trade initiative, despite environmental concerns. It had also come in for criticism from the National Audit Office. Dale had sat on the Public Accounts

Committee and felt that there were major discrepancies in its reports. So we flew out to India to find out more.

The Rihand project was awesome in its scale. There was an open-cast mine right next door providing the fuel to the project, connected by rail to the power station. I couldn't get over how easily the coal was being extracted from the deep open-cast mine, used as I was to the arduous process British miners faced. Here it was like paring cheese. The detrimental impact on the environment was clear, but it provided a livelihood for thousands of people living in the neighbouring villages who came out to greet us enthusiastically and hung garlands around our necks. From an economic point of view, the criticism of this project seemed unfounded.

We had been told that the Orissa health project was a successful aid venture. It was a primary care and nurse training initiative linked to a family planning project designed to address the issue of population growth. When we arrived we found an old school building with no modern sanitary facilities. There was rubbish dumped in the central courtyard, the whole thing was unkempt and squalid. The centre's director, dressed in a smart pinstriped suit, came to greet us and show us around, seemingly oblivious to the indescribably filthy conditions. We were escorted around a local family planning facility where a sterilisation programme was underway. There were women seated in a waiting area in the most rundown of conditions and some, who had just had sterilisations, were lying on the dirty floor. We were shown into a room, a so-called theatre, at the back where conditions were appalling and an operation was in progress. It was horrible. We also went into the countryside to look at some of the health centres in the project only to find that where they did exist, they were empty buildings.

After we came back, Dale's researcher Jim Mahon dug deeper. He found two versions of the project evaluation report and discovered that a highly critical section had been removed from the published version. He tracked down the person who had written the report who told Jim he had been asked by the Foreign and Commonwealth Office (FCO) to amend the report, removing a section which they felt was unduly critical of the project. So there was a sanitised version for publication and another which told the truth.

Given my international interests, I have always spent an inordinate amount of time on airplanes and in airports, but the most intense time was this period when, it seemed, I was permanently on the move. I am not a good traveller inasmuch as I don't enjoy it; the cramped conditions and the recycled air. During this time I also became aware of the number of people who appeared to suffer food poisoning. I commissioned a survey into airline food. The results were shocking. Tests carried out by the local authorities near Heathrow showed that a quarter of airline meals were found to contain potentially dangerous bacteria. I used the statistics to lobby for airline food to be included in food hygiene regulations, something it had so far escaped because it was 'given away' rather than sold.

It soon became clear that the overseas aid department was the Cinderella within the FCO. Unfashionable and unappreciated during the Thatcher years, morale was low and it failed to attract top-calibre people. The UK was rapidly slipping down the table of aid provision and, equally worryingly, was pursuing an Aid For Trade policy linking aid to purchase of goods from Britain – often arms. The department had no voice in Cabinet and when John Major made a speech about wanting more women, I seriously suggested he started with Lynda Chalker, my opposite number. Despite our disagreements she was a very able woman.

The overseas aid department had, in its various incarnations, been in and out of Cabinet and in and out of the FCO. Judith Hart, former Paymaster General, had overseen its creation as a ministry during her tenure in 1969 only for it to be downgraded by a subsequent Conservative administration, made a separate ministry again by Labour, and then transferred back to the FCO again under Thatcher in 1979. No wonder that by the time I took up the opposition brief, departmental morale was low.

In addition to the administrative merry-go-round, the government had little sympathy for the moral justification for aid to the world's poorest countries. No concept of the rich helping the poor. For them the key driver was: 'What's in it for us?' and those years represented a bleak time for people working in the sector.

This was a brief I knew quite a lot about before I started. I had long-standing links with Oxfam and other non-governmental organisations, and had a personal interest in the development of countries like Cambodia. I spoke to staff within the department and also NGOs and others working in the sector and it was clear that things needed to change.

Over the years I had come to know Lord Joffe, a major benefactor of the Labour Party. He was a human rights lawyer, had defended Nelson Mandela at his trial, and was a member of the House of Lords and Chairman of Oxfam. I liked him very much. He was quiet and unassuming while at the same time very principled and knowledgeable. At the instigation of Neil Kinnock he had funded my fact-finding trip to Kurdistan and I always found him supportive and interested in overseas aid. Our paths would cross regularly and at one event or another we got talking and I bemoaned the lack of support for overseas aid. He suggested I develop a policy for restructuring the whole operation. He even offered to fund a couple of researchers from the Institute of Public Policy Research to help.

As we moved ahead with the project we found considerable support, including within the Civil Service. Finally, we were able to publish the work in a document called 'A World of Difference'.

We advocated a separate government department, free of the FCO, with a clear strategy that reduced the amount of aid tied to purchase of British goods and services. It was a substantial piece of work that covered the whole gamut, including transition and recruitment and resources. I lobbied hard for it to be made Labour policy and included in the manifesto for the 1992 election. The day we heard that the then shadow Foreign Secretary, Gerald Kaufman, had agreed was a happy day for the team. All we had to do now was wait to become the government.

There was a confident mood in the party as 1991 merged into 1992 and the general election approached. My office was situated on the shadow Cabinet corridor and there was an increased energy and vibrancy as we prepared for government. As polling day approached we were increasingly confident, despite the hostility levelled at Neil Kinnock by the Murdoch press. The coverage was personal, degrading and totally unfair, culminating with the infamous lightbulb front page in *The Sun*: 'If Kinnock wins today will the last person to leave Britain please turn out the lights'. *The Sun* wasn't shy in claiming credit for the Tory win either: 'It's The Sun Wot Won It' was the following weekend's headline.

Throughout the campaign, I had been shadowed by a BBC TV crew preparing for a documentary on a year in the life of a new minister. A week before the poll, we were in Sheffield for the final party rally. It was an electrifying meeting, there were excellent policy speeches and we were all flying high. The perceived triumphalism would later be cited as one of the reasons why we lost on polling day, but again a small moment was seized on by the media and taken out of all proportion. I never did understand the level of hostility levelled at Neil. It was unwarranted. I believe he would have made a good Prime Minister. I was back in my constituency when the national results started coming through. We were watching in a pub with a growing sense of disbelief. By the end of the evening I think we were all in tears, including the documentary team which was seeing its programme going down the drain.

By the time we did eventually get into government in 1997 I had moved on. However, implementing the overseas aid strategy was one of Clare Short's first actions as Secretary of State, which was deeply rewarding. Since then the Department for International Development (DfID), as it became known, has been reborn and raised its game. Today it attracts quality civil servants and has a distinctive culture and a much higher profile than the FCO. I am optimistic that in the future it will be able to resist inevitable attempts to transfer it back to the FCO on some spurious cost-cutting grounds.

Neil stepped down after the election and John Smith became leader of the Labour Party. He called me in to tell me he was moving me to shadow Welsh Secretary. I was not happy, although many in my constituency were delighted. I had loved my brief at overseas aid, but John explained that following the last shadow Cabinet elections I was now the party's only elected Welsh member. He promised to move me as soon as another Welsh MP was elected. When the time came I campaigned wholeheartedly for Ron Davies and when he made it I breathed a sigh of relief.

My deputy was Paul Murphy, with whom I enjoyed working. The only thing we felt very differently about was the Welsh language. He was not a Welsh speaker and we came from totally different backgrounds. I did take him to his first Eisteddfod, but I don't know if that made him change his mind. The Labour Party had been supportive of the language for some time, since the days of George Thomas, who had been a hard-line opponent of devolution and any attempts to gain legal recognition for the Welsh language.

Having had a confrontation with my leader when appointed to the role, I was to have another one while in post. My opposite number, David Hunt, had been chosen by the government to close a major debate on the future of the coal industry. As the shadow Welsh Secretary, and furthermore an MP for a mining constituency, I fully expected to be winding up. John Smith, however, chose shadow Energy Minister Martin O'Neill to close. I was furious and strode off to John's office where I made my views known in no uncertain terms. Other MPs and the media quickly seized on it, describing it as a snub and speculating as to whether I did not have John's confidence. He denied it and later apologised for what he described as an 'error of judgement'.

As soon as Ron got elected, Gerald Kaufman told me that he went to see John to suggest I take over National Heritage from the departing Brian Gould, saying I was the only member of the shadow Cabinet who had credibility in the role. So, less than a year after arriving in the Welsh Office, I was off. I had a background in the arts, having served on the Arts Council of Great Britain and the Welsh Arts Council. I started the job during the middle of the introduction of the National Lottery. Labour Party policy was in favour of the lottery. I was not. I always felt it was legitimising gambling and disproportionately targeted people who could not afford to buy tickets, offering the illusion of an easy way out of the poverty trap. Nevertheless, I toed the line and got on with it.

An area where I had failed to toe the line was that of car parking. Parking places are at a premium at Westminster and I would often park my car on an empty patch of tarmac outside the Speaker's residence. The speaker, Betty Boothroyd, went berserk, and to everyone's astonishment made a formal announcement from the Speaker's Chair that she would have my car clamped if I ever parked it there again. She was rather prone to taking great exception to any perceived challenge, especially from a woman, and once switched off Ann Widdecombe's microphone mid-speech to shut her up. Apparently, she complained about my action to John Smith during a meeting about Scottish Nationalists and he replied that he found it easier to deal with them than me!

I only had the Heritage brief for about a year but it was an interesting time. There was a lot of disquiet about the 1990 Broadcast Act which the Tories had brought in, effectively deregulating independent television. I, and many others, believed it led to a dumbing-down. I tried to get an amendment to the act through the House of Commons as it was clear that smaller companies were getting swallowed up by larger rivals. And they were not honouring the pledges they made at

Waving at a train in Aberdyfi with my mother.

With my sister Gwyneth.

Attending Elizabeth Taylor's birthday party with Owen. My dress was from An-An!

Campaigning with suffragette Leonora Cohen in the 1970 general election.
© DAILY POST WALES.

Posing on the walls of Denbigh Castle as Labour candidate in the 1970 general election. © DAILY POST WALES.

A prospective MEP on a familiarisation trip to the European Parliament.

Owen and I celebrating winning the Euro seat for Mid and West Wales in 1979.

Unemployment protest at European Parliament with Barbara Castle.

A peace protest at Capitol Hill, Washington, with Julie Christie and others.

ABOVE With Neil Kinnock on the campaign trail during the Cynon Valley by-election in 1984.

BELOW Saturday in Aberdare. Canvassing with Beth Day in 1984. © JONATHAN JAMES, PINEGATE.

Victory at last! Cynon Valley by-election in 1984. © PRESS ASSOCIATION

One of many cartoons celebrating my PMQ ambush of Margaret Thatcher. © RICHARD WILSON, TIMES NEWSPAPERS LTD.

Miners' strike with Arthur Scargill and miners from Tower Colliery.

The Phurnacite plant in my constituency with Alan Williams, shadow Secretary of State for Wales, and Arthur Pearce, the plant manager. © MEDIA WALES

My flooded House of Commons office. I'm wearing Brian's boots!

Neil Kinnock's shadow Cabinet.

Visit to Ethiopia as shadow Secretary of State for International Development.

A trip to Guangzhou, China in 1990 with Brian and Dale.

At the front bench in the House of Commons while shadow Secretary for International Development – my Rottweiler is behind me!
© UK PARLIAMENT

Retirement presentation to Cledwyn Hughes, former Secretary of State for Wales, on behalf of the PLP. With Jim Callaghan, Michael Foot, Donald Dewar, Gordon Brown and Harold Wilson in 1992.

Emerging from the Tower Colliery sit-in.
© DRAGON NEWS LTD

Protesting at Porton Down.

Iraqi President Jalal Talabani.   President Karzai of Afghanistan.

Tony Blair and a group of Kurdish women who came to thank him for his intervention in Iraq.
© PRESS ASSOCIATION

At an Iraq post with British troops.
© PRESS ASSOCIATION

At the retirement of Jean, my constituency secretary. Luckily she came back to work.

ABOVE Seated front-centre with the Parliamentary Labour Party celebrating Keir Hardie's centenary.
© TERRY MOORE

LEFT My great-nephew and great-niece, Twm and Mali, with constituent Brian Fear, former president of the Welsh Football Association.

the time of winning their franchises. When Tyne Tees was swallowed up by Yorkshire Television a great deal of regional output was lost. Helped by the late Brian Sedgemore, an ex-employee of Granada, I also investigated Granada Television's franchise claims. Brian put me in touch with employees who were angry about broken promises. There were numerous points on which it had breached its franchise application. It had committed to developing fourteen films – but dismantled its film department. It pledged to deliver two or three drama-documentaries to the network each year but barely managed one. It made a great play of the fact that it was an important centre of technical research and development but after winning the bid closed the laboratory. The North East MPs were supportive on the subject of Tyne Tees; some of the Manchester MPs were anything but. When I came to investigate Granada, they were so incensed they orchestrated my removal at the following year's shadow Cabinet elections.

The other issue that was to loom large on my watch was the Windsor Castle fire which broke out on 20 November 1992, causing around £50 million worth of damage. Although the Queen's home, the castle is owned by the state, and Prime Minister John Major promptly announced it would pay for the repairs. As with most things to do with the Royal Family the issue was shrouded in secrecy. The report into how the fire began was suspect, there were reports that fire extinguishers had not worked. There were also allegations that lessons learnt from a previous fire at Hampton Court had not been implemented. It also emerged that the Palace itself had cancelled the insurance. I stood up and challenged my opposite number, Peter Brooke, on much of the detail, but never received a response. It was not a good year for the Queen; she later described it as her *annus-horribilis* and the monarchy was seriously slipping in the public's regard, with questions being raised about her exemption from income tax and the numbers of minor royals paid for from the public purse.

I opposed the government's proposal to foot the entire repair bill.

In response, the Queen agreed to meet 70 per cent of the restoration work and open parts of Buckingham Palace in order to generate funds. From today's perspective, it's truly shocking that parts of it weren't open earlier, particularly the Queen's Gallery, given how much money the public pays! In future that would change and the public would have access, albeit limited to certain times of the year. I consider that my contribution to public access to art!

The episode caused many to describe me as a republican but I am not. I think the monarchy has its role, it attracts a great deal of tourist revenue to the country, and I have a great deal of personal respect for the Queen's sense of duty. I did not therefore have an issue when I was made a Privy Councillor. Due to a skiing injury I was excused from kneeling in front of the Queen for the initiation. Plaid Cymru's Dafydd Elis-Thomas was made Privy Councillor on the same day. He was forced to kneel and it is something I have teased him about remorselessly ever since. His sharp response was: 'I always knew you were a republican.'

After a year at National Heritage, I was voted out of the shadow Cabinet. I was rescued by John Prescott who appointed me as his deputy – I was now deputy to the deputy leader! A part of his portfolio was employment and I became frontbench spokesperson on Employment. A new and tricky brief to master. My main priority was to develop our policy on the minimum wage. I worked closely with trade union colleagues, who were funding the research, especially Maggie Jones, Director of Policy and Public Affairs of UNISON. Everything had been completed and the draft policy was ready to present to the Labour Party Conference, when the word came down that the actual minimum wage should not be specified. I felt that made the whole project somewhat academic and the trade unions were apoplectic. Labour HQ sent a researcher to argue with me. I have no recollection of the meeting but Jean tells me it was a young David Miliband, not then an MP. Despite all the objections the amount came out.

I was used to moving after a year into a new job, but this time it was a matter of months. I was to be a shadow minister for the FCO. At the time Chris Patten, former Conservative Minister for Overseas Development and minister at the FCO, told me it was the best job he had ever had. I have to agree with him.

In the way these things work I was not given the Middle East region which was where most of my expertise lay. I suspect that it was largely at the instigation of the then shadow Foreign Secretary Robin Cook, who never liked the people around him to be more knowledgeable than him. Luckily, I enjoyed far better relationships with other foreign secretaries; David Miliband, who valued other people's expertise, and Jack Straw, who was always more interested in getting things done than his own ego. Nevertheless, I made it clear to Robin Cook that I wanted to maintain my interest in Iraq and the Kurds and he said he was OK with that.

I kept up my contacts in the region. Turkey was in the middle of carrying out yet another incursion in Iraqi Kurdistan. I was, by then, a friend of Erdal İnönü, acting Prime Minister of Turkey. I phoned him and asked for permission to observe the incursion. He answered, 'You can go anywhere you like.' It was late on a Friday and I phoned Labour's pairing whip. There was no answer, but I left a message. I phoned my colleague in the foreign affairs team who said he would like to come with me, since he had never been to the region. The outcome was that we went, but the repercussions were huge. It ended with myself and Jim Cousins being sacked for going on 'an unsanctioned trip'! On our return I was summoned to see Tony Blair. I knew what was coming as soon as I saw Chief Whip Derek Foster. I was returned to the backbenches.

It was not the end of my active interest in foreign affairs. Freed from front bench responsibility I took an increasing role in the Inter-Parliamentary Union. The IPU is an enormously influential international organisation that provides opportunities for dialogue and co-operation between parliamentarians and fosters the establishment of democracy. I have twice chaired its International Human Rights Committee. In Westminster I have been the chair of the All-Party Group on Human Rights since 1997.

International Development was much more than a job. Long after leaving the front bench position I continued to play my part as a member of the House of Commons Select Committee on International Development. The committee oversees the workings of the DFiD and I felt that, after years of campaigning, I had a great deal to contribute. Not to mention my desire to continue pushing for the resolution of unfinished business.

It was in this capacity that, in the spring of 2002, I found myself surrounded by Israeli tanks. At the invitation of the BBC Radio 4 *Today* programme, I was with a UN convoy trying to gain access to the Palestinian refugee camp at Jenin. The Israelis did not want us there and were trying to intimidate us. Many of the UN contingent were nervous, after all their colleagues had already been attacked. I picked up my mobile phone and called the British Foreign Secretary, Jack Straw. I managed to make myself heard above the deafening growling of the tanks and told him what was happening. He immediately called in the Israeli ambassador and instructed our embassy team in Tel Aviv to go to Israeli Prime Minister Ariel Sharon's office to protest. They called off their dogs but we still were not allowed in to the camp.

The atmosphere in Israel and the West Bank was tense, even by Middle East standards. The Second Intifada, the Palestinian uprising, was in progress. Suicide bombers had targeted Israeli towns and cities, killing civilians. The Israeli government responded in the only way it knew how – brutal reprisal. Troops, tanks, bulldozers and helicopters invaded Palestine. It was called Operation Defensive Shield.

It was not long before harrowing stories of human rights abuses began to circulate. Pitched battles were being fought in the Jenin refugee camp. Conflicting accounts emerged; not only did the Israeli and Palestinian accounts differ, so did those of the Europeans and Americans. It was impossible to work out what was actually happening on the ground. So I did what I always try and do in these situations, I set off to see for myself. That way, when I came to talk to the House of Commons, I would be doing so with first-hand experience.

British aid money had been spent developing infrastructure in Palestine; I wanted to find out what had happened to the projects and to learn more about what would need to be done in terms of dealing with the unfolding crisis. While I was there I was asked to broadcast eyewitness accounts through BBC Radio's flagship *Today* programme. An opportunity to act as parliamentary observer and journalist – I was on the first plane out.

When I arrived in Jerusalem I was taken aback by the obvious military presence and the tension in the air. I had last visited twelve years previously but matters had clearly worsened, the communities more polarised. The city still exerted its magic. I saw Jews pressing their faces to the Wailing Wall, reading aloud from scripture, some weeping. Next to it was Islam's third holiest site, the Noble Sanctuary. Nearby was the Mount of Olives, a sacred place for Christians, although to me it was somewhat devalued by the knowledge that Robert Maxwell was buried in the Jewish cemetery, where plots sold for $11,000.

The strained atmosphere in the city was summed up by a van I saw with a slogan on the back proclaiming: 'No Arabs – No Problem'. The hostility and intransigence seemed to sum up the problem.

Colin Powell, US Secretary of State, was in town on a whirlwind tour of the Middle East. I asked the British Consul General to help me get an interview with him. Nothing happened so I found out where the American delegation was staying. I made my way to their hotel and introduced myself. They were friendly, told me Colin Powell was resting and that an interview might be possible later. It never happened.

I wanted to ask the Secretary of State why he wasn't visiting the Palestinian territory. He'd seen the effect of the suicide bombers in

Jerusalem but, unbelievably, failed to visit Jenin and other areas where the Israeli army had terrorised Palestinian civilians. To me it did not make sense. Surely if you expect to bring two sides together you need to appreciate the suffering on both sides.

There was nothing else I could do in Jerusalem so I tried to get to Ramallah where the Palestinian leader, Yasser Arafat, was pinned down in his compound. I knew that I would have problems getting in but I was not expecting to be challenged at an open checkpoint outside Jerusalem. 'Where are you going?' the soldier demanded. 'To visit Yasser Arafat,' I replied. I was informed that I could not travel in that direction for my own safety.

While at the checkpoint I met a man from Médecins du Monde who told me that he had been hearing sounds of shooting and bombardment from the town all night. He was desperately worried about his colleagues.

Meanwhile, the international media were reporting on the deteriorating situation in the Jenin refugee camp. The Israelis claimed that many attacks were originating from there and took uncompromising action. They went in with heavy armour, destroyed the opposition they met, and proceeded to bulldoze homes – apparently with inhabitants still inside them. There were also harrowing stories of massacres, bodies shovelled into mass graves or taken away by troops. The Israelis denied such accounts as Palestinian propaganda. However, they would not let in any external observers, so the truth of the matter was hard to determine.

I set off for Jenin with a UN convoy. Our vehicles had UN clearly painted on their sides and flew the UN flag. Despite this we were continually stopped by tanks and roadblocks. There was no one else on the road but it took us over six hours to deliver relief supplies to the women and children who had been allowed out of the refugee camp. They were not really interested. They were in a state of real distress, desperate to know the fates of their husbands, sons, brothers and fathers. Through the Arabic speakers in the convoy they told us how their men had been called out of their homes with their hands above their heads and shot. Their bodies left in the street.

Not long after hearing this we saw a sea of men walking down the road outside the town of Jenin. The Israeli army had called out every man over sixteen years of age for a roll-call. It was a chilling moment but on this occasion they marched back half an hour later.

One of the men was the mayor of Jenin. He was extremely angry and contemptuous of the UN and the international community. He said there were 1,000 dead or injured inside the camp and no one was providing any assistance or holding Sharon to account.

We were trying to help but we couldn't get in to the refugee camp. Enormous tanks blocked our way and even after Jack Straw's intervention, they did not budge.

At nearby hospitals we heard they had had their electricity cut and been denied access to medical staff and supplies. We were able to help with staff and supplies but although they could see in to the camp – people were even waving for help out of their windows behind the barricade – they had not been able to treat a single person.

All the humanitarian agencies were desperate to get independent observers into the camp. Even the UN were refused access; their emergency teams of doctors, nurses, medicine and food were held up for days while people died.

It is hard to describe the anguish of organisations like the Red Cross. They knew people were dying but could not reach them. Their ambulance tyres were shot out, their staff pulled out of cabs and humiliated. Tanks deliberately crashed into the ambulances. As one official told me, 'It's impossible to do our work.'

The Director of the UN Relief Agency, Richard Cook, told me one member of his staff had been killed in an ambulance. He had also had a doctor, a nurse and two ambulance drivers shot. 'That's nothing compared to the Red Crescent,' he said. It had 122 members of its medical staff shot, seven of them killed. I personally saw a UN ambulance riddled with bullet holes.

I had witnessed some desperate and harrowing situations in my time but I had never seen such deliberate targeting of medical personnel and ambulances. The deliberate denial of access to humanitarian aid and medical treatment was leading to death and unnecessary suffering. It had to be a breach of international law by anyone's reckoning.

And yet the world largely stood by. All the feeble calls of the international community for Israeli restraint had no effect. I sympathised with Israeli communities which had been attacked but surely, more bloodshed could not be the answer.

On my return I spoke in the House of Commons. I wrote articles, gave interviews and made speeches. I said it was simply not enough for European countries to condemn. We needed to make a stand: withdraw ambassadors, impose arms embargos, impose economic sanctions, suspend preferential trade terms. It was a moment when the EU should have shown its mettle and implemented this type of action regardless of the objections of the Americans.

It did not, of course. Despite international condemnation, Israel was allowed to continue its actions without being penalised in any way. And by doing so it gave birth to the next generation of angry and vengeful Palestinians.

CHAPTER ELEVEN

CAMBODIA

The blood stains lay on the bare tiles of my hotel room in the shape of a human body. 'What is it?' I asked. 'Oh, someone was probably killed here,' said the man from Oxfam. He also warned that I would only have water available for a few hours each day.

There was raw sewage floating around what had once been one of the finest establishments in Phnom Penh, but the Khmer Rouge had seen the porcelain washbasin and toilet as decadent and smashed them up. They had also smashed up the water treatment plant which was why we only had water for a few hours a day.

I was exhausted after twenty-seven hours of hard travelling but reluctant to crawl into the grimy bed. Eventually I lay down fully clothed, sweltering in the humidity and trying my best to get some sleep. Strange scuttling noises disturbed me – I turned on the light to find I was sharing the room with an army of cockroaches marching across the floor. Ugh! I kept telling myself to get a grip; it was my first official overseas trip since becoming an MP and I was here for ten days. What on earth had I let myself in for?

Just as I drifted off to sleep again I was woken up. There was an 'urgent' telephone call. It was the wretched Ray Powell from the House of Commons. Despite the fact I was on a fully sanctioned trip, representing the Labour Party, he insisted I had to return immediately for an important vote in the House. His voice got louder and louder as he tried to shout down my perfectly rational explanation of why I could not – that there was only one flight a week. My Tory counterpart, Jim, himself an ex-Tory whip, thought the man a total imbecile. He had never come across such behaviour.

If you had asked the young Ann Clwyd why she wanted to be in politics she would have told you that it was to speak out for those that were not being heard, to protest on behalf of the underdog. For all the faults in our society, we are privileged to live in a democratic society governed by law; millions of people are not so lucky. The plight of people ruled by dictators or ravaged by abject poverty and disease, whose access to education and medicine is tenuous at best, has always connected to the missionary in me. I grew up with the Christian socialist belief that the fortunate among us have a moral duty to help those who need it. It is not fashionable to speak of morality in politics now, let alone religious beliefs, but I was raised with these core beliefs and they are part of me.

So, when I eventually took my seat at Westminster, I was keen to represent not only the Cynon Valley but to bring attention to human rights abuses and injustices elsewhere in the world. After over thirty years of my championing often unfashionable causes my colleagues would joke, 'She doesn't go on holiday; she visits the hellholes of the world.' They were not too far from the truth. I now found myself in my own personal hellhole in Phnom Penh.

It was 1987 and Donald Anderson MP was supposed to go to Cambodia as a Labour representative with an Oxfam delegation. He could not go and, at the last minute, asked me to take his place as Oxfam had already paid for the air fare. When we arrived in the Cambodian capital of Phnom Penh it was like no other city I had ever known, it was eerily silent. The Khmer Rouge regime, who had murdered or starved to death 1.5 million Cambodians, may have been recently defeated by the

Vietnamese but they were still fighting a rear-guard action in the Cambodian jungles. Pol Pot had believed in a return to an agrarian utopia and all Cambodian cities were forcibly evacuated into the 'killing fields' in the countryside, Phnom Penh's 2 million inhabitants were marched out at gunpoint and forced to live off the land as best as they could – catching rats and even eating dead people to survive.

During the trip I met the inspirational Eva Mysliwiec, a Polish-American Quaker working for Oxfam. She wrote a booklet for Oxfam called 'Punishing the Poor' which, stupidly, had to be pulped. The charity commissioners, apparently under pressure from the Tory government, claimed it was 'too political'. She made her home in Cambodia, running training farms for young people, and became the only American to be given Cambodian citizenship. I would try and explain to her how guilty I felt for not having been aware of the shocking suffering under the Khmer Rouge during its reign in the 1970s, the cruelty and the extreme poverty. I thought, good Lord! How had I missed this? I felt so guilty. Eva would give her gentle smile and comment that it was the future that now mattered. I returned regularly after that first trip and we became good friends.

Cambodia became one of the major international issues I would take up over the years as I fought for a more sympathetic policy from Britain towards one of the poorest countries in the world. They needed aid and we gave none. As far as Mrs Thatcher was concerned they were 'communist' and that was that. No aid for them.

This did not sit well with me so I kept a watch on what was happening there, working closely with Oxfam and other agencies. Cambodia had been liberated from the Khmer Rouge by the Vietnamese. Although the Vietnamese army subsequently retreated and the Cambodian government pursued a policy of non-alignment, it continued to be isolated by the West, freezing any UN support or aid. I went on heartbreaking visits to hospitals where children lay dying in corridors because there were no doctors, no beds and no medicine. The Khmer

Rouge had killed anyone they perceived as a professional; sometimes deciding this on the basis of whether they wore glasses. One in five children died from preventable diseases such as diarrhoea, caused by drinking contaminated water.

Accompanying me on this trip, and several subsequent ones, was Tory MP Jim Lester. On our return we both sought to change the British government's policy towards Cambodia. Our FCO briefing before our first visit had turned out to be completely out of touch with the reality on the ground; we reported on the reality but no one wanted to know. We were accused of being stooges of the Cambodian government, although we repeatedly raised human rights abuses on behalf of Amnesty International.

Wherever we went we felt the chilling fear people had of the Khmer Rouge returning to power. As the years progressed and the civil war continued, they occasionally made inroads, coming in from the jungle to capture Pailin, Cambodia's second city which was rich in gems. Pol Pot, in exile in Thailand, was backed by the governments of the US, China and the UK. Our government voted to seat the Khmer Rouge at the United Nations in 1979, 1980 and 1981, giving them diplomatic credibility. In Cambodia there were constant rumours that Pol Pot was back in the country.

Even more worryingly there were reports that British advisers were helping train the Khmer Rouge guerrillas. Susan Eliot, an independent observer who had worked for many years with Cambodian refugees, wrote to me saying she had seen British and American trainers working with the guerrilla forces.

The respected British periodical *Jane's Defence Weekly* reported that British troops had been training guerrilla troops in secret camps for the past four years, making a nonsense of ministerial assertions that we had not and would not offer any such support. Foreign Secretary Douglas Hurd's statement to the House of Commons in 1990 that 'We have never given, and will never give, support of any kind to the

Khmer Rouge' was nothing less than a deliberate attempt to mislead the House.

Two years later, Jim and I again visited Cambodia to witness the final withdrawal of Vietnamese troops. We were invited to a liberation party given by the King of Cambodia where Jim introduced me to two British men who, he said, were in Cambodia 'on holiday'. As soon as I heard that I was suspicious. Surely no one in their right mind would choose to go on holiday to Cambodia at that time. I soon became aware that they were hostile to their host country and were either ignorant or were playing at being ignorant. I suggested that if they wanted to know more about Cambodia they should speak to non-politicians, or people in the aid agencies, who had worked in Cambodia for many years. I pointed them in Eva's direction. I watched out of the corner of my eye as they stayed with Eva for only a few minutes. They clearly were not really interested in what she had to say.

The following day the King invited us to fly to the legendary Angkor Wat for a major Buddhist celebration. Now it is a major tourism centre, but then it was just a clearing in the middle of the jungle, a rough camp in among the trees. We were quite a big group, a lot of international journalists and photographers, and keen to see one of the wonders of the world. Most of us stood looking in awe and photographing the magnificent temples, but among the group were those two same men. They were carrying the most sophisticated photographic equipment in the party and taking pictures of the undergrowth! They did not look like botanists.

Meanwhile, I had started to feel very unwell. I am like a limp lettuce leaf in extreme heat, and went to search out some shade. An Indian journalist came to sit down next to me and for a while we watched the others in the distance. Unprompted, he said to me, 'Those two over there stand out like sore thumbs; it's quite obvious what they're up to.' I asked him what he meant and he replied: 'They're spooks.'

Later that day we were flown back to Phnom Penh for a press

conference in the palace. The air conditioning had been turned off, for the sake of the broadcasters, and I could feel my face turning red like a tomato about to burst. I knew the symptoms, I had heatstroke. I told Jim and headed back to my room. Later, there was a knock on the door, it was Jim. He said the two English guys were worried and had asked him to check on me, offering medical remedies such as Dioralyte. They had also asked Jim and me to intervene with Prime Minister Hun Sen, to get them to the front to see the action. I very much doubted that anyone would spend a holiday in Cambodia, one of the most beautiful countries on earth, watching people kill one another or blow one another up, unless they had another agenda. I refused to get involved.

Back in London I met up with the renowned investigative journalist John Pilger. He was deeply immersed in what was happening in Cambodia and later wrote one of the defining books of the Khmer Rouge's years of repression. He was preparing for his film *Cambodia – The Betrayal* at the time and when he had heard I was going on the trip he asked if we could meet afterwards to let him know what I had found there. He was banned from travelling there at the time. Anyway, I told him that the only suspicious thing I had to report was these two men.

Many of us suspected British government involvement, but MPs' questions were either blocked on the grounds of 'national security' or ministers lied, including Margaret Thatcher, who wrote to me in 1990 categorically denying any British involvement of any kind 'in training equipping or co-operating with Khmer Rouge forces or those allied to them'.

Meanwhile John's film had set the cat among the pigeons, leading to newspaper headlines like the *Daily Mirror*'s 'Thatcher orders the SAS into Cambodia's killing fields.' John had uncovered evidence that British forces were training people in Cambodia, under the so-called non-communist resistance.

I had been pursuing British aid for the Cambodians since my return from there. I believed Parliament and the British people had a right to know the truth. I obtained the official guest list of those invited to witness the Vietnamese troop withdrawal from Cambodia. On it were the names of the two 'holidaymakers' I had met. I used parliamentary privilege to name Anthony de Normann and Christopher Mackenzie. They were described on the guest list as Fonctionnaire de l'Institut de Recherche Défense. Given that we did not recognise the government of Cambodia there were no 'official' British visitors present, so who were these men? I needed to find out. I asked the House of Commons library to contact the Royal United Services Institute, funded by the Ministry of Defence, which they were claiming to represent, and find out whether the men worked there and if so what their roles were. The RUSI demanded to know who wanted the information and when they were told who had asked, they replied that the information was classified. Why, I wondered, if there was nothing to hide.

Meanwhile writs were served on Central Television and John Pilger. It was only a few days before a High Court action that the actual and shaming truth emerged. The British government admitted, after lying for years, that it had been involved in training the non-communist resistance (which included the Khmer Rouge) and, presumably, helping to arm it. Indeed, since 1985 British and American Special Forces had been on hand to provide advance training in weapons such as land mines. But once again the British government was caught in a web of official deceit. Eventually I received a letter from Mrs Thatcher contradicting her earlier letter and admitting British forces' involvement. I went live on the BBC's *Nine O'Clock News* to read out the letter.

It did not stop the two characters, who John had also named in the film, from suing him and Central Television for libel. I offered to appear as a witness for the defence and duly arrived at the High Court only to find that the defence were not allowed to give evidence in public. The government had successfully argued that the evidence could not be heard in public because it was 'against the national interest'. I recall sitting in the High Court thinking: 'Is this British Justice at work?' At the end of the week those men walked away with £250,000 apiece in libel damages.

Our policy in Cambodia was just plain wrong. These were some of the very poorest people in the world who had been subject to one of the most evil and repressive regimes of the twentieth century. Our policy to back the bad guys, just because they were fighting communism, held no moral weight whatsoever and I was pleased at having played some part in exposing it but also frustrated at not being able to do more. When we lost the following general election in 1987 I remember feeling gutted at having to explain to a visiting delegation from Cambodia that we could not help them, because we were not in a position to do anything. I could have cried.

I have returned to Cambodia many times and have been astounded to see how much progress they have made. It is a beautiful country and its tranquillity and spirituality belies its violent past. When I first visited there was so little in terms of infrastructure or democracy. There were pigs and hens running around the French mansions in the main streets. Now the economy is improving; the streets of Phnom Penh are bustling with life again and everywhere is a riot of colour and noise. I feel as if I am taking my life in my hands in the crazy traffic, where motorcycles and rickshaws flit in every direction often carrying whole families!

On my trips I have seen projects that have made a real difference to the lives of ordinary Cambodians, especially in education and health in rural areas, and I have been able to highlight them and put pressure on people to give more assistance to similar projects. Over the years Hun Sen, the Prime Minister, has come to consider me as a friend of Cambodia. The place is much more stable now but there remains a great deal of work to do.

The Inter-Parliamentary Union plays an important part in encouraging emerging democracies. On an IPU trip I met members of the opposition groups who were struggling to make their voices heard. They felt they were being treated as a nuisance and alienated from the business of government. In meetings with the ruling group I was able to point this out and, as diplomatically as possible, I suggested that they give the chairs of some committees to the opposition, to show their magnanimity. When they were starting out they had lots of problems and I tried to advise them. When people know that you have helped in the past, they are more receptive to your views when they are in power. Then, behind closed doors, you can often get things done.

One of the ongoing issues I have worked with the Cambodian government on is that of landmines. I had campaigned against the use of landmines since my first visit in 1987. When you see row upon row of limbless men, women and children lying in hospital, their lives destroyed in a meaningless instant, you cannot ignore it. Travelling around the country you cannot miss the numbers of amputees begging pathetically on the streets of Phnom Penh, or hobbling on one limb in dusty lanes in the villages.

Cambodia has the highest ratio of mine amputees in the entire world. An estimated 5 to 7 million mines were planted there and Britain helped supply and assist the evil Khmer Rouge regime to lay them. It is to our eternal shame and made me so angry. I believed our complicity gave us a special responsibility to invest in demining and also to lead the world in banning landmine use.

I was determined to do what I could to bring world attention to this problem and on one trip I ventured out with a mine-clearing team for first-hand experience.

We left the chattering tourists behind at Angkor Wat and now it was the monkeys chattering, accompanied by the squawking of exotic birds. I walked gingerly through the undergrowth, keeping to the footprints of my guides. We were in a partially cleared minefield and I was dressed in light body armour and a visor; neither of which would protect my legs if I stepped on a landmine. The guide in front was carrying a metal detector, the sort used on a British beach to unearth lost coins. Here the 'treasure' was lethal. Now and again it would emit a high-pitched sound and the guides would point out the metal fragments responsible. Although vigilant, they seemed relaxed. A few minutes later all that changed, a loud continuous screech emitted from the detector. Both my arms were grasped firmly and I was briskly escorted back along the path to the safety of a clearing. While I waited there the team dealt with the live mine, or anti-personnel device as military types would have it. The loud explosion reverberated through the jungle, sending birds into the air and animals into panic. It was only too easy to imagine the pain and horror that device would have caused if an innocent farmer or child had stepped on it.

We were only a few minutes from the Buddhist shrines at Angkor Wat. There, all was green, serene and contemplative. The area had been cleared of landmines but as I had found out, you did not have to stray far to put yourself in danger. Landmines had been designed to destroy tanks. The reality was that they were destroying the lives of innocent people. Wars finish, regimes change, but long after the fighting is over the mines lie in the ground waiting for unsuspecting passers-by to step on them before blowing them sky-high. The casualties are farmers working their fields, or children, who like children the world over, are looking for adventure away from their parents' gaze. And my country was partly responsible.

The Cambodians are a wonderfully resilient people. Despite their tortured history they are positive and hopeful of the future. On subsequent trips I have visited specialist prosthetic centres where, supported by British aid money, young Cambodian nationals are being trained to assess injuries caused by landmines and fit prosthetics. Some of these centres are becoming world renowned and have students from other war-torn countries such as Iraq learning how to deal with the human consequences of landmines.

I have also visited a group of remarkable young women working for an organisation called the Mines Advisory Group (MAG) who are working on clearing minefields. They told me how proud they were to have the opportunity of doing this important work for their communities, but also the chance to earn good money which is unusual in a country where women's status is low. I spent a long time talking to them about their dangerous work and also about their personal aspirations for the future. They told me that their concerns were about education and opportunities for their daughters and wherever I have travelled, almost without fail, the women will say the same. After the Iraq war I travelled with Latif Rashid, the Iraqi Minister for Water Resources, to the marshlands. He asked a group of women what they wanted from their new government. They banged the floor, where we were all sitting cross-legged, and demanded, 'education, work and a better life for our daughters'.

My outrage at the loss of innocent life and hope caused by landmines was shared by many and by 1995 there was an international movement to ban the production and export of landmines. A leading campaigner, newspaper editor and parliamentarian Lord Deedes, described them as a crime against humanity and said civilised nations should not touch them with a bargepole. I spoke out in Parliament many times, calling for an immediate ban on exports. Although other countries such as Canada, France, Sweden, Australia and South Africa agreed to back an export moratorium, the British government, yet again deferring to the arms lobby, dragged its feet, introducing semantic arguments about alternative 'smart' landmines.

In Britain, and internationally, one campaigner stood head and shoulders above everyone else. Diana, Princess of Wales, searching for a new role following her divorce from Prince Charles, became a leading campaigner against landmines. The most photographed woman in the world, she was able to use her celebrity to highlight the campaign and, boy, did she do it. There are iconic images of a visit to Angola where, dressed in body protector and visor, she walked through a minefield,

others of her consoling victims. Those of us who had been working
in this field found her support invaluable and while she was in Angola
I tabled an Early Day Motion congratulating her for 'highlighting
the tragic humanitarian consequences of the government's refusal to
completely ban the production and use of landmines'. Seventy-three
MPs signed their support. I am not a royalist but like many others I
could appreciate her commitment to the cause, unlike some government ministers and other members of the establishment who sought to
rubbish her efforts at every turn. They were terrified of her popularity,
now she was no longer a member of the Royal Family.

When she returned from Angola I sent her a copy of the EDM as
well as two reports I had written on the topic of landmines. A few
weeks later, in February 1997, an unexpected phone call to my office
from her staff invited me to meet her at Kensington Palace. It was an
offer I could not refuse. It was an opportunity to gain further support
for the campaign of course, but also on a personal level I was intrigued
to see what she was like in real life.

When I got to the door of Kensington Palace I was surprised to be
greeted very enthusiastically by the Princess's butler, Paul Burrell. He
told me he had grown up in a coal mining community and that many
of his family had worked underground. He said he had admired my
'sit-in' at the Tower Colliery and went on to say how delighted he was
that the Tower situation had worked out so well.

He took me up to the first floor, to a large sitting room full of
flowers and family photographs in silver frames. Diana came into the
room dressed in a dark brown pin-striped trouser suit with a pale pink
sweater and strode, smiling, towards me. My first thought was how
thin she actually was and how television and magazine photographs
made her look much rounder.

I told her, quite genuinely, that many of my friends in the House
of Commons admired her courage and her humanitarian work and
said she had done more than anyone to highlight the importance of

the landmine issue. She smiled her trademark shy smile and said she would like to travel more extensively to publicise the issue. She laughed and added, self-deprecatingly: 'Have passport, will travel.'

She said she wanted to go to Cambodia, but the Foreign Office had blocked the trip on safety grounds. I told her that I had been twice with Oxfam and it had been the first time I had seen first-hand the innocent victims of landmines. She was fascinated and wanted to hear my detailed description of the visits. We discussed the role that Britain had played in planting some of those landmines in the first place when we trained the anti-communist resistance in Cambodia – including the Khmer Rouge. I told her that before we went to Cambodia the Foreign Office had provided us with briefings which had turned out to be totally inaccurate.

She jumped out of her chair. 'The Foreign Office briefing I got on Angola was totally useless, I must show you.' She went into the next-door room and returned with the briefing in her hand. She showed it to me and I read it and we both laughed as she told me how the ambassador in Angola knew nothing about landmines; he had never seen one.

I told her about my own campaigning on landmines including northern Iraq, where again thousands of undetected landmines claim their innocent victims. We talked about the importance of bringing war criminals like Pol Pot and Saddam Hussein to justice for their war crimes against humanity and she asked me lots of questions about the INDICT campaign. I was struck by how well briefed she was and how seriously she took her campaigning. The media portrayed her as an airhead, but that was a long way from the young woman I met that day.

She was remarkably open and frank. She was interested in hearing the latest speculation on the possible date of the forthcoming general election and said she thought the Prime Minister, John Major, was feeble and had difficulty in making up his mind.

Given my Welsh background I asked her why she did not spend more time in Wales, after all she was the Princess of Wales. She said it was difficult, she did not want to step on Charles' toes and spoil things for her sons. She talked about how difficult it was to find a role in life and how she wanted to use her celebrity to achieve something worthwhile. Freed from the constraints of being a member of the Royal Family – 'thank goodness' is how she summed it up – she felt she now had some freedom to pursue causes that interested her. Not that she would ever feel wholly free, she told me. She recounted how the Queen, after a visit to GCHQ, said that she would never use a phone again. Diana talked about how all her phones were bugged and that she had found a small tracking device, about the size of a button, on the hub of her car.

We discussed her visits to see the homeless and the sick and compared our experiences of being out on the streets. She had been very recently to talk to the homeless directly and found the conversations very sad. One man had not recognised her and asked her if she was a social worker and was being paid to visit them!

We also talked about the forthcoming Earth Summit and the gap between the rich and poor. I was taken aback that, despite her own privileged background, she was quite fierce on the issue, saying that the world's problems would never be resolved until rich countries transferred more of their resources to poor countries. She then said, 'Rich people just want more and more,' adding vehemently, 'It makes me sick.' We went on to talk about the growth of drugs and the attraction of these cash crops for the poorest farmers in the world, and the responsibility of the developed world to offer alternative crops if they were serious about combatting the drugs trade.

I returned to the House of Commons impressed by her grasp of issues that interested her and believing we would meet again. We talked about meeting with other women MPs, particularly those who had signed the EDM. A few months later the All Party Group on Landmines invited her to come and talk at one of our meetings, but some Tory MPs objected vociferously, causing her to back out. In July she wrote to me explaining how the controversy prevented her attendance.

A month later I was on holiday in Italy, high in the Tuscany hills. It was a sparkling sunny day, about nine in the morning, and I idly switched on the BBC World Service news. At first it was not clear what had happened or to whom it had happened. Then I heard the name Diana and people being interviewed. I then realised there had been an accident. I assumed it was a water-ski accident, since the last I had heard Diana was cruising off the Ionian coast. It must have been a full five minutes before I heard the word 'dead'.

I felt the same sense of shock that millions of people felt all over the world. I cried. I had only recently received a letter saying she hoped we could meet again soon. Diana was certainly not paranoid, as Tory MP Nicholas Soames once said. Neither was she stupid as some other detractors would have us believe. I was impressed by her knowledge, her intelligence, her friendliness and her capacity for self-deprecation. I, like millions of others, felt she was a great champion of good causes. She could have moved mountains and her death was a great loss.

The Ottawa Treaty banning the production and export of landmines was signed in 1997. It is a lasting tribute to her. A total of162 states signed that treaty, including, under a new Labour government, the United Kingdom. Despite the omission of the USA, Russia and China, the world was, to a significant degree, a safer place.

CHAPTER TWELVE

AID FOR TRADE

F ew things in my parliamentary career have made me as angry as
the misuse of the overseas aid budget to fund the British arms
industry. It was bad enough that my country had blood on its hands in
some of the worst human rights abuses of the twentieth century. It was
equally galling that it was using funds earmarked for desperate people
to fund its activities. The final straw was that Margaret Thatcher, John
Major and their ministers repeatedly misled Parliament under the
guise of public interest in order to conceal their complicity.

Chickens have a habit of coming home to roost and William Waldegrave should have been mindful of the fact when he commented that
all government departments will use secrecy for convenience – if they
can get away with it.

Along with other concerned colleagues I was not prepared to accept
the machinations of the Tory government and the abuse of Parliament. Our persistence eventually paid dividends and although the true
extent of the Tory government's manipulation of funds earmarked for
aid has yet to emerge, enough came to light to cause serious disquiet.

Many of us campaigning on human rights abuses in Iraq had long
suspected the British government of breaking the UN embargo on the
sale of arms to Saddam Hussein. In 1991 I stood on the treacherous

snow-covered mountains between Iran and Iraq and saw thousands of pitiful men, women and children fleeing the killing guns of Saddam Hussein. And still we sold Iraq the components and the technology to make more guns. After Halabja the government fed us the fiction of a concerned humane government and they denounced Saddam Hussein. But in the same year they doubled his trade credits to £388 million. There was little mention of the gassing of the Kurds or of the regime's human rights abuses. Instead we sent ministers to the Baghdad Trade Fair, where they were pictured warmly shaking hands with their counterparts from the Iraqi regime.

Questions were asked. Indeed, I was one of the people raising the issue in the House of Commons only to be told that UK policy had not been changed.

The issue became toxic when, in 1992, directors of a British engineering firm, Matrix Churchill, were charged with illegal exports. The company responded by saying it had the backing of the security services and that Alan Clark, the then Trade Minister, had implied that the government would turn a blind eye if British machinery was being used to make weapons. The government produced public immunity certificates to suppress critical evidence in court, but the trial judge overruled the decision. The trial collapsed after Alan Clark told the court he had indeed encouraged the company to export equipment with military uses.

Held to account in Parliament, Alan Clark was forced to admit he had been 'economical with the *actualité*' in answer to parliamentary questions, including those tabled by me. Prime Minister John Major was forced to order an inquiry. It took three years for the Scott inquiry to report, but when it did it rocked the establishment to its foundations.

Parliament, on the eve of the report's publication, was buzzing with rumour and speculation. The government had reviewed the report but no news had leaked out. It was clear from the tone of the inquiry that the report was likely to be critical of government policy. The issue was how far it would go and to what extent it would hold individuals culpable. Like many others, I was caught in rounds of endless speculation with colleagues such as Jeremy Corbyn and Alice Mahon. Dale, who had by now gone to the House of Lords because of his health problems, made constant forays on the 'other side' to find out what the word on the ground was. He virtually set up camp in my office. We all sensed we were on the verge of a triumph for democracy and landing a significant blow on the industrial-military cabal and the tentacles they had deep into this government. We took comfort from seeing ministers scurrying through the corridors tight-lipped and stressed, and planned our strategies post-publication. My office was inundated with requests from the media for post-publication interviews. We did not even know what was in the report yet!

Finally, on the morning of publication, Robin Cook, shadow Foreign Secretary, was given just two hours in a room to read the 2,000-page report. He was not allowed to make copies or take notes before challenging his counterpart in the House that afternoon, a man who had time and the full resources of the Foreign Office to formulate his defence. I was never a fan of Cook as a man, but his intellect was never in doubt. His performance that afternoon was little short of brilliant, especially when you took into account the way the debate had been weighted in favour of the government.

The Scott report criticised the government for failing to inform Parliament of reforms to arms export law, fearing a public outcry. At the core of the report was a simple big lie. Britain, whose people believed it to be a decent democracy, does not sell arms to tyrants. We did so and we still do so.

The Economist summed up the report perfectly: 'Sir Richard exposed an excessively secretive government machine, riddled with incompetence, slippery with the truth and willing to mislead Parliament.'

In many ways Alan Clark summed up the arrogance of ministers when he dared to suggest that Labour MPs were a bit dim not to understand that, from 1987 onwards, they were being misled by the government and that we should have known Britain was selling arms to Iraq. We did suspect it, we did try and expose it, but he and his colleagues lied to cover it up. His colleague, William Waldegrave, had denied misleading Parliament but the report found him guilty also. He had repeatedly insisted the guidelines had not changed in response to PMQs tabled by MPs including me. The Scott report left both their reputations in tatters.

The issue of arms exports was in no way limited to Iraq. When I was the shadow Overseas Aid spokesperson I got wind that everything was not quite what it seemed with the contract for building the Pergau hydro-electric dam in Malaysia. I was not really able to get to the bottom of the matter until, one day, my PA found a copy of a confidential ODA (Official Development Assistance) report left in the photocopier. Truth can indeed be stranger than fiction. The report was in a brown cover rather than the usual blue one, suggesting it was not for distribution. In it was the explosive allegation that British companies had paid bribes to secure the contracts.

I could not quite believe our luck, but the information we had stumbled on now allowed me to start asking piercing questions. Caroline Ashley, my assistant, kept a pad of the forms for parliamentary questions on her desk and we began filling them in at a rate of knots. I also called on the National Audit Office to investigate.

The ensuing publicity paid dividends when a letter arrived in my office. It purported to be from a senior employee at Balfour Beatty – one of the contractors on the dam project. It claimed that the degree of corruption on the project was far worse than anyone had imagined. I got in contact with him, ascertained that he was who he said he was, and arranged to meet. His information was dynamite and supported our case.

I was uncomfortable with the whole ethos of linking aid to trade. Surely aid should be given to those most in need and not only areas which benefitted British exports. Sir John Bourn, Comptroller and Auditor General, ordered a value-for-money investigation into the government's Aid for Trade programme, leading to fresh allegations and shame for the Tory government.

The Malaysian government had been promised money for the dam in 1989 by Thatcher as a 'sweetener' for a £1.3 billion arms order she personally negotiated with Malaysian Prime Minister Mahathir Mohamad. Aid had been directly linked to arms sales by a mathematical formula; in other words the more arms Malaysia bought from Britain, the more aid we would give them. This was in contravention of the British law governing overseas aid but, despite Civil Service advice that the aid was an abuse of the aid programme, Foreign Secretary Douglas Hurd approved the first instalment.

Like hounds on a scent, my colleagues and I closed in on the administration. I remember jubilantly watching a Public Accounts Committee meeting as Alan Williams, the Swansea MP, questioned Tim Lankester, the senior civil servant on the project. He got him to admit that he had been directed to sign the contracts by Douglas Hurd against his personal judgement. Another parliamentary inquiry followed, along with protests and intense media coverage, but the telling blow was when the High Court awarded a landmark judgement against Douglas Hurd. Aid for the Pergau dam project was deemed 'unlawful'.

Our scrutiny into the project had uncovered three separate scandals: UK policy linking aid to sales of defence equipment contravened international agreements. The project's economics were fundamentally flawed, as Malaysia could have produced cheaper electricity from other sources. There were also unproven allegations of corruption as profiteers cashed in on privatisation of shares in the project.

The Scott inquiry and those into the Pergau dam project were taking place more or less concurrently in the first half of the 1990s, and at the same time another arms for trade scandal was brewing, one that once again I was to become deeply involved in.

The island of East Timor had won independence from Portugal in 1975 only to be invaded by its larger neighbour, Indonesia, nine

days later and illegally annexed in 1976. Although the action was condemned as unlawful by the UN, the Indonesian military dictatorship
enjoyed the support of many Western governments who valued economic ties, to the exclusion of any ethical responsibility. By 1978 it was
estimated that some 200,000 Timorese had died, but reports of this
and of human rights abuses were slow to percolate. In the early days
it was only the Australians who publicised what was happening. The
scale of abuse eventually brought the situation to the attention of the
UN's Decolonisation Committee.

I first visited the island of East Timor in 1989 as part of a cross-party
parliamentary delegation to Indonesia. The trip did not get off to a good
start when the leader of our delegation, a Tory, proved a sycophantic
toady in the presence of President Suharto. It is not protocol to argue
with other members of the delegation in public, but as soon as we were
out of earshot I gave him a piece of my mind, pointing out Suharto was
a military dictator with myriad human rights abuses to his name.

Needless to say, I was not playing the appeasement game, and when
Suharto asked us where we wanted to go I immediately piped up 'Dili',
the capital of East Timor. The request caused a flurry of activity
among his entourage but, fair play, we were taken there. Suharto said
it was an open book, 'We have nothing to hide.' Only a massacre of
the local population, I thought.

When we arrived on East Timor we were taken into an enormous hall
and addressed by the governor in Portuguese. It went on interminably
and I think we had all had enough. In mid-flow I put up my hand. He
stopped. I asked to visit the prison in Dili. Then people started scurrying
out of the room. Within half an hour I was in that prison. If I remember
correctly none of my fellow travellers wanted to come with me!

I always talk to Amnesty and other human rights groups before going
on trips and ask for specific information, people they want me to check
on and so forth. I went to East Timor armed with a list of people who
had been imprisoned and then documented by Amnesty. At the prison

I asked for people by name including a man Amnesty had asked me to look for, a leader of the rebel Fretilin movement. When he was brought from his cell I asked the governor and his staff to leave the room to enable me to talk to the man freely. To my surprise, they agreed.

So I got first-hand confirmation of Amnesty's allegations. He told me that he had been tortured before coming to the prison but was being treated alright there. We talked generally about the fight for freedom and of his plans for the future. He said that if he were to get out he would go straight back to fighting for the liberation of East Timor. He was a very brave man.

Whenever I visit repressive regimes I usually put a prison visit at the top of my agenda, not typical tourist fodder. I think it is so important to get first-hand accounts of what is going on. I was grateful to the Indonesian authorities for allowing me access, because it enabled me to confirm that some prisoners had been tortured when they were first captured but that, once in prison, the torture had ceased.

We were supposed to meet other people there, but either they didn't turn up or they were terrified to talk in case they were overheard by the authorities. Groups were brought to us and we were told they could speak their mind. They spoke in very soft voices, and even when a member of the church came in to speak to us he could not say what he felt because the door was open and somebody from the security forces was listening, rather obviously, to our conversation. Our programme had originally included a meeting with the outspoken Bishop Belo but it never took place. We were told later that the bishop had not even known of our presence. There was such a climate of secrecy and fear that you could almost taste it.

After returning I was put in touch with a group of Timorese women who had escaped to Portugal and I went out to interview them in Lisbon about their experiences. Many of them had been raped by the Indonesians and had horrific tales to tell. I forwarded my evidence to Carmel Budiardjo, who ran a pressure group called TAPOL. She is an extraordinary woman with boundless energy and hope. I also shared it with the Portuguese authorities in the hope they would pursue the issue, but years later I met a Portuguese MP in London and asked what had happened. I became very angry when it became clear it had all been swept under the carpet.

I left East Timor after that first trip, determined to champion the cause of the Timorese. I gave evidence to the United Nations' Special Committee on Decolonization in New York on the subject, urging them to recognise the rights of the East Timorese to hold a referendum on the way in which they wished to be governed. I began to speak out on the issue in the House of Commons and campaign for an arms embargo against the Indonesian dictatorship.

The more I looked into it the more it became clear that, once again, the British government had blood on its hands. As in Malaysia, aid had been linked to arms sales. In 1993 Douglas Hurd had agreed a £65 million soft loan to build a power station in Samarinda, Indonesia, just two months before the Indonesian dictatorship agreed to buy twenty-four Hawk trainer aircraft. The full aid package subsequently increased to over £80 million and *The Observer* newspaper revealed that an order for tanks suited for use in East Timor was also in the pipeline.

Over the next decade aid to Indonesia was to more than double, despite the fact its economy was improving rapidly. Aid money also went to projects in East Timor – projects designed to reinforce Indonesia's illegal occupation. Some £2 million of British taxpayer's money went to a project attempting to colonise East Timor with Javanese peasants, loyal to the Indonesian regime. Yet the government continued to lie to Parliament when telling it that no British aid went to East Timor.

The use of British aid money to train the brutal Indonesian police force was a moral disgrace and a reckless waste of taxpayers' money. One of their colonels, who received training in UK and was later implicated by the East Timorese for human rights violations.

I accused the government of inconsistency and disingenuousness about its Aid For Trade programme which was typified by support for aid projects in East Timor and Indonesia. It was increasingly obvious its overriding objective was to promote big business. Projects were not properly appraised and there were no established criteria. The aid could go to civil or military business, or even arms for internal repression.

There was also more than a whiff of cronyism. GEC, under the chairmanship of Tory grandee Lord Prior, provided shortwave transmitters to the Indonesian Information Ministry, which were used to suppress democratic freedoms. Richard Needham, a minister at the DTI, made frequent visits to Indonesia and joined the board of GEC within two months of leaving office.

The UK became Suharto's largest arms supplier after the US. We were told that British jobs were dependent on the Aid for Trade programme and I was challenged on television and elsewhere as to whether I could justify arms embargos if they cost British workers jobs. I could. Britain, I pointed out, was one of the world's largest arms exporters and the Defence Export Services Organisation, a part of the Ministry of Defence, was funded by the British taxpayer to the tune of over £40 million a year. The British construction industry employed three times as many people as the defence industry, but received a fraction of its publicly funded export support. Arms exports accounted for a quarter of all Export Credit Guarantee Department activity. If we had put the funding and effort that we put into arms exports to other sectors, I believe we would have created alternative jobs elsewhere.

When I heard that three women had broken into a BAe site and disarmed a Hawk jet, I felt nothing but admiration for them. And when I heard that they had been acquitted by a Liverpool jury on the basis that they had acted to prevent a greater crime, genocide, I could not have been more delighted.

Providing torture equipment is big business and some British companies were caught in the act. The activities of British Aerospace were exposed by the *Dispatches* programme on Channel Four in 1995. The company was prepared to sell electro-shock weapons to countries found to practise torture. Posing as an undercover arms dealer, producer Martin Gregory was offered $3.5 million worth of electro-shock weapons by BAe. The next morning, we were fully expecting the government to announce an inquiry at the least, but the DTI response was extraordinary. Gregory was accused of entrapment and threatened with prosecution. Channel 4 backed off, but Gregory bravely responded by launching defamation proceedings against three ministers at the DTI.

I felt strongly that all of us who were involved in campaigning against the arms trade had to step up and support Gregory. I tabled an Early Day Motion urging a review of legislation on export of torture equipment and another, signed by nearly 100 MPs, supporting Martin Gregory in his libel actions and again calling on government to investigate allegations. I wrote to the Prime Minister demanding an inquiry only to be fobbed off. Many of us also took to the airwaves to defend the programme makers and, with the media generally inclined to defend its own, the storm of controversy forced the government to climb down and pay £55,000 in damages.

After the *Dispatches* programme was shown I resolved to dig deeper into British export licences to Indonesia. I asked over 100 parliamentary questions on arms export licences, but trying to get an answer on this issue was like drawing teeth. Prevarication and obfuscation were the order of the day. Lynda Chalker, the Overseas Aid Minister, became increasingly tetchy in our exchanges in the House of Commons.

I borrowed a researcher from Dale, Jim Mahon, to work with me. We spent six months compiling evidence linking aid and arms sales, and I tabled another fifty or so questions. As a result we produced a comprehensive report called 'British Aid to Indonesia: The Continuing Scandal'. The report also detailed a number of human rights abuses, including the 1991 Santa Cruz Massacre in East Timor, when 300, mainly young people, were killed when government troops opened fire on a peaceful procession in the Santa Cruz cemetery.

In launching the report I called for an investigation by the National Audit Office and for the Attorney General to investigate illegal use of British aid to Indonesia. Lynda Chalker denied everything and rubbished the report, claiming that the government had supplied copious information including the answers to over 100 parliamentary questions. She was also dismissive of my repeated demands that Britain should monitor the end-use of its arms exports. She said that it would be impossible to corroborate despite the fact that other countries, including the US, managed to do so.

Parliamentary questions can be a highly effective means of extracting information from the government, but they can also prove incredibly frustrating as I was finding out. In November 1995 I had asked Michael Heseltine, the grandly titled President of the Board of Trade, if he could list the companies to which export licences were granted for the export of electronic batons in the last five years. A straightforward enough question you would have thought, but the reply was that the question could only be answered at disproportionate cost and therefore the information was not provided. This caused widespread amusement. During a public meeting on East Timor in Dublin, an Irish senator walked up to me as I finished speaking. He pushed ten pounds into my hand. 'Towards the cost of answering the question!' he said to loud applause.

As ever I was not prepared to back down, so I proceeded to ask the same question separately for each of the five years. At the very least I thought it would embarrass the government and make a point but, to my surprise, my questions were answered. In each of the years, except 1993, no licences were granted for these goods and in 1993 only one. I never did work out why it was more cost effective to answer year by year.

During this period I travelled to Indonesia on many occasions; few of these trips can be described as uplifting. But on one trip something quite remarkable happened, which was to bring enormous solace to my family and others too.

Jo Owen, my mother's cousin, had died in a Japanese prisoner of war camp in Java, but the family knew very little about his death. It was a tragic story. The only son of the large Hendre farm in Abergynolwyn, he did not have to serve in the war but, after a family argument over a girl he was courting, he joined the RAF. After training, he was shipped out to Singapore, arriving days after its fall to the Japanese. The next flight out was cancelled. The family did not know what became of him until they were informed that he had been captured by the Japanese. His mother wrote to him every week but only ever received standard reply cards. Jo died in a POW camp three months before the end of the war. Other than a brusque communication of his death no one in the immediate family knew what had become of him.

By a strange quirk of fate a niece of the last person to see him in the village before he left went to work for the British Council in Jakarta. She came across his grave in the large war graves cemetery there. She had mentioned it to family at home and the word got back to us.

On my next trip to Jakarta I made contact and went with her to visit the grave. It was incredibly moving. There was only a simple marker with his name, Jo Owen, and the date of death. I commissioned a new headstone which gave his name, his parents' names and a rhyming couplet in Welsh:

> *O Walia I Jafa aeth Jo*
> *Ffeirio'I wlad a ffarwelio;*
> *Ateb her â dewrder dau,*
> *A gwrol uwchlaw geiriau.*

Jo went from Wales to Jafa
Changing country and saying his goodbyes;
He answered the challenge with great courage
And was brave beyond words.

The day afterwards I was at an official banquet in Jakarta and found myself sitting next to a Japanese man. I knew logically that none of it was this man's fault but I was finding the situation very difficult. I thought it best just to address the issue and told him straight that my uncle had died as a prisoner of the Japanese and that I had just been to visit his grave. The man was kind and sympathetic and although part of me felt it inappropriate to raise the issue I also felt that it would have been a betrayal of Uncle Jo to have sat there and said nothing.

The discovery was particularly emotional for his immediate family and friends. On my return I wrote about my experience. That brought about meetings with other men who had been in the camp with Jo and they told me great stories about him, about his sense of humour and his bravery. They told me that he was once severely beaten for standing up to their Japanese captors.

Before I left I had spoken about my planned trip on a BBC Wales radio programme and invited anyone who had similar experiences, losing someone in that war, to get in touch and I would see if I could find the grave. Where I succeeded I photographed it and took cuttings from shrubs in the cemetery, keeping them damp in tissue. When I got home I sent the photographs and cuttings to the families.

In the run-up to the 1997 general election, the Labour Party had published its defence strategy paper which included the commitment not to 'sell weapons to regimes which would use them for repressive purposes or to threaten or invade neighbouring countries'. When, in 1997, Labour won the general election, my colleagues and I had high hopes of improvement in the field of arms exports, a hope that was encouraged when Robin Cook made a speech in the FCO about human rights and the arms trade, highlighting the new government's commitment to an 'ethical foreign policy'. He specifically said we would not be sending arms to countries for 'internal repression' or 'external oppression'. I remember going up to him after the speech and saying how very pleased I was to hear a British Foreign Secretary make that statement. I also said, 'I'll be watching you,' and he replied, 'I know you will!'

Within weeks Cook rose to his feet in the House of Commons to make a statement on arms sales criteria. I, and other campaigners, were dismayed that there was not a single reference to human rights. He went on to announce that another sixteen Hawk aircraft, over 300 armoured vehicles, as well as water cannons, were to be exported to Indonesia. I was livid. This was not what I had expected of our government, and furthermore, Cook's announcement was in direct contravention of Labour Party policy. I was not prepared to take it lying down and made my views about the policy and the Foreign Secretary known on the floor of the House and in the media.

One day I remember Cook, who had little physical presence, arriving rather apologetically in my office. I called in Jeremy Corbyn, my closest ally on East Timor, and we both berated Robin for his betrayal. He tried the line that the contracts were already signed and he was legally committed to following through. We asked to see the legal advice because we had been advised that that simply was not the case. Of course, it was not forthcoming. Cramped into my small cubby hole of an office the whole meeting was stilted and embarrassing and Cook did not really have any convincing answers. He really scraped the barrel when, in response to Jeremy's assertion that there was clear and undisputed evidence of Hawks being deployed in East Timor, he said the British ambassador had not seen them. Given that the ambassador rarely left Jakarta that was hardly surprising. It was to prove one of my greatest disappointments with Tony Blair's government. An 'ethical foreign policy' had promised so much but turned out to be a hollow promise. Fine words but little substance.

The final chapter of my campaigning on East Timor proved a much happier occasion. In 1999 I travelled to Dili with Jeremy Corbyn and Alice Mahon as part of an international group of electoral observers for a UN-sponsored referendum. I have performed the same task in Iraq, Cambodia and South Africa and they are always joyous occasions.

I particularly recall the excitement of the first post-apartheid elections in South Africa. I visited polling stations in Orange Free State, the Afrikaner heartland. The Afrikaners' polling station was in the centre of town and well organised, it completed its business by late morning. The rest of the population had to trek out to temporary stations in the fields, so inadequately staffed that elderly people and pregnant women had to queue in the hot sun for hours. The lines were still there well into the night. They didn't care. There was a carnival atmosphere and everyone was full of hope for the future.

I had been fortunate to meet Nelson Mandela when he visited London shortly after being released from Robben Island. Neil Kinnock had kept in touch with him when he was in prison, sending him books and campaigning for his release, so when Mandela visited London he came to meet Neil's shadow Cabinet, of which I was an elected member. He and Winnie talked to each of us, shaking our hands, and it was a memorable moment. We were all seasoned politicians, not easily impressed, but I suspect our reactions were not unlike those of adolescent fans meeting their boyband heroes. Although I managed not to scream with pleasure!

Mandela was special. It is hard to describe how humble and inspirational he was at the same time. And all with a twinkle in his eye. While I was out for the elections I set my heart on bringing back one of the iconic election posters. I went to the ANC headquarters but they had run out. My taxi driver took pity on me and said he knew where he could find one. When we got there he shinned up a lamp-post and got me the poster. It now has pride of place in my office in London.

The same spirit of excitement and hope was palpable in the East Timor referendum. Many people were voting for the first time in living memory. They were coming down from the mountains, carrying their elderly and disabled family members on makeshift stretchers, determined not to miss out on this historic occasion. This was all despite a lot of violence from supporters of the Indonesian regime. Polling stations were attacked and burned down and there was sporadic fighting, all of which caused our hosts to nervously insist we stay together where they could protect us. They had not reckoned on Jeremy, always a free spirit, who would wander off on his own regardless, causing great consternation. One day we were visiting a polling station up in the mountains and Jeremy just got out of the car and walked off by himself. He was gone for hours. Goodness knows where he went; he loved just going off and talking to people. As the delegation's leader, I was furious with him for disrupting the whole schedule.

Unsurprisingly, there was an overwhelming vote for independence from Indonesia but the joy was short-lived. Anti-independence militias, supported by the Indonesian military, launched a campaign of retaliation and killed some 3,000 Timorese. The UN moved in peace-keeping troops and finally, in 2002, East Timor realised its hard-won independence and was recognised as an independent state. Xanana Gusmão became the first President of East Timor, a man I had first met in a prison cell in Jakarta. The next time I met him was in a suite at London's Dorchester Hotel. He had invited me to discuss the country's progress and greeted me with a huge smile. He was a leader I had a lot of time for, very much in the Nelson Mandela mould. He was quietly spoken and self-effacing, yet charismatic and committed to reconciliation in his country.

One of the things I have learnt during my long service in politics is that time moves on, governments change, and the same issues raise their ugly heads again and again. I served on the Commons Arms Export Committee for fifteen years under Sir John Stanley. He was a highly principled man and an effective chairman. On his watch we repeatedly embarrassed governments, none more so than the coalition government on its sale of chemicals to the Syrian regime. However, in 2015 Sir John retired and, rather scandalously I felt, after the general election the CAEC was not reconvened for about six months until ten others joined me in campaigning for its reinstatement.

Hilary Benn, in his role as shadow Foreign Secretary, called for its re-establishment citing the urgent need to review sales of arms to Saudi Arabia. In March 2015, the Saudis had brutally intervened in the Yemen. There was a public outcry as the civilian death toll mounted and a humanitarian disaster loomed. A UN report cited 'widespread and systematic attacks on civilian targets' and the Labour Party called for an immediate suspension of arms sales to Saudi Arabia pending a UN investigation.

The CAEC duly reconvened and instigated an inquiry. CAEC is unusual in that it is made up of representatives of four select committees – Business, Defence, Foreign Affairs and International Development – which can make it unwieldy and achieving a quorum difficult. We were due to publish the report at the end of July 2016, just before Parliament broke for the summer, but when the date was arranged it clashed with another meeting in my diary. I said I could change my diary if necessary but was assured the meeting was quorate. When CAEC did meet, it was not quorate as it was short of a Foreign Affairs member. If only I had been there. I immediately smelt a rat because my view, that arms sales to Saudi should be halted, was in direct opposition to the chair of the Foreign Affairs Committee, Crispin Blunt.

When Parliament returned in September the issue had become more pressing. Human Rights Watch and many other NGOs were calling on Britain, and others, to halt weapons sales to Saudi. New Foreign Secretary Boris Johnson tried to pre-empt the report by assuring Saudi Arabia the UK would continue to sell it weapons. But a draft report, tabled by the chairs of the Business and International Development Committees, took the view that such sales should be suspended immediately until the UN could lead an investigation into alleged violations of international law by Saudi Arabia.

The meeting to discuss the draft report was bad-tempered. We went around the table for hours, well into the evening, as the unholy alliance of Crispin Blunt and John Spellar tabled over 130 amendments in an attempt to filibuster. Hours later, when it became clear they were not going to succeed, the pair of them walked out, leaving the meeting inquorate and powerless to act.

Within the next few days Saudi Arabia mounted a diplomatic offensive, sending over its Foreign Minister, Adel al-Jubeir, to reassure MPs that they were investigating and could find no evidence to back the claims being made. Hilary Benn, who was sitting next to me, said there was plenty of evidence and I and many other Labour members backed him. Of course, hand in glove with the rebuttal of the allegations came the promises of support and financial aid. It was sickening to watch members, including those from my own party, fawning at the Saudis' feet, hoping to use the occasion to secure trade deals.

Days later we met again and Crispin Blunt tabled an alternative draft report, asking the government to support an international inquiry into the allegations but not an arms embargo. I proposed we should vote on the original draft report but was defeated. A few days later the Foreign Affairs Committee put out a misleading press release, implying the conclusion was 'unsactioned'. I raised the issue with the Speaker, pointing out most people only read press releases, not full reports, and that it was unacceptable for a Commons Committee to deliberately mislead in this way.

Once again the UK had bowed to vested interests; any hope of an ethical foreign policy remained a distant dream.

CHAPTER THIRTEEN

WALKING A TIGHTROPE

arly one morning a black taxi pulled up unexpectedly outside my London flat. Its driver hand-delivered a letter which summoned me to meet the leader of the Labour Party, Neil Kinnock. Having voted against the party whip on the defence budget, I could guess what was coming next. Sure enough I arrived at Neil's office at Westminster to find the Chief Whip, Derek Foster, with him. It was a certain portent of doom. Neil said, as leaders always do, that he was reluctant to sack me but that party discipline … blah, blah, blah. As I left his office, a backbencher once again, his parting comment was: 'Don't worry, I'll be watching your back.' A strange statement to make in the circumstances; a bit like closing the stable door after the horse had bolted, I thought. Was he warning me that the whips were out to get me again?

Few people outside Westminster truly appreciate the extent of the whips' power. I am not sure I did at first, although it certainly became apparent after being sacked by two leaders who protested that they did not want to sack me. For party discipline read Whips' Office. Officially, the whips, MPs themselves, exist to organise their party's parliamentary business. This ranges from allocating offices to assigning people to committees, ensuring people attend votes and vote the way their party wants them to. In reality their power is widespread. They reward 'good behaviour' with superior accommodation, desirable committees and 'pairings' with opposition MPs to allow them time off. They have the power to make and break careers, an instrument they wield mercilessly. No one, it seems, is immune from their power and that includes party leaders, for whom upsetting their own whips is tantamount to a suicide note.

I was doomed from the start as a result of a vendetta harboured by the late Ray Powell. It dated back to the Ogmore by-election when I fought him for the nomination. Perhaps he blamed me for the bad publicity he attracted over the murky dealings within the constituency party but if so, he was wrong. I was aware of the allegations, but once I failed to get the nomination I moved on. I think he was probably a misogynist; he certainly never had a good word to say about any female politician, although he may have changed in later life when his own daughter was elected to the Welsh Assembly. He was legendary for imagining slights and harbouring resentments. I was later told that he had erupted when, as an MEP, I supported Tony Benn's bid for the deputy leadership at an event in his constituency. Even after entering Westminster as MP for the safe Cynon Valley seat – which surely put paid to any chance of my reappearing in Ogmore – his vindictiveness continued to fester.

Physically, he was a little, fat man, but he was also a bully. His belligerent temperament made him a natural for the Whips' Office, where he enjoyed wielding power. He seemed determined to make my life a misery. It was Ray who had deliberately put me on two important committees which met at the same time, the Gas Privatisation Bill and the Felixstowe Docks & Harbours Bill, ensuring that I could not do either properly. When I asked him what he expected me to do, he advised me to run up and down the corridor between the two, a huge grin on his face at what he perceived as his witticism. Not content with making practical difficulties for me, he then launched a smear campaign.

I was aware that he was bad-mouthing me to other MPs, particularly the Welsh group, but I saw red when he went public with accusations that I was not doing my job properly with relation to the select committees. He had a friend in the Welsh media, Mike Steel, who worked for HTV. Mike placed articles in the Welsh newspapers and also wrote a script for HTV. It was full of misinformation and innuendo, classic Ray Powell. I was not going to take it lying down and demanded corrections to the script and made it clear that any misrepresentation would result in legal action. It eventually blew over, but not before my constituency party took umbrage and wrote a formal complaint to the Ogmore constituency party, insisting they tell their man to lay off. I was damned if I was going to let Ray see that he was getting to me, but on the inside, as a newly elected MP, I felt it was threatening and unfair.

His reaction to the Oxfam trip to Cambodia was the tip of an iceberg. Again and again I would detect his malevolent hand when I got into trouble with the Whips' Office. The man was a total shit and both my sackings had his imprint all over them, not least the way they were plastered all over the media within minutes. Every party has a Ray Powell and it was my bad luck that he chose me as a target.

To be fair, my own independent streak certainly did not help matters. I think the most difficult challenge I have faced in my political career is balancing support of the party line with doing what my conscience dictates. It is like walking a tightrope, one that I have repeatedly fallen off.

As an MEP I had often found myself at odds with our leader in the European Parliament, Barbara Castle, but never voted against the Socialist group. I also found myself out of kilter with the party over membership of the EC, as it then was. As I mentioned earlier, I had been elected on an anti-Euro ticket in 1979 and changed my mind two years later. I had felt the only honest thing to do was to be open about it. It took the party a few more years but eventually our views converged again. To be honest though, I am not sure that many people cared about how I felt, European politics was marginalised. When, as an MEP, I was surprisingly elected to the Labour Party's National Executive at the first attempt, I was greeted as something of a pariah.

I thought standing for the National Executive would be a constructive way of integrating our European and Westminster parliamentarians, but I was told that MEPs were not eligible to stand, which was total nonsense. The policy changed a couple of years later and at the first opportunity I put my name forward. I had big backing from the unions, particularly the Transport and General Workers Union and my old friends on the NUM. The National Executive had several specialist sections to ensure it represented the whole party, including a women's section. The women's section was later replaced by a 50 per cent quota across all sections but it was as a women's section nominee that I was elected, along with Betty Boothroyd.

It was an eye-opening experience. At my first ever meeting the one and only Dennis Skinner was his trademark blunt self. 'What are you doing here?' he snarled and did not speak to me again for several months. Eventually, we got on very well. One of the few friendly faces was Lord Doug Hoyle, an old hand, and he guided me through the arcane workings of the National Executive. These had to be seen to be believed. Rather than the stimulating debate on party policy which I had looked forward to, the reality was a meaningless exercise where a motion would be put; everyone would raise their hand according to their allegiance to the left or right of the party and that would be it. We were expected to behave like a lot of puppets and I was never anybody's puppet.

I was only on there for a year. I think I disappointed the right of the party by voting with the left wing too often. Anyway, at the next party conference much of the union support, including the NUM, shifted to someone else during a late-night horse trading session and I was thrown off. I was disappointed, the South Wales NUM and my constituency party were furious, but I soon got over it. I never tried again, I found the whole thing tedious and plodding – it was no place for a free thinker.

I arrived in Westminster during a by-election less than a year after we had been heavily defeated in a general election, again. The Thatcherites were destroying communities across Britain, my own constituency being particularly badly hit, but there seemed to be nothing we could do. The Labour Party remained in the political wilderness.

I had joined the party and fought my first election under Harold Wilson's leadership. I had spoken at my first party conference in 1970 urged on by Eirene White, MP for East Flint, who advised me to make myself seen and heard, advice I took to heart. I loved going to conference; it was just like an Eisteddfod! They were great fun, a gathering of old friends. You met up with people you had not seen for the intervening year and caught up for a coffee or at the bar. There were interesting fringe meetings and occasionally you would listen to key speeches in the main conference hall. I have to admit though that they could be awfully tedious and, on one occasion, I spent the afternoon with Dale and Brian playing the slot machines in a Blackpool arcade instead.

The leadership seemed remote, a different generation. Wilson was succeeded by Jim Callaghan, MP for Cardiff East, who had come to support me in Denbigh in 1970. He was Prime Minister in what would be the last Labour government for eighteen years. He was succeeded as leader by Michael Foot, a time that coincided with my spell as MEP.

I had the utmost respect for Michael as a man of modesty, conviction and integrity. I had first met him and his wife, Jill Craigie, in my capacity as a journalist and CND campaigner. When the Wilson government announced the closure of the steelworks at Ebbw Vale in 1975, Michael, as the local MP and Employment Minister, insisted on going and explaining to the men himself. He took John Morris, then

Welsh Secretary, with him but John soon disappeared out of the back door. I wrote about that in my *Guardian* article and John was angry, demanding an apology. Michael's wife, Jill, was a well-known film and documentary maker. 'Michael,' she would say plaintively, 'can't you find Ann a seat somewhere?' However, the British electorate did not appreciate Michael and the party looked to a new generation to lead it.

A lot of people assumed Denzil Davies, the young and talented MP for Llanelli, would be in the running as the next party leader. Sadly, Denzil's ambitions to lead the party came to nothing. Neil Kinnock travelled the length and breadth of the country building up support. Denzil blew his chance one hot summer evening on the terrace of the House of Commons when he said he was going to resign as shadow Chancellor. His abrupt 'throw-away' remark, after a boozy night waiting for a vote, was picked up by a Press Association reporter. Michael eventually anointed Neil his chosen successor and the rest, as they say, is history. I liked Denzil, he was a great support when I was the MEP for his constituency and we shared an agent in Jeff Hopkins. We were on opposing sides of the devolution debate with Denzil a prominent campaigner against devolution for Wales, while I was very much in favour.

By the time I entered Westminster, Neil was leading the party. As an MEP our paths had rarely crossed, although I did persuade him, with some effort, to come and visit the Socialist group in Brussels. That was before the Kinnock family took to European politics. At Westminster our paths would inevitably be more interlinked. I think he had initially seen me as someone he could mould, a potential ally. After all we were both Welsh, even had neighbouring industrial constituencies and were both associated with the soft left of the party. I had nothing against Neil but I had my own ideas and spoke out, regularly. Presumably he also had the Whips' Office muttering in his ear; my alleged inability to juggle two select committees; my absence from a 'key vote' while in Cambodia; my flair for publicity. Who knows what other poison went in?

In contrast to the view from the Whips' Office, my stock within the parliamentary party was rising. Although I do not blindly toe the party line, as a member of the shadow Cabinet I accepted collective responsibility and as a backbencher I fully understand the need to support party policy. But I also believe there are times when you simply have to act with your conscience. This inevitably puts you on a collision course with the whips. I was not the only member of the 'awkward squad' on the backbenches, by any means, but I received far more than my share of opprobrium from the whips. I did realise they had a job to do, I also appreciated that it was not always an easy role. None of which excuses some of the behaviour I was subjected to.

Neil was trying to re-shape the party in order to get us back into government. We were still in the political wilderness having been heavily defeated in two general elections. The first real inkling I had that he was also going to change long-held Labour policy positions was in the House of Commons dining room. It was 1988 and Dale, Brian and I were sitting at a table with Roland Boyes. Roland, a close friend in the European Parliament, was now on the shadow defence team. He told us Neil was planning to change the party's policy on nuclear weapons, including our position on Trident. He must have seen the stunned expressions on our faces. The party had for some time been a unilateralist party and this was difficult to digest.

I had been at the Labour Party conference where we had passed a resolution against increased spending on nuclear weapons. But I think the leadership felt they had to be seen as 'macho' when it came to defence issues if we were to be electable. A three-line whip was imposed in support of the government's defence spending plans, which predictably included more money for nuclear weapons. It made no sense to me and when the day came I voted against the proposal and against my own party whip. I did not walk into the 'No' lobby with the intention of embarrassing the leadership, but unfortunately, unlike the US and other legislatures, you cannot vote on the defence budget line-by-line. It is all or nothing.

Of course, the whips seized on my act of rebellion and demanded I be sacked from my front bench position as shadow Minister for Education and Women's Rights. It was hardly a surprise, in fact I had been expecting it since finding myself pretty much alone in the division lobby. I did not let Neil get away scot-free though and took the opportunity to remind him of his unilateralist past and the days when he himself had rebelled against his party leadership.

So, I was cast into the wilderness, my career prospects looking decidedly ropey. But there is more than one way of skinning a cat. Until 2011 the majority of the shadow Cabinet was determined by a ballot of the parliamentary party. It was a good system and I think Ed Miliband made a big mistake when he got rid of it. Now the front bench members need only to please their leader to keep their job, they are not accountable to the parliamentary party as a whole. To get on to the shadow Cabinet you needed the support of one of the main parliamentary groups of which Campaign, Tribune and Manifesto were the key players.

The Campaign group were to the hard left of the party and supported by many of my friends including Alice, Jeremy and John McDonnell. Membership was, until recently, considered career-limiting, with the exception of Dawn Primarolo. Dawn, Alice and I became good friends and would often squeeze into the back of Dale's Volkswagen convertible for some jaunt or other. After winning the 1997 general election, Dawn was, as Alice put it, 'colonised' by Gordon Brown's team. Gordon was ever the operator and we felt he had rather cynically brought her into the Treasury team to protect the government from a backbench revolt. Dawn was a formidable politician in her own right and she may well have risen to the top quite naturally. The cynical way in which Gordon's team deployed her at the despatch box, however, wheeling her in for news our wing of the party would find unpalatable, meant she drifted away from the rest of us.

I did not have many friends at Manifesto, which later became Solidarity.

They were the right-wingers, people like Stuart Randall, Stuart Bell and Roy Hattersley. Perhaps it was his membership of this group that gave Roy the reputation of being to the right of the party. When he stood for the leadership as deputy to Neil Kinnock, it was widely regarded as a dream ticket; Neil representing the left and Roy the right.

I have been a member of Tribune, described as a soft left group, since my early days in Parliament. I was its first woman chair during which time I attempted to bring Tribune and Campaign together under one umbrella but did not quite manage to pull it off. With their support though I topped the ballot for the shadow Cabinet in 1991 – just three years after Neil sacked me. He was not exactly thrilled to bits to have me back.

I comfortably retained my position the following year but was then voted off after upsetting the Manchester MPs over Granada Television's broken franchise commitments. Tom Pendry, in particular, was very upset and I was told he and his friends plotted to remove me from the shadow Cabinet, although Tom denies it.

The real villain of the piece was Dale though! For some reason, best known to himself, he chose to back Gavin Strang, even ran his campaign. I never rated Strang and I was not the only one who never understood why Dale championed him. Unsurprisingly, Strang came way down the list, meanwhile I missed out by three votes. I was bitterly disappointed to be voted off and refused to speak to Dale for about a week. Harriet Harman was also kicked off at the same time but, in her case, with Gordon's backing, she was nevertheless brought back in as shadow Chief Secretary to the Treasury.

By this time Neil had moved over and John Smith was leader. He was a warm, witty and inspiring man and became a reforming and unifying force in the party, making us electable again. He was very supportive when I lost out in the shadow Cabinet election and told me to bide my time. He also apologised for Harriet's elevation. 'I am so sorry about that,' he said, 'but what could I do – Gordon insisted.'

I was devastated by his sudden death the following year. I heard the news in the House of Commons cloakroom and could hardly believe it. Only twenty-four hours earlier we had all been celebrating record local election success. I was not alone in failing to hold back the tears. John had managed to introduce 'One Member One Vote', removing direct union representation in parliamentary selection, a move which I supported. He could have been a great leader and Prime Minister, his death was an enormous blow to the party.

Discussing what makes a good leader is one of those conversations everyone likes to take part in. There are all sorts of intellectual opinions but for my friends and I, it was always the 'tea-room test'. This is not as odd as it sounds; appearance in the tea room, where most MPs tend to gather, is an indication of the degree to which the leader is comfortable with his or her own MPs. And John was the arch exponent of accessibility. He would be in the tea room every morning enjoying breakfast with his Scottish colleagues and he was also partial to inviting people back to his room for a 'wee dram' after late-night debates. Neil made regular appearances but was usually flanked by his entourage; Allan Rogers, MP for the Rhondda, was like an extra tail. Tony Blair would make some forays but you always suspected there was some sort of agenda and I can never remember seeing Gordon Brown there. Ed Miliband was quite shy so although he was seen he did not engage naturally with people the way John Smith did.

John's death opened the leadership debate again. I had decided to support Gordon Brown, perceiving him as the strongest and most radical candidate. Brian, in particular, rated his intellect and grasp of finance. But then a bombshell dropped.

It was a beautiful evening, the sun setting over Cardigan Bay, and I was looking forward to a relaxing supper. Aberdyfi was my refuge from a hectic life so when the phone rang Owen called out for me to ignore it. I answered. The caller was Gordon. I confirmed that Dale Campbell-Savours and Brian Sedgemore were with me and the ensuing conversation, somewhat one-sided, was short and to the point.

I returned to the kitchen in a state of surprise; Dale, Brian and Owen had picked up some of the conversation and now looked at me expectantly. 'He's not going to stand for the leadership,' I said. 'He wants us to vote for Tony Blair.'

Whenever Dale and Brian came down to stay in Aberdyfi we would spend our days sailing, walking or reading, but our evenings were a time for political chat. We debated policies, plotted campaigns and, of course, gossiped. We were not short of things to talk about that evening.

We were stunned at Gordon's withdrawal. We were all aware of his ambition to lead the party so the withdrawal came as a bolt from the blue. It was all very well speculating about the reason behind Gordon's decision but we had to decide who we would now support, Tony, Margaret Beckett or John Prescott. Gordon wanted us to support Tony, the shadow Home Secretary. He was clearly able and had proved himself an excellent performer in the House of Commons and appeared the best of the remaining candidates. We took Gordon's advice.

It later emerged that the two of them had reached a pact whereby Tony would stand for leadership with Gordon as his Chancellor and, after a suitable time, hand over the reins. Millions of trees have been pulped to accommodate media speculation about the exact terms of the agreement but no one except the two men will ever know.

Under Tony my career looked to be turning in a positive direction as I was appointed opposition spokesperson for Employment and then Foreign Affairs. The New Labour project was in full swing; party discipline was tighter than ever and we all carried pagers which alerted us to the party line on every subject imaginable. We all had to sing from the same hymn-sheet and myriad other clichés. And I did.

Finally, it looked as though we could return to government. I had my disagreements with Tony, but he delivered three terms in government for a party that had been in the political wilderness. As a committed socialist and to the left of the party I had issue with many New Labour policies, particularly the rolling back of benefits. At the end of the day though what was the alternative? More years of Tory government would have caused greater hardship to the people in my constituency and given tacit support to some invidious regimes around the world.

Personally, I always found him approachable and a good listener. On Iraq I say that he eventually came round to my point of view, that there was no alternative to the physical removal of Saddam Hussein. After the war he appointed me his Special Envoy on Human Rights in Iraq; it was a fascinating time and enabled me to continue to be involved with the Kurds and the country as a whole. During that period we met regularly and I always found him engaged and supportive of my work. He was genuinely interested in rebuilding the country, which is more than could be said of Gordon. He behaved as if he had inherited a mess that had nothing to do with him despite being the second most powerful man in government at the time the critical decisions were made.

I make no apology for my support of Tony Blair as Prime Minister and I am angered by the vitriol directed towards him by people who have conveniently forgotten their earlier support. Some members of the party were never fans of his, the New Labour project, or the Iraq war, and I respect that. Those who infuriate me are the hypocrites who were happy to serve in the administration, never spoke out against policy at the time, and now seek to airbrush their history.

After the war Tony would often point to my role in Iraq over the years, praising me in public. I would then remind him that I was the first member of his front bench team that he sacked! He had not been a leader long when that happened. It all blew up over my 'unsanctioned visit' to Iraqi Kurdistan. Once again the Whips' Office chose to make my visit a test of party discipline and make an example of me. I was called in to see Tony on my first morning back. Jonathan

Powell, his Chief of Staff, and Derek Foster, the Chief Whip, were with him. I was told that I would have to go; it was a matter of 'party discipline'. He had been backed into a corner by the whips and I bore no resentment towards him. I could, once again, detect the hand of my arch nemesis Ray Powell. I pointed to the Chief Whip, who was supported by USDAW, and said: 'He's your problem. He's old Labour. He's the man you ought to get rid of. '

I kept my head down for a while and then sought to get re-elected to the shadow Cabinet. I narrowly missed out in 1994 and in 1995. In 1996 I was unsuccessful and never stood again.

In the 1997 general election we won a landslide majority and returned to government. Finally, we were able to roll back the excesses of the Conservative governments at home and abroad. I enjoyed the celebrations and the new mood in Parliament that followed, but I was disappointed not to be a member of a Labour government.

I threw myself into committee work, campaigning for human rights and, of course, regime change in Iraq.

I became chair of the PLP in 2005 having previously served as vice-chair for a number of years. Time was passing and Tony was showing no signs of leaving. Gordon was becoming increasingly frustrated and bad-tempered. He was a difficult man, one of obvious talent and intellectual ability, but on the personal side he was morose and a bully. It was clear to everyone at Westminster that the relationship between them was poisoned and their respective teams geared up for action.

Team Brown's tactics started to get out of hand with regular media briefings as the whole affair played out in the press. The party was becoming a laughing stock and the final straw came when, in 2006, Labour MPs Chris Bryant, Wayne David and others wrote an open letter demanding that Blair go. Our MPs were being caught in the cross-fire; some pledging their support for one of the two warring factions, most wishing the issue would go away and not damage our ability to govern or our electoral chances. It was a difficult, nasty period and, of course, it was replayed when Gordon became Prime Minister and the factions within the party plotted to get rid of him. Today the party is again in the grips of a civil war, more pernicious than any that preceded it.

Back then, with no sign of the civil war abating, I felt I had to do something about it. As Chair of the PLP I asked for a meeting with Gordon. It would have been easier to gain an audience with the Pope. Excuse after excuse, delay after delay, he would agree a date and then cancel but I persisted. Eventually, he agreed to see me, late on a Thursday afternoon when like other MPs I would normally be leaving for my constituency. I headed for the Treasury at the appointed time, and waited. Eventually he appeared with his PPS Ann Keen and, somewhat reluctantly, sat down.

I explained that I had asked to see him to discuss the briefing against the Prime Minister that was coming, if not directly from him, certainly from his team. He prevaricated and blustered and said he did not know what I was talking about. 'Gordon,' I said, 'you must be the only person in the country that doesn't.' The media was full of it day after day. He affected a bemused expression and continued to protest his ignorance. I told him to stop it, that whatever his feelings, this washing of our dirty linen in public had to stop, it was irrevocably damaging the party. 'Call your dogs off,' I said to him sharply. 'Otherwise the party will never forgive you.'

It was a short meeting and I saw no discernible change in Team Brown. Behind the scenes their lobbying continued and now I was in the headlights as well. It was not long before I lost the PLP chair, it was rumoured that it was because I had become 'too close to Tony Blair'.

Being accused of being in the pocket of the party leadership, moreover a leader who was now perceived to be to the right of the party, was a new experience for me. Until then I had been labelled a thorn in the side of successive leaders.

CHAPTER FOURTEEN

WALES

Denzil Davies looked at me as though I had grown a pair of horns. He and I had spent many years in happy opposition over the issue of devolution for Wales. I had campaigned as vociferously for devolution as he had campaigned against it. The Commons sat long hours as Denzil and Ted Rowlands kept us up to three in the morning attempting to talk out the legislation. We had agreed to differ.

After Denzil's retirement from the House of Commons our paths rarely crossed but, when the National Eisteddfod came to Llanelli in 2014, it was inevitable that we should meet again. The town's former MP was happily holding court among his old constituents and the great and good of Wales. His bonhomie and skill as a raconteur were still clearly visible. I was pleased to see him and conversation turned to the consideration of new powers for the Welsh Assembly. Denzil, predictably, expressed his opposition. I think he was expecting me to counter him, as I had done repeatedly over the years, but I did not. 'Denzil,' I said, 'you were right and I was wrong.'

His face was a picture and he was lost for words, a rare occurrence. I explained that not only was I opposed to further powers for the Welsh Assembly, I now had second thoughts about the whole devolution project.

I had been devastated when we lost the first devolution referendum in 1979 – I had even taken leave of absence from *The Guardian* to campaign for a 'yes' vote. Like most of our friends Owen and I believed passionately that it was time for the Welsh people to have more say in our own destiny.

The defeat when it came was overwhelming, only 12 per cent voted in favour, but it was hardly a surprise to me. Even the Labour Party had been divided on the issue. Day after day I stood in shopping centres and knocked on doors debating the issue with my compatriots and getting very little support. Things were different in the West, the Welsh-speaking heartland, but in Cardiff and South Wales the answer was overwhelmingly 'no'. The confidence just was not there. 'It will just be jobs for the boys,' was one constant refrain. People saw it as another, unwanted, layer of government that would be a drain on the public purse.

Two months later, at the May general election, the Conservative Party came into power and stayed for the next eighteen years. Under Thatcher the people of Wales suffered. Coal and other heavy industry was wiped out, unemployment became endemic, the public sector – schools, hospitals, libraries and so on – was cut back as was the state safety net for the old, the sick and the poor. Welsh Office bureaucracy was spiralling out of control and the country seemed to be governed by hundreds of unaccountable quangos. Little wonder then that people began to wonder whether they had made the right choice.

The Wales Group of Labour MPs, many of whom had resisted transfer of powers, were now coming around. When I first became an MP I had found this group a hostile place. It was very much a boys' club and I was its only woman member. As time passed my gender became less of an issue, as I earned my spurs battling for my constituents. By the '90s I was a relatively senior member of the group – an on-and-off frontbench spokesperson. Peter Hain and Paul Flynn were in the front-line of pro-devolutionists and future Welsh Secretary of

State, Ron Davies, and our leader, Neil Kinnock, had changed their minds and now actively supported the cause. Not all Labour MPs were on-side though and Denzil stuck defiantly to his guns.

A broader coalition involving Labour, Liberal and Plaid Cymru had meanwhile formed a Parliament for Wales Campaign and I was one of several MPs involved. We campaigned hard all over Wales but also had great fun. At the Royal Welsh agricultural show and the Eisteddfod our team wore masks of people like Prime Minister John Major, Prince Charles and Mr Spock from *Star Trek* to attract people to our stand.

The party had its reservations, viewing the campaign as too closely aligned to the nationalist Plaid Cymru. With all the polls indicating that the majority of Welsh people were now in favour of devolution Tony Blair announced that an incoming administration would introduce legislation for a Welsh Assembly within the first year. But, for many, Labour's proposals did not go far enough. Dr John Marek, MP for Wrexham, put the cat among the pigeons by introducing a Bill giving the devolved government primary law-making powers, introducing proportional representation for election of members and, after four years, the ability to raise or lower tax. I joined Paul Flynn in defying the whips and sponsoring the Bill, believing that if we were to devolve power it had to be meaningful and that the official proposals were a wishy-washy compromise.

Of course, the Bill got nowhere and after we won the 1997 general election the official Bill went through despite the efforts of Denzil and others to talk it out. Night after night they kept us up into the early hours of the morning and I would go home bleary-eyed as the sun rose over the Thames. It was worth the lack of sleep when Wales managed a small majority in favour of devolution and Owen and I celebrated long into the night in Cardiff. All of which explains how my comments in Llanelli were a bit of a shock for Denzil.

To say the reality of a Welsh Assembly did not live up to my expectations is understating the case. I feel bitterly disappointed and let down by an institution I campaigned so passionately for. No one is prouder of their Welsh heritage than I am, but I can recognise our weaknesses as well as our strengths. One of our greatest weaknesses as a nation is the giant chip that we carry on our shoulder, a symptom of the centuries of being a poor relation to England. As a result, we view any criticism, even the constructive kind, as an attack and immediately pull up the drawbridge. Translated into institutional behaviour this becomes dangerous as it means organisations do not learn from their mistakes or the experience of others.

Given that my party has been in power at the Assembly, either out-right or in coalition, since its inception, it pains me to observe that it has a poor track record. In health, education and other areas we are lagging behind the rest of Britain. Meanwhile the Welsh Assembly government refuses to accept people's concerns, spending more time defending the indefensible rather than fixing what is wrong. What makes it worse is that people who genuinely care about what is happening, and speak out, are accused of betrayal if we dare to voice any concern or criti-cism. 'Go back to Westminster and leave us alone' is the subtext.

As far as I am concerned I am elected to represent the people of the Cynon Valley. I do not see why my constituents should die earlier and receive worse care because they live there. I will raise issues wherever and to whoever is responsible regardless. The demarcation line between the two governments is a sensitive area and we are still finding our way in how representation on issues works on the ground.

My own relationship with the leadership at Cardiff is another matter. When the Health and Social Services Committee at the Assembly invited me to speak to them about work I had done on health complaints the lead-ership tried to block my attendance. Leighton Andrews, who at that time was AM (Assembly Member) for the Rhondda, said it was not appropriate for a Westminster MP to give evidence to an Assembly committee.

And as for Mark Drakeford, he is continually in denial that there is anything wrong in Wales. Things came to a head in the run-up to the 2015 general election as the Conservative Party attacked Labour on its performance in Wales. I actually thought Cameron was right to attack its performance. Drakeford, then Minister for Health and Social Service at the Welsh Assembly, and others who were defending what was going on in Wales were misleading people.

The extent of this myopia hit me when I was verbally attacked by a local Assembly Member at a constituency party meeting. We were discussing health issues and I was saying how the Assembly needed to get a grip on waiting lists because Wales was lagging well behind England and Scotland. 'It's a lie,' said Christine Chapman. They were strong words and a hush descended over the meeting. I was not going to take that lying down. I produced the statistics which proved the case and also referred to a 2015 report by the Royal College of Surgeons, *The State of Surgery in Wales*, which warned that 'unacceptably high waiting times in Wales need to be urgently tackled'. Although I demanded an apology it was not forthcoming. She went on to say that I was betraying my colleagues in the party with my outspoken criticism. 'I've always spoken out against my party in Parliament when I think it's been in the wrong and I'll do the same now,' I said. 'Someone needs to speak up for the people around here.'

I have reluctantly concluded that if the devolution referendum was held today I would probably be in the 'no' camp and I certainly will not be supporting any transfer of additional powers to the Assembly. Not until it shows it can effectively carry out its existing responsibilities. I do not wholly blame the AMs – many of whom are hard-working and able – or even the ruling Labour Party. I think a large part of the problem is that the Civil Service in Cardiff is inexperienced and out of control, leading to successive scandals. Many of the civil servants, even at a senior level, have never worked outside Wales and the high-fliers in Whitehall cannot be tempted out of London. What I do blame the Welsh government for is not recognising the issues and being big enough to admit mistakes and do something about it.

It is not always doom and gloom. There are very many issues on which we do see eye to eye in the interest of our common constituents. One such was the battle, sadly unsuccessful, to save Remploy.

Remploy (re-employ) dated back to before the post-war Attlee government, set up in 1944 to provide work for disabled returning servicemen and miners. The very first factory was in Bridgend and it soon developed into a network of factories across Britain. Cwmbach in my constituency was typical. I first visited it as a newly elected MP and watched with amazement at the skill and love with which its employees went about their work making special clothing and surgical boots.

I had been involved in disability issues since my MEP days and knew both how important meaningful work was to disabled people and how hard it was to come by. People at Cwmbach told me how working at Remploy enabled them to retain their dignity. It enabled them to provide financial support for their families and take a meaningful place in the community.

For many, alternative employment was not an option. There were already too many able-bodied people competing for available jobs. And often, when they did secure a position their disability was not understood or catered for, leaving them feeling humiliated and bullied.

Remploy provided a place where they could work safely. But, despite its long and proud history and the excellent quality of its output, the future of Remploy's 100 factories became uncertain. In 1994, the Major government scrapped a scheme which gave Remploy supplier-priority for certain government contracts. I suppose if you do not accept the concept of 'society' – as Thatcher herself famously declared – then you are not going to have any sympathy for an organisation like Remploy.

Management was centralised, sales staff nationalised, and the business quickly lost direction. It was inevitable, then, that factories would be shut down. By 2007, Remploy's management had announced forty-two closures. There was an outcry at the Labour Party Conference and the TUC and those of us who had factories in our constituencies were at the forefront of the campaign to save them. A year later several factories did close but others, including Cwmbach, were reprieved.

Ongoing instability did nothing for the organisation and, in 2011, under the coalition government, once again rumours of more closures began to circulate.

I set up and chaired a parliamentary group of interested MPs and persuaded John McDonnell to become its secretary. I have an enormous amount of time for John; he is one of the best MPs I've come across in my time in Parliament. He's principled, committed and very clever. He also had a track record on disability issues having served on a TUC committee tackling discrimination in the 1980s.

My Cwmbach constituents talked to me about their fears for their future, how they were frightened about employment prospects. They, and colleagues across Remploy, were convinced the government was deliberately allowing the organisation to be run at 50 per cent capacity in order to make the case for closure.

There were highly paid consultants crawling all over the business but no one was listening to the workers, who were pleading for a cut in management overheads and an increase in local marketing.

We handed in a 100,000-signature petition to Downing Street and I secured a Westminster Hall debate. We believed Remploy had a perfectly viable future if it could have a decentralised procurement system.

I went to see the Secretary of State for Work and Pensions, Iain Duncan Smith, and Culture Secretary, Maria Miller, to argue the case. They went through the motions, but really did not want to know. They kept referring to Cwmbach as being part of the furniture business to which I replied, 'That's news to me!' In reality it makes products for the surgical market. The quality of their information in general seemed poor. I knew there was no economic case for closing Cwmbach, it was meeting all its production targets. The highly skilled people working there deserved better.

The real issue was procurement. I spent the whole summer visiting Welsh local authorities and NHS purchasing departments, trying to bring them together with Remploy. I was trying to persuade them that they could make a real difference. It was an uphill battle though. The public sector was under attack from every direction and although the people I met made promises, only a few of them delivered.

Neither Duncan Smith nor Miller gave Remploy a fair chance. Duncan Smith infuriated workers after a comment he made suggesting that they 'go out and get proper jobs' was printed in the *Daily Express*. Did he have neither the imagination nor empathy to understand that in a savage labour market these people would be at the back of the queue? I was horrified. Surely it is the hallmark of a civilised society that it ensures its most vulnerable are protected.

In 2012, following a review, Duncan Smith withdrew all subsidies and Miller announced that thirty-six of the fifty-four factories would close by the end of the year with the loss of 17,000 jobs.

After a major protest rally in London the factories earmarked for closure were cut to thirty-three. Cwmbach escaped the bullet, but Abertillery, Bridgend, Croespenmaen, Merthyr, Swansea and Wrexham were closed along with their counterparts elsewhere in the UK.

The staff at Cwmbach told me they had christened Maria Miller 'Remploy Killer'. When I referred to this in Parliament she looked very hurt, her lip wobbled and Iain Duncan Smith had to lay his hand protectively on her shoulder. His sympathy would have been better reserved for the disabled workforce at Remploy.

In October 2013 the last three factories – at Neath, Blackburn and Sheffield – were closed and Remploy Employment Services was privatised, ending nearly seventy years of sheltered employment for the disabled.

Despite the government's claims that the employees would be better served through the Access to Work programme it ultimately proved hollow. In March 2016 I tabled a question in Parliament asking how many former Remploy workers remained out of work. The answer was 43 per cent.

What the government had failed to allow for, despite all our arguments, was that the factories were largely situated in former industrial areas like the South Wales valleys where jobs were very thin on the ground. There simply was no alternative employment for these people. My fellow MPs, Welsh Assembly Members, local councillors and trade unions all appealed to the government and attended rallies. All to no avail.

Despite my frequent arguments with the government in Wales I remain passionately patriotic. I was born in Wales, my constituency is in Wales, and my home is in Wales. I enjoy playing as active a part as possible in Welsh life as my Westminster schedule allows. And although I have little or no interest in sport I was even driven to congratulating the Wales football team on Twitter following its 2016 European campaign.

I was honoured to be inducted into the highest order of the Gorsedd of Bards, a white robe, at Mold in 1991. It was a matter of immense pride for all my family. It is an institution which completely flummoxes my friends outside Wales! Despite its pseudo-druidic appearance, the Gorsedd was created by the Welsh poet Iolo Morganwg and first convened at Primrose Hill in London in 1792. Its aim was to make the world aware of Wales' links to Celtic culture and heritage. Today membership is made up of poets, writers, musicians, artists and people who have made a significant contribution to Welsh life and language.

The main event of the year is the procession at the crowning and chairing ceremonies at the National Eisteddfod. We dress up in our robes, headwear and boots and walk in order behind the Arch Druid through the Eisteddfod field into the main pavilion and on to the stage. It is a great sight but one which, since my induction, I have not taken part in. My propensity to heatstroke was not helped by having to wear extraordinarily scratchy and uncomfortable nylon robes on a hot August day in a pavilion seating 5,000 people. The stage was like a sweatbox. It was torture.

Having said that, I love attending the National Eisteddfod. Billed as a national festival of the arts, people from all over Wales compete in music, poetry and prose, dance and art. Even in the twenty-first century it continues to have a relevance to Welsh life, especially for the Welsh-speaking community. The standards are normally high but a visit each August to the peripatetic site is always a celebration as people stroll around the '*maes*' (field), browsing the stalls and bumping into old acquaintances. I think my father took me to my first Eisteddfod when I was about six years old and I have always held it in great affection, which is why, indirectly, it was responsible for the break-up of my first serious relationship.

I was young, engaged to be married and in love, but one day I looked at my fiancé and realised that he could not understand me because he was not Welsh. He had planned something for us for the first week of August and I was absolutely adamant that I would rather go to the Eisteddfod. He simply could not understand my position and, predictably, an argument ensued. It was an agonising moment that highlighted the differences in our backgrounds, something we had glossed over until then. But now I was forced to realise how deeply ingrained my 'Welshness' was. I prided myself on being an internationalist but the language, the culture and the history of my tiny country was deeply rooted, it was in my DNA. The engagement became history.

Some years later I was desperately looking for a parliamentary seat. I was asked by some party members to apply for Birmingham Stechford, Roy Jenkins' old seat, and made the shortlist. I was heavily supported by the unions and one of the frontrunners for what would be a safe seat but I then realised that I could not go through with it. The seat lay on the wrong side of the border. I needed a constituency that I could connect with, a Welsh constituency, so the wait had to go on for some time longer.

Today the Cynon Valley is resolutely English-speaking as is the case in most of industrialised South Wales. The Welsh language and traditions, and there was no greater bastion than Aberdare, have been largely worn away by the enormous influx of migrants from England and further afield. Those migrants brought with them other traditions – Italian ice cream being particularly popular – and new ways of thinking that challenged what was perhaps the more narrow vision of the indigenous people. Society as a whole has benefitted. Today the Valley exhibits a different 'Welshness' but ask anyone and they will define themselves as Welsh.

I am fortunate that my work allows me to support all I love about Welsh life. I enjoy the stimulation of my workday life in London but nothing beats the feeling of crossing the Severn Bridge back into Wales at the end of a hectic week. I take every opportunity I can to support the arts in Wales, a passion that dates back to my student days and was reinforced by a spell on the Arts Council of Wales in the years before I became a politician. It was an exciting and vibrant time as we championed emerging artists like filmmaker Karl Francis and helped the National Museum of Wales build its art collection, for example acquiring much of David Jones' collection.

A campaign that has given me great pleasure is an ongoing attempt to win a royal pardon for Dic Penderyn. As every Welsh schoolchild knows, Dic Penderyn, real name Richard Lewis, was a martyr. In 1831, growing dissatisfaction with wage cuts, aligned with the rising price of bread, culminated in a protest which became known as the Merthyr Rising. The authorities were unnerved as the scale of protest began to get out of hand, with properties ransacked and the red flag flown as a sign of rebellion. They responded by sending in armed troops who opened fire, killing sixteen people. One soldier was wounded, stabbed in the leg, and although he could not identify his assailant, Dic, a young miner, was arrested and charged. Despite a petition of 11,000 names, Dic was found guilty and subsequently hanged in Cardiff still protesting his innocence. He was vindicated many years later when the real assailant made a deathbed confession and the witness who testified against him also admitted to lying under oath.

In October 2015 I presented a petition to the House of Commons, calling on the Secretary of State for Justice to grant a pardon. Of course, nothing is that simple and the minister referred us back to the Court of Appeal to quash the conviction. The discussion is ongoing and other Welsh MPs have added their names to the petition including Stephen Kinnock who, in his maiden speech, referred to this famous son of his Aberavon constituency.

I am proud to have been born Welsh and extremely grateful to my parents for having brought my sister and me up in the Welsh language in an English-speaking part of Wales. It is a big part of my identity and it has had definite advantages in my political life as I get two bites of the cherry when it comes to television and radio! I do my best to support the protection and development of our ancient language. For example, I am supportive of the Welsh medium education movement, which allows children to be educated through the Welsh language. The schools' popularity is growing, they have excellent results, and they are therefore encouraging more and more Welsh speakers. I do have reservations about insularity though. Like much else in Welsh life the tendency is to be inward-looking rather than embracing the best from elsewhere and adapting it to our world.

Of course the Welsh language movement is inextricably linked with the nationalist cause. This is partly why I had a fleeting association with Plaid Cymru as a student. The other reason was its exciting social programme at the university. These days I am wary of nationalism in all its forms; I have seen first-hand the devastation that has been caused in its name. There is a very fine line between nationalism and xenophobia and it worries me that it is being used to stoke up right-wing populist movements across Europe.

While I am proud to call myself Welsh, I am also proud to be British and European, I see no contradiction in that. I am proud of being Welsh because of the traditions and the language that have been passed down to me through my family, and I feel the same about being British. I think we have much to be proud of, such as our democracy and tolerance, and our history of standing up against repression.

CHAPTER FIFTEEN

IRAQ - THE BEGINNING

I was sitting with Hero Talabani, wife of the Kurdish leader, enjoying tea and a chat. Suddenly the most terrible sound of gunfire rang out outside. In many ways it was an unlikely friendship, the blonde politician from Wales and the dark-haired Peshmerga warrior, wife of the leader of the Patriotic Union of Kurdistan. However, we shared many political ideals and enjoyed each other's company. It was a hot day in the hills of Iraqi Kurdistan and in the distance was the incessant sound of heavy bombardment by Saddam Hussein's military. Hero was telling me stories about her childhood. How one day in Baghdad her father, the revered Kurdish leader Ibrahim Ahmed, came home and told the family they had to leave that night. That meant leaving everything behind including Hero's sister Shanaz's much-loved doll, which her father had brought back from Russia.

When the shooting started she got up very calmly and stuffed her gun belt on. 'Stay here!' she commanded. Then she was out of the door. I thought, 'This is it!' and my eyes frantically searched the room for somewhere to hide. There was nowhere. My mind was a jumble of conflicting thoughts: how Owen would manage; whether my family would be sad or infuriated that I had put myself in danger again, and how CARDRI – the Committee Against Repression and for

Democratic Rights in Iraq – might be able to make political capital out of this. Just as suddenly the shooting stopped and Hero reappeared. The noise had been the Peshmerga troops training; they had not told her about it and were punished with a few days' imprisonment. I had to admit I was frightened and could feel my heart pumping.

The struggle for democracy in Iraq would one day become my defining cause as a politician and human rights activist. It began long before my political career, with a telephone call from Dai Francis, General Secretary of the South Wales Miners' Union. Dai had become something of a mentor and would often point people who had a story to tell in my direction. As a freelance journalist and producer I was always grateful. This time he wanted me to meet a couple of students from Cardiff University who were making the rounds of politicians and trade unionists to spread the word about human rights abuses in Iraq. Dai knew of my interest in human rights and told them I was a good person to talk to. So, one November evening in 1979, I went to the NUM's office in Cardiff and met a couple who were to have a major influence on my life.

Jamal Hafid and his wife Selma were a gentle couple, dedicated to their postgraduate studies and to each other. We chatted for a while about how they were finding Cardiff, which they loved, and our shared passion for cinema and drama. We gossiped briefly about people they had met and then the conversation turned to events in Iraq. Dai and I listened with growing horror as they talked of disappearances, imprisonment, torture and summary execution. Some of the stories were so horrific I could hardly believe them. I questioned them in detail and they produced names, dates, photographic and written evidence, as well as data from Amnesty International. The more we talked the more grotesque it became.

This was their world. Jamal explained that as a student activist at Basra University he had been interrogated and tortured by the regime including enduring a fake execution. At that point he and Selma felt they had to flee, and decided to study abroad as postgraduates. They joined a wave of Iraqi students studying in Britain at that time and when they left for Cardiff, in 1976, they reassured their families that they would return once their studies were complete. However, as the political situation at home deteriorated, their families warned them not to return. I remember them explaining to me how their families had publicly disowned them to protect themselves. They understood the rationale but it was upsetting nevertheless.

I was captivated by this young exiled couple and their determination to stand up and be counted, and I offered to do what I could to help them expose the atrocities taking place under Saddam Hussein's dictatorship. I suggested other journalists they might talk to and at the end of our meeting we promised to keep in touch.

Although I would soon be elected to the European Parliament, I kept in touch. Owen and I would sometimes be invited over by Jamal and Selma for dinner. I signed the petition founding CARDRI and attended their conferences. I still have a small embroidered picture of a woman and child with the words '*Iraqi Women's League*' given to me by Selma about this time. When I later became an MP in 1984, the then chair of CARDRI, Stan Newens, went to the European Parliament and I was asked to succeed him in the role. Little did I suspect how it would come to dominate my life. As always my motiv-ation was born out of a sense of injustice. I was increasingly angry at what was happening to the minorities in Iraq, but there was more to it than that. I witnessed first-hand how, even in a modern democratic nation like Britain, Jamal and Selma feared for their lives.

It sounded melodramatic: such things did not happen in Britain, let alone in Cardiff, but it became clear that Saddam Hussein's henchmen were targeting activists in Britain. Indeed, in 1988 a plan of assassin-ations here was exposed by the press – one of the targets was Jamal Hafid. Jamal was physically attacked many times on the Cardiff Uni-versity campus, once requiring hospital treatment for broken ribs. The local police were reluctant to get involved. On one occasion Jamal called me from a police cell. I immediately rang around and amassed a group of local politicians, trade unionists and members of the media, and we descended on the police station and got Jamal released. The following day he appeared before Cardiff Magistrates Court, along with one of his attackers, and was bound over to keep the peace.

The most frightening incident was the attempted kidnap of Jamal and Selma's son, Thaker. Seven years old at the time, he was playing on his bike in the street outside their home in Cardiff's Pontcanna. His father Jamal watched from the window and became suspicious of a Mercedes car with tinted windows driving slowly down the street. He ran down to his son, arriving just as the car returned, pulling alongside the young boy with its doors open. Jamal screamed and a neighbour, aware of the family's position, came running out of his garden with a spade and scared off the would-be kidnappers. Jamal and the neighbour were able to give descriptions and the registration number to the police, and later that evening plain-clothes police came round to the house and told Jamal they had stopped the car on the M4. And that, publicly, was the end of it. No court appearance, nothing. The police advised Jamal to move from Cardiff and 'get lost' somewhere like London or Manchester, which they did with heavy hearts. The family did later return to Cardiff and our friendship has endured. Selma is usually the first person to appear with soup if anyone is ill and Thaker has helped me with research.

There was never a satisfactory explanation from the authorities, indeed any explanation at all. I honestly do not know how and why it was hushed up. It was not an isolated incident; I later learnt that there were regular attacks on Iraqi students by their fellow countrymen on university campuses across Britain. Ayad Allawi, future interim Prime Minister of Iraq, was a doctor in Britain when he was attacked with an axe in the middle of the night in 1978 in his Surrey home. He was left for dead by his assailants, believed to be representatives of the

Ba'athist regime. He and his wife miraculously survived the attack and were forced to hide in Cardiff under assumed names.

The Iraqi embassy in London was the nerve centre for repression in the UK. It had been implicated in several crimes on British soil, including the assassination of former Iraqi Prime Minister Abdul Razzak Al-Naif in London in 1978, and the poisoning of Abdullah Rahim Sharif Ali with thallium after a dinner with Iraqi agents in Kensington. It was Iraq, not Russia, and therefore received a fraction of the coverage which Alexander Litvinenko's death would receive some years later.

My first visit to the embassy was with a women's delegation from Cardiff. We travelled up by train together, but when we approached the embassy in Kensington, the Iraqi members of our group refused to go near the building itself because they saw the cameras outside. They were afraid they would be identified, with resulting repercussions for their families in Iraq. The rest of us went ahead to enquire about a group of missing women and children. At first it was all smiles. An official representing the ambassador met us and offered cups of tea. Then I said my piece about our concern for the women and children and asked for information on the names of the missing people on our list. At first he refused to acknowledge the list but then turned nasty. The more I insisted the angrier he became before standing up and screaming, 'Out! Out!' at us. We tried to remonstrate with him, but there was nothing more to do. He continued to scream, so we turned around and beat it up the street, met our Iraqi friends and took the train back to Cardiff.

My next visit to the embassy came after the regime's reported use of chemical weapons at Halabja in 1988. This time I was accompanied by Brian Sedgemore and we were received by the ambassador himself, oozing charm. He said he was delighted to meet us. Hardly likely given my position with CARDRI and a track record of asking questions about the regime's atrocities in the House of Commons. He disappeared into a back room, returning with a big glass dish of Quality Street chocolates. Now, he may have been aware of my partiality to all forms of chocolate but I was certainly aware of the embassy and the regime's track record of poisoning people and had a well-founded fear of accepting any forms of food or drink from Iraqi officials. I declined the chocolate. He declined to accept any knowledge of events at Halabja. Before we left he invited me to a trade fair in Baghdad and I said I would only go if I could also visit the Kurdish North. He said, 'That might be slightly more difficult,' but that he would put my request to the Iraqi government. I heard nothing more from them. It would take many years and a regime change before I visited Baghdad but I made a number of covert visits to the north, eager to see things at first hand and speak to people directly.

As chair of CARDRI I became increasingly involved in the campaign for human rights in Iraq. We took on the task of publicising the atrocities being committed by the Baghdad regime, aided by a worldwide network of Iraqi nationals. Some of these old colleagues have since become high-profile politicians in Iraq. Barham Salih became Prime Minister of Iraqi Kurdistan in 2009 and Hoshyar Zebari was appointed Iraqi Minister of Foreign Affairs in 2003. The years of working together have established a bond of mutual trust and respect that has been invaluable in seeking solutions in post-war Iraq.

We had an excellent volunteer secretary, a student from Najaf, who was too afraid to let me know his second name. He came to see me in the House of Commons every fortnight, but it was only years later, after the death of Saddam Hussein, that he felt secure enough to let me know his full name. He went on to become Iraqi ambassador to South Korea. He would come with reports from inside Iraq including lists of prisoners executed at the Abu Ghraib prison. The information was comprehensive, specifying names, dates and methods of torture and execution. He used to say: 'After Saddam is gone we will name a street in Baghdad after you.'

Our role at CARDRI was to collect evidence of the atrocities taking place in Iraq and publicise them in a bid to get the world to take action. We published books, pamphlets and newsletters; we held conferences and lobbied politicians in the USA, UK and elsewhere. It seemed as if the world was not listening. We were not alone in our work. Amnesty International, Human Rights Watch, even the UN, were reporting the most horrific abuses but still no action was taken.

There was a history of brutality in the region, but as the Iran–Iraq war drew to a close Saddam Hussein turned his attention, as well as his weapons, on his own people. The Ba'athists had always hated the Kurds, Assyrians and other non-Arabs and wanted to drive them out of the oilfields of Iraq and Kurdistan around Kirkuk and Sulaiman-yah. The policy of Arabisation, al-Anfal, was brutal. The campaign, using ground offensives, aerial bombing, destruction of settlements, mass deportation, firing squads and chemical warfare, was overseen by Ali Hassan al-Majid, earning him the nickname 'Chemical Ali'. More than 4,000 villages were destroyed, some 4 million people displaced and Human Rights Watch estimated that between 50,000 and 100,000 civilians were massacred. It was a major human rights catastrophe and still the world did nothing. I tabled questions in Parliament, harried the Foreign and Commonwealth Office, spoke at numerous meetings at home and abroad. Nothing was done.

Stories of atrocities continued to pour in and they made tragic and harrowing reading. The regime used just about every imaginable – and unimaginable – form of torture and abuse. One of its instruments of torture, reported by Amnesty International, was a machine called the *manganna*, which crushed the victim's heart and chest. As crimes increased in their inventive barbarity, we heard accounts of the ex-ecution of more than 400 war objectors in Abu Ghraib prison. The victims' bodies were drained of their blood while still alive.

We also reported the atrocities in the Kurdish city of Sulayman-iyah. Thousands of citizens were arrested including 300 children. In

February 1987 we reported that the bodies of seventy children had been handed back to their families. In an added evil, characteristic of the Hussein regime, the families had to pay for the cost of the execution of their murdered child before the body was handed over. The following month, Helga Graham reported in *The Observer* that Iraqi forces had delivered fifty-seven boxes of dead children to Sulaimanyah. Each child had been drained of blood, and had had their eyes gouged out.

Some years later the Kurds showed me extensive documentation they had discovered when they liberated Sulaimanyah. It seemed that, like the Nazis before them, the Iraqi regime could not resist cataloguing their genocidal atrocities. It was routine policy for people to be lined up and killed. Tortured prisoners left their last messages scrawled in blood on their cell walls at the secret police HQ. A military order from Chemical Ali's Northern Affairs Office, dated 20 June 1987, demonstrated the brutality of the regime stating: 'Anyone found in these villages will be detained and interrogated by the security apparatus. All those aged 15–70 inclusive to be executed after making use of any information obtained off them.' Among the evidence were soldiers' identity cards. One was chillingly described as the 'official rapist'.

It was a tide of despair and occasionally I would feel overwhelmed by it all. It made me wonder about human capacity for evil. Even worse was the feeling of total impotence. People would ask me whether I could turn off and remarkably I found I could. A nightly episode of *EastEnders* or a weekend walk in the country helped, but in all honesty I never had trouble sleeping. It was a case of 'Keep calm and carry on' and I was also conscious that however horrifying I found the stories it was 100 times worse for those who had families living in Iraq.

In April 1987 Saddam Hussein achieved the notorious distinction of being the first head of state to use chemical weapons against his own people. Iraqi air force warplanes swooped over villages in

Sulaimanyah, Erbil and Kirkuk, dropping chemical bombs and leaving hundreds of dead and injured in their wake. Affected areas were littered with the bodies of animals. One village, Sheikh Wassan, was completely destroyed, with 107 of its inhabitants dead and a further 350 injured. The bombing of Halabja, in 1988, finally made the international community sit up and take notice. This time an estimated 5,000 people were killed, but it was probably the fact that the attack was captured on film that did the trick.

Halabja had been a bustling Kurdish town, with a busy commercial section, set in a green valley surrounded by poppy fields. It was also a stronghold of the Peshmerga and the PUK. Eyewitnesses told us how the attack had started with a traditional bombardment mid-morning. Then the planes came, unleashing napalm or phosphorus, which burned everything and everybody it touched. The people moved into primitive air-raid shelters as the attacks came in waves. Claustrophobia and the creeping smell eventually drove them out. In the dim twilight they saw nightmarish scenes: dead bodies slumped over steering wheels, huddled in doorways, or lying in the street. Dead women with their dead babies in their arms.

It did not take long for the news to get out. The Iranian authorities took international press across the border to witness what had happened. The West, which had a pathological hatred of Iran and leant heavily towards Baghdad in the regional battle for supremacy, chose to believe the Iraqi regime. I went with fellow MP Jeremy Corbyn to see William Waldegrave and David Mellor, ministers at the FCO, to protest about Halabja. Waldegrave said, 'There is no proof.' I told him bluntly to get it.

Of course it was CARDRI who eventually unearthed the proof, in the form of soil samples collected and analysed by Professor Alistair Hay of the University of Leeds. The samples established conclusively the presence of the chemicals at Halabja. Mellor told us that he had seen an official at the Iraqi embassy to express the British government's 'disapproval' of the reported use of chemical weapons at Halabja – as though that was going to change anything. He even went on to tell us quite bluntly that despite being acutely aware of the nature of the Iraqi regime, the British government's thoughts were geared to increasing legitimate trade with Iraq in preparation for the end of the Iran–Iraq war.

I was not surprised when, a few months after Halabja, Mellor, in his ministerial capacity, accompanied a British delegation to the annual Baghdad trade fair and was pictured shaking hands with leading members of the Iraqi regime.

Some of the Halabja survivors were brought to Britain and I took a cross-party group of women MPs with me to the Cromwell Hospital in South Kensington to visit them. Among the group were two grandmothers and a fourteen-year-old girl, badly burned and hardly able to speak because of the damage to their lungs. We stood helplessly by their bedsides trying to communicate our care and concern. We had an interpreter who relayed their messages, so agonisingly whispered. They told us of their family members who had not survived, of how they had found their dead bodies and had to leave them where they lay because there was no one to bury the dead. My colleagues were shocked. It is one thing to hear second, third-hand reports from a far country, another to come face to face with the victims. As we talked to the press afterwards I could hear the shock and anger in their voices. People were beginning to wake up to what was going on.

By 1989 I had been elected shadow Secretary of State for Overseas Development. As part of my remit I repeatedly raised the issue of Iraq in the House of Commons, challenging the then Foreign Secretary Geoffrey Howe and his ministers. The response was evasive and weak, condemning the use of chemical weapons while constantly emphasising the need for trade links. I was joined in my condemnation by my colleague George Robertson MP, future Secretary of State for Defence, who said: 'Surely there is something indecent at the sight of the Foreign Office condemning the use of chemical weapons, followed by that of a Cabinet minister going to Baghdad touting for trade and business and doubling trade credits to Iraq without any linked condition that Iraq desist from the vile slaughter of so many people in the northern provinces.' The government's attitude can be summed up in Howe's answer when he referred to the 'allegations' of use of chemical weapons and the need to 'maintain trading relations with a large and important country'. A sentiment that clearly continues to resonate with the Conservative Party, as the current debate over supplying arms to the Saudi regime illustrates.

When I look back now at what transpired afterwards, including the Gulf War of 1991, the subsequent repressive campaigns by Saddam's regime, the continuing contempt for human rights and his obfuscation regarding weapons of mass destruction that led ultimately to war, the British government's response seems unbelievably feeble. I cannot begin to convey the frustration felt by those of us in CARDRI and other organisations raising these issues until we were hoarse. But Halabja was not an isolated incident. From February through to September of 1988 there were many more reports of similar incidents as the al-Anfal campaign raged. The Kurds estimated that about 182,000 of their people were killed. The man responsible for the campaign, Chemical Ali, protested that it was 'only' 100,000.

At CARDRI our efforts to campaign against Saddam's atrocities were numerous. We highlighted the regime's use of chemical weapons and made it known that Iraq had begun experimenting with poisonous gases in the late 1970s. Political prisoners in Abu Ghraib prison and abducted Kurdish men were used as guinea pigs. We called for specific action from the British government and the international community, but the recurring theme was that although action was proposed, very little was actually done and our demands ultimately fell on deaf ears.

CHAPTER SIXTEEN

PLIGHT OF THE KURDS

The British and Western love-in with Saddam came to an abrupt end when he invaded Kuwait in August 1990. Britain and America were in the vanguard of a drive to assemble an international coalition, including many Arab countries, to expel Iraq. The UN issued an ultimatum, which came and went. Then Operation Desert Storm was launched, leading to the liberation of Kuwait in an awesome display of Western armed superiority. Iraqi forces were quickly defeated but the coalition interpreted its UN mandate literally and did not march on Baghdad. A crucial opportunity lost.

Saddam's brutal suppression of his peoples continued. After the Gulf War every region of Iraq rose up and attacked the visible symbols of Ba'ath power such as Saddam's palaces. But despite President George Bush's tacit calls on the people of Iraq to rise up, he and his Western allies' failure to support the uprisings were to prove disastrous. Saddam took his bloody vengeance, particularly on the Kurds in the north and the Shi'as in the south.

By Christmas 1990 reports were coming in from Iraq that the Kurds, afraid of another chemical attack, were fleeing across the mountains into Iran and Turkey in their tens of thousands, pursued by Saddam's helicopter gunships. When Parliament reconvened in the New Year

I raised the issue with my party's leader, Neil Kinnock. He urged me to go and investigate the situation for myself. I made plans to go into northern Iraq covertly from Iran. Through my CARDRI contacts and Ahmed Chalabi, I arranged for members of the Kurdish PUK based in Iran to help. When I arrived in Tehran I found I was not the only person trying to get in; there had been several British journalists on my flight and, on arrival, I found that members of the diplomatic community were also trying to find out what was happening. Despite years of campaigning it was my first visit to the region and I made sure I dressed appropriately in loose black clothing and a scarf on my head. The Iranian hotel staff were not impressed and asked me to put even more clothes on!

We were all kept kicking our heels at the hotel while we waited for permission to travel to the border. I was lucky enough to meet the Bangladeshi ambassador. We discussed what was going on and I told him how desperate I was to see events at first hand. One evening he contacted me and told me to go to the airport the next morning because Tehran-based ambassadors were being taken to the border. Believing that the best thing anyone could do to help the Kurds was publicise their case I passed on the news to the journalists I knew and we all went to the airport.

It was mayhem. There were dozens of people milling around trying to find out about the rumoured flight. I had to jostle through the crowds, elbowing my way, until I caught sight of the Bangladeshi ambassador. I stayed close to him until the flight was called and he was as good as his word and pulled me through the throng towards the gate. Everyone was pushing and shoving but we were eventually rushed outside on to the tarmac where a helicopter was waiting. My new friend managed to get me on board. The journalists were, of course, excluded but as the rotors started whirring they charged after us on foot and I managed to pull some of them on board; a fact I still remind them about occasionally!

The flight took over an hour and as we flew over the Zagros mountain range, near the border, we could see the lines of Kurds snaking up the hillside on the Iraq side. It must have gone back over thirty miles. It was a miserable and desolate sight. As we swooped low over a field we could see hundreds of refugees running towards us, holding their hands to their mouths. They were literally starving and we had nothing to give them. They were at the top of a mountain in winter conditions, freezing at night and bitterly cold during the day. They had no proper cover; the makeshift tents they had constructed were made of the thinnest plastic, the kind in which clothes are returned from the dry cleaner. Our helicopter landed on top of the mountain and we were able to see for ourselves the condition of the refugees. A woman pushed through the sleet and snow and biting wind. She had a baby in her arms and tried to push it towards me, but the baby was already dead. I was the only woman up there and more mothers came up to me and tried to push their babies at me, wanting me to take them out. It still brings tears to my eyes. The ambassadors and aid workers, most of whom had witnessed famine, flood and earthquakes all over the world, were appalled.

The ambassadors were soon returning to Tehran but I fell into my natural community and joined the group of journalists, hoping to hire a car and travel to the border point. It was snowing and conditions were terrible. Lorries loaded with tents and clothing were trying to reach the refugees but there seemed to be little or no co-ordination and the vehicles were slipping and jack-knifing across the mountain roads in all directions. Desperate people were begging for food. I did a quick interview with Sky TV in the sleet and snow on the mountain top and then made for a nearby town. There were thousands of people milling around, but as we pushed our way through them I heard someone shout 'Ann!' It was a Kurdish doctor from the UK, Dr D'alawa Aladin, who was searching for his brother.

My media friends and I decided to call a taxi to take us into Iraq.

Of course, we couldn't tell the driver our final destination in case he refused. We just asked to be taken to the border. Even that was hours away. Of course, the border between Iran and Iraq was a heavily militarised zone and there were lots of roadblocks along the way. We had no official papers but I had a piece of paper from the Iranian Red Crescent. I think it was just a blank letterhead. But it had the semblance of an official document so each time we reached a roadblock I thrust it out of the window and, surprisingly, we were let through. I usually find that a combination of courage and doggedness goes a long way.

We saw virtually no one else on the roads. We went without food for twelve hours – it was Ramadan – but we did quite well with the paper and sheer bravado until we reached the last roadblock before the border. One of the guards snatched my bit of paper and went away to telephone someone higher up. We had a bit of an argument when he came back, but he eventually waved us on, only for us to face a mountain of earth barricading our way. There was no way we could move it by hand, so we returned to the checkpoint for help. Eventually a bulldozer came and shifted the earth. On the other side was a man bleeding profusely in a car, trying to get to hospital. I hope we saved his life.

We persuaded the taxi driver to keep going into Iraq. I was very anxious about the time because I had arranged to meet a representative of Jalal Talabani, the PUK leader. It was now dark. We drove along the rough, narrow mountain road for a long time, passing endless Kurdish villages razed to the ground during the al-Anfal campaign. Wanton destruction is the phrase that comes to mind. There was just nowhere left standing. It was quite dark when we came at last to a village where there were lots of campfires and people dressed in traditional Kurdish costume. Unbelievably, in the glow of the fire, I suddenly saw a face I knew. He was a doctor I had previously met in Paris where he had dressed Western-style. Now he wore the full baggy uniform of the Peshmerga. He smiled broadly. I have never been so glad to see anyone in my life. He then took me in a vehicle for what seemed, again, like miles along the steep mountain paths to where Jalal Talabani and his wife Hero were camped out with the Peshmergas. During the journey we could hear the constant boom-boom of heavy guns. I thought of all those Kurds still trying to flee across the hills in their thin clothes, without shoes or shelter, and with the helicopter gunships bombarding them from above.

When we eventually arrived at the Talabanis' hideout in the hills we received a fantastic reception. As always the hospitable Kurds, somehow, in the shell of a building with no roof, managed to greet us with barbecued lamb and other delicacies spread out on rugs on the floor. After a day of travelling without food or drink, it was a very welcome sight.

As we ate we discussed the plight of the Kurdish people, the refugees in particular. Our conversation was punctuated by the distant sound of the thumps of the aerial bombardment of Sulaimanyah and the gunships attacking the fleeing refugees. Jalal Talabani argued passionately for Kurdistan to be made a safe haven and exempted from the UN embargoes. These, he felt, were punishing the Kurdish people twofold: they were paying the price for Saddam's actions even as he was taking action against them. It is hard to emphasise how important it was to the Kurds that a foreign politician had come to listen to their story. It formed a strong bond between us that would become vital in the years to come.

I promised to bring their plight to the attention of the West and planned to leave quickly. They tried to dissuade us, afraid we would be attacked, but the journalist and politician in me was in a hurry to get back and report what I had seen. Even up in the hills, in the glow of firelight, I had a fierce conviction that this was what I had to do.

We set off and I insisted on sitting in the front seat of the jeep: if an attack was coming our way I wanted to see it coming. It was one of the few occasions in my life when I have genuinely felt fear. We could hear the bombardment but not see it, so we did not know how close it was. We made it back to the Iranian border only to be arrested as soon as we reached the airfield. The military commander insisted we wait until morning, until the governor of the province could be contacted. I had had enough. Valuable time was slipping away and after several hours of waiting I started shouting very loudly. That did the trick. They decided to get rid of us as fast as possible and we started on the long journey back to Tehran and then home.

During the journey home I started to compose the account I would give to the House of Commons. I wanted it to be an eyewitness account. I wanted parliamentarians to feel some of the desperation that I had felt and, above all, I wanted the British government to take action. My colleagues listened in total silence as I asked for the international community to take action. I appealed to the Foreign Secretary for desperately needed aid, and also to pursue a political solution to the genocide that was taking place. I asked for support for Iran who were struggling to cope with the influx of refugees. Afterwards I was congratulated by parliamentarians on both sides. Journalists picked up the story and the next day people all over Britain heard about the Kurdish refugees' plight.

The government's response was to send my opposite number, Lynda Chalker, to the region with Mars bars and then do precisely nothing. My comments in the Chamber on her return summed up all the anger and sadness I felt at the government's wholly inadequate response to the catastrophe. I pointed out that weeks of miscalculation and poor organisation had left perhaps as many as 2 million people dying on the bitter cold mountain slopes. Chalker had said on the BBC that I must have been clairvoyant to have anticipated the need for relief. 'It did not take clairvoyance to realise what was happening: we knew,' I replied.

The exception was Prime Minister John Major. After my speech, I was told that he would like to meet me. He asked me lots of questions about what I had seen and heard on my trip and listened closely, clearly engaged. Asked what Britain could do to help, I explained that what the Kurds wanted most was protection from the air attacks. To his credit, within a week or two he had established a 'Safe Haven' and a 'No Fly Zone'. People on both sides of the House now wanted to help and Jeffrey Archer – a man with whom I otherwise shared few political beliefs – played a big part in raising money and awareness for the Kurdish cause.

Jeffrey is a complex man, but on the whole we had a good relationship. He would always point to me at meetings with Kurds and say, 'That's the woman you ought to thank!' Nevertheless, he was less than pleased to see me when I turned up at his penthouse apartment one evening. A group of Kurds had approached me, saying Jeffrey had arranged for them to be interviewed on the BBC's current affairs programme, *Newsnight*. He had also given them a script which they were not happy with: it was too effusive in its praise of him, they felt. So I went along with them and as we were shown in to his apartment he muttered, 'I wasn't expecting to see you, Ann.' I then went on to scupper the television piece, so it was quite generous of him to continue to credit me in the circumstances!

Over the coming years, as my parliamentary life took several twists and turns, I continued to make regular trips to Iraq, probably averaging about one every couple of years. Sometimes I would be asked to take specific items with me. On one occasion I took a vital part for the Kurds' radio transmitter. On my second trip I was overwhelmed by the reception I received out in the towns and cities of Iraqi Kurdistan. Tens of thousands of people came out to welcome this Western woman who had fought their cause. I was hoisted up onto a makeshift platform and given a loudhailer to address the crowds. I have no idea how much they understood of what I said, but I think they understood that there was someone out there who sympathised with their plight and was trying to get something done.

It was just as well Saddam did not get wind of my visits as I was probably high up in the regime's public enemy stakes and I would not have given much for my chances if I had been taken prisoner. I had publicly denounced him on the embryonic Kurdish television station and he had returned the compliment on Iraqi television. I was now 'most wanted'!

I suppose I was at risk, although I never gave it much thought. The police visited our home in Cardiff and we had extra locks installed. They also visited my old family home in Aberdyfi when I was on holiday there and recommended I did not allow any Iraqis into the house – not a particularly viable suggestion given how many Iraqi friends I had. They also offered me a course on defensive driving as apparently one of Saddam's preferred assassination methods was a motorway 'accident'. I declined and just got on with it. On the whole I felt safe in the UK. In Iraqi Kurdistan, I had Peshmerga protection, and felt relatively secure.

Whenever I visited I was always taken aback by the scale of the country. It would take so many hours to get from one centre to another, and there were miles and miles of ruins. Everywhere we travelled in Iraqi Kurdistan we saw deforested, devastated and abandoned villages and towns, the result of Saddam's policy of Arabisation, the forcible destruction of non-Arab communities. It has been estimated that over 4,000 villages were destroyed; all that remained of those once vibrant communities were piles of stones. Over and over again we heard of people taken away and never seen again, and of survivors living in caves. I met a young boy who was one of only two survivors when his entire village was rounded up. The people had been loaded into lorries and driven to big burial pits, where they were shot and thrown in.

The use of rape as an instrument of war was commonplace in Iraq at this time. On a visit to a tented hospital and pharmacy in one of the refugee camps, one of the nurses asked to speak to me privately. In the darkest recesses of the tent she told me that she had been the last nurse to remain in her town's hospital when the Iraqis invaded. She had hidden in one of the toilets, but the soldiers found her and she was repeatedly raped throughout the night before one of the soldiers came to her and gave her his coat. He also helped her to escape. 'They're not all bad,' she whispered to me. It had taken a great deal of courage for her to talk to me. Rape is particularly damaging in Muslim societies, where victims are reluctant to speak out for fear of being shunned.

Jalal Talabani had warned me that the plight of the Shi'as in southern Iraq was probably worse than that of the Kurds. Although it was much more difficult to get people into the south to find out what was happening, some information did come to us through the CARDRI network. To say that Saddam's Republican Guard had brutally suppressed the rebellions that had erupted in the aftermath of the Gulf War would be an understatement. Even those of us hardened by years of accounts of atrocities found these reports chilling. We heard about the bombing of the Shi'as holy places, including the death of 1,000 people at Immam Ali's shrine at Najaf. More than 22,000 people were killed fleeing from Karbala to Najaf. All the patients and health workers at Huseini Hospital Karbala had been killed. Eyewitnesses told of people being thrown out of helicopters over rebel towns. Between fifty and sixty men and women executed daily in Saad Square, Basra. Republic Guards forcing victims to drink petrol and then shooting them, setting their bodies on fire.

Once again I felt increasingly impotent in the face of horrendous atrocities. It seemed the international community was abandoning the Kurdish people. Turkey embarked on a number of cross-border campaigns into Kurdistan, ostensibly to hunt PKK guerrillas who were attacking the Turkish military. No doubt there were clusters of activists, but the results of the incursion did not warrant the scale of military action. It was undoubtedly a show of force, designed to intimidate the Kurds. No one was speaking out. Part of the problem was Turkey's policies towards its Kurdish minority, denying them basic democratic rights, which had created a breeding ground for terrorists.

By April 1995 it was clear that Turkish troops were massing for another incursion into Kurdistan. I picked up the phone to Erdal

Inönü, the acting Prime Minister of Turkey, and asked if I could go and observe. Out of courtesy I informed the shadow Foreign Minister responsible for the region, Jim Cousins. He said he wanted to come too as he had never been to the area. It was a Friday afternoon by the time the trip was confirmed by the Turkish authorities. We left messages with Robin Cook's office and the Whips' Office and set off along with CARDRI's secretary, Clive Furness.

First we flew to the Turkish capital, Ankara, where we met with Frank Baker the deputy British ambassador. He was very surprised we were being allowed in to observe but felt it was very helpful; there were no other press or other international observers of the incursion. From there we travelled on a military helicopter accompanied by a General of the Turkish Army. First stop was a Kurdish school high up in the mountains and, as we arrived, the schoolchildren came out waving, of all things, Turkish flags. Unimpressed by the 'spontaneous' display, I said to the General: 'Please don't insult my intelligence.' He laughed and after that we got on just fine.

We were then taken to the village of Gorum, just on the Turkish side of the border, which had, he claimed, had been victim to a PKK atrocity. We arrived to be greeted by a large crowd which accompanied us into the village. We climbed up some steps and then several men emerged from a house carrying rolls of carpet. I was puzzled and felt this was hardly the time to try and sell us carpets. They were unrolled at our feet to reveal dead bodies. These were the first dead bodies I had witnessed at such close quarters. One child had an arm crooked, as though trying to protect her face. There was dried blood everywhere. The oldest must have been about seventeen, the youngest just seven. The journalist in me quickly whipped out my camera to record the moment. By now I was a pretty seasoned traveller to war zones and I found the most effective way of dealing with it was to put away any squeamishness and get on with being a professional observer: questioning, note taking and photographing.

Next, we visited caves where the PKK had supposedly holed up but they, along with the armchairs and television sets, had been abandoned. A nearby field was full of Turkish military hardware and a captured PKK soldier with a broken arm. He was very young, about seventeen, a Syrian Kurd. I asked for his parents' address so that I could let them know he was alive.

For most Kurds inside northern Iraq the focus of concern was very much on Baghdad and the two main parties, the Kurdistan Democratic Party (KDP) and Patriotic Union of Kurdistan (PUK), were careful to distance themselves from the Kurdistan Workers Party (PKK), who were separatist guerrillas. The next stop on my trip was to meet the KDP leader, Massoud Barzani. As usual, he kept us waiting to the extent that we eventually had to be accommodated overnight at his guest house. Next morning, after a meeting with Barzani, who called for a political rather than military resolution to the PKK problem, we set off with armed escorts to reach the PUK headquarters.

However, the Kurdistan capital city of Erbil was being bombarded by Iraqi forces and although excitable Kurds were urging us forward on the car radio, assuring us we would be safe, Jim was adamant that he was not going one step further. He wanted to return to Ankara immediately. I tried to reassure him that we were safe. But against my better judgement, and not wanting to show up a fellow British shadow minister as a coward, I gave in. It was a long journey back, exacerbated by total stonewalling from Jim and a stream of calls from Chalabi, whose final words on the subject were: 'We need help. Please tell the world.' When we eventually landed in Ankara, en route to the UK, a ministerial car was waiting to take us for a de-briefing. Jim refused, insisting on getting the next flight back to the UK, despite the fact we were booked for the next morning anyway.

The reason for his behaviour soon became clear. Throughout the trip he had insisted on a daily phone call to his wife and it appears she had warned him of the whips' wrath at our 'unsanctioned trip'. He had been advised that if he returned ahead of me and apologised he would not be sacked – dirty tricks at the crossroads. When I got back it was clear the dark forces, otherwise known as the Labour Whips' Office, had it in for me. Jim and I had missed a Foreign Office question time in the House and also a number of votes and the Chief Whip had issued press notices saying I was going to be sacked. On my first morning back, I was asked to see Tony. His Chief of Staff, Jonathan Powell, and Derek Foster, the Chief Whip, were also present. I was told that my trip to Iraq was 'unsanctioned' and as a result I would have to go. It was a case of party discipline. The whips had forced Tony's hand and I bore him no ill will, but once again I could sense the machinations of Ray Powell.

The press revelled in the story and it attracted a huge amount of column inches fuelled by Jim Cousins' claim that he only went on the trip to protect me and describing my trips to Iraq as 'Clwyd Loony-Tours'. I do not know what I was most incandescent about; the trivialising of the work that CARDRI and I were doing, or the patronising insinuation that a woman could not possibly do this sort of work without the benefit of protection from a wholly inexperienced male. Maybe the story would have died sooner if I had kept my counsel but I was not going to take it lying down and, feeling that I no longer had to worry about showing up Jim's cowardice, I gave as good as I got.

I was also furious with Ray Powell and the Whips' Office. Serious international events were being subsumed by the whips' petty politicking. I believed my excessively harsh treatment was motivated by personal agendas and I let rip with a typically spirited response.

The only good thing about the whole sordid process were the letters of support that came in. Some came from unexpected sources, none more so than a letter to Tony Blair from the Turkish government, asking him to reconsider sacking me. Several Kurds also wrote to Blair, saying that far from sacking me he should have been proud that my actions had enhanced the reputation and image of the Labour Party.

In my Cynon Valley constituency there was a lot of support and the constituency party wrote to the leadership in my defence.

There were plenty of people licking their lips over the fall-out, although they were far less interested in the issues at stake. Our magazines, conferences, letters and protest marches seemed ineffect-ive but we continued in an attempt to draw attention to what was happening. Support came from the then Liberal Democrat's Foreign Affairs spokesman David Steel and Tory MPs David Howell and Sir Bernard Braine, but it was all to no avail. Calls for the overthrow of Saddam's dictatorship, however justified, fell on deaf ears. Even as late as 2002 the UN and its Security Council would have been willing to reach a compromise deal with Saddam in exchange for more rigorous monitoring of his 'disarmament', France's preferred solution. The British government's position was, broadly, that Saddam could remain in power as long as he disarmed Iraq of weapons of mass destruction. Despite the campaigning of CARDRI and others, the idea of actually toppling the regime was anathema to the government.

During my visits to Iraq I would always seek to speak to both Talabani and his PUK and also Barzani of the rival KDP party, scru-pulous not to take sides. The pair were very different men. Talabani was well educated, well travelled and a socialist, and I soon developed a close rapport with him. His party was generally in favour of parti-cipating in a multi-ethnic Iraq. I found Barzani less approachable and more difficult to work with. The KDP was far more inclined towards independence and prospered from its control of border crossings with Turkey. However, as far as the Kurds were concerned, we had a common cause and we worked well enough together. The links with both men were to prove invaluable as the region marched inexorably towards the abyss.

The refugee crisis was far from over. Over a million Kurds remained in Iran as well as those in Turkey and displaced within Iraq. Despite the attempts of MP Emma Nicholson, less was known about the Marsh

Arabs who had taken refuge in the marshes of the south. Aid agencies put their figure at around half a million. All were frightened of returning to their homes. I supported calls for UN troops on the ground to protect safe havens but, to their eternal shame, the Americans under George W. Bush opposed it. Saddam Hussein did, however, offer to negotiate a degree of autonomy for the Kurds. In return he demanded that the Kurds cut direct ties with the West; denounce the UN, Iran and Zionism; and seek the Ba'ath party's permission to contact outside governments and organisations. Both the KDP and PUK rejected the deal.

Meanwhile, as a result of the ill-fated invasion of Kuwait, the United Nations had imposed stringent financial sanctions on Iraq with the aim of compelling Saddam to pay reparations to Kuwait. Iraq was also meant to withdraw its support for terrorist organisations and disclose its weapons of mass destruction. Under UN resolutions 661 and 687 all trade with the regime was banned, although exemptions were made for medicines and, 'in humanitarian circumstances', food. It was hoped that making life uncomfortable for the Iraqi people would encourage them to topple the regime. In 1991, I warned the House of Commons that large numbers of civilians were dying needlessly from disease and starvation and a major international aid effort was required. The UN offered the Iraqi government an opportunity to sell oil in return for food and medicines, but Saddam refused. In 1996 UN special rapporteur Max Van der Stoel then condemned Iraq, claiming that in addition to its continuing abuse of human rights, the regime's refusal to sell oil to increase the volume of medicine and food available to the suffering people of Iraq was inexcusable.

Pre-Kuwait, Iraq had imported some 70 per cent of its food. Now virtually none was coming in. We were also being told by our contacts that water and sewage services were in a critical state and there was a real danger of a major epidemic. Sewage was flowing in the streets of Baghdad and the children's hospital reported that diarrhoea-related disease among children was rampant. UNICEF reported that the death rates for children under five in 1991 was more than twice the level it had been ten years previously. Eventually, in 1995, the Iraqi regime agreed to the UN's Oil for Food programme, under which 72 per cent of the proceeds of its oil exports would fund humanitarian relief. 25 per cent would go to pay reparations to Kuwait and the rest would fund UN monitoring of both relief and weapons inspections. When finally implemented in 1997, the programme did go some way to alleviate the suffering of some Iraqi people, but relief supplies often failed to get through outside the major centres because of the lack of fuel, the final irony in an oil-rich state. And, of course, the Baghdad regime did its utmost to manipulate and confuse matters.

Did sanctions work? The general consensus is that, in military terms, they did prevent Saddam from rebuilding his army after the first Gulf War. In humanitarian terms things are not so clear cut. I believe sanctions were justified but totally useless if not policed. I crossed the border from Turkey into Iraqi Kurdistan many times over those years. Lines of heavy goods trucks would be queuing to get into Iraq and, over the years, the lines got bigger and bigger, so it was quite clear sanctions were being broken. The major problem was that the UN did not have enough people on the ground to monitor what was coming in or where it was going, and that the whole programme was badly thought through.

There were numerous allegations of corruption. After the 2003 invasion the UN set up an independent inquiry under the chairmanship of Paul Volcker. Philip Truitt, a key member of the team, had previously been a researcher for INDICT, an organisation I chaired with the purpose of attempting to get Saddam and his key team indicted for human rights abuses. The report concluded that the behaviour of the UN Iraq Programme (OIP) Executive Director, Benon Sevan, had been 'ethically improper' and he had received large cash payments each year he had headed the programme. Many others were implicated, including the Swiss inspection contractors Cotenca. The inquiry did not pronounce on the role of Kofi Annan's son Kojo, who had been accused of being up to his neck in the Oil for Food programme by the *Sunday Times*.

As sanctions hit people across the whole of Iraq, and in particular the Kurds, both Talabani and Barzani would implore me to raise the issue of exempting the Kurdish region. The Iraqi government took great delight in diverting any aid from their 'internal enemies'. In one case it was reported that twelve food lorries were sent into Iraqi Kurdistan to feed the refugees; six of them ended up feeding Iraqi military personnel and the other six ended up feeding government supporters. I raised the matter time after time, supported by colleagues who also felt passionately about the injustice to the Kurds, but to no avail. It was perfectly possible to have exempted Kurds from sanctions; I never understood the UN's logic.

I attempted to make the case to the British Foreign Secretary, Robin Cook; he could and should have spoken out. I found him very difficult to deal with. I knew more about Iraq and the Kurds than most but he did not want to know.

The Kurds struggled against terrible hardship for years. There were an estimated tens of thousands of people dead, villages destroyed, factories closed and an entire infrastructure in need of repair. Slowly they began rebuilding their villages by hand. The establishment of safe havens had provided the Kurds with the opportunity for democratic self-government. Free elections were held in 1992 and an imposing parliament building erected in Erbil, symbolising an emergent nation's sense of hope, a belief in a better future. However, the appalling economic conditions, exacerbated by sanctions, eventually led to factional conflict among the Kurds.

As ever, the infighting had its roots in power and money. Barzani's KDP had allowed the Iraqis to smuggle oil out through its strongholds, a highly lucrative venture that caused considerable jealousy. Tensions between the two main parties increased further when a CIA-backed plan to assassinate Saddam Hussein ran into trouble. The KDP withdrew from the agreement, leaving Talabani's PUK to fight Saddam alone. Talabani, meanwhile, fostered close relations with Iran which the KDP saw as a threat and Barzani responded by asking for Saddam Hussein's protection. Seizing an opportunity to divide and conquer, Saddam's troops invaded Kurdistan once again, attacked the PUK and executed its captured soldiers. When Saddam was forced to withdraw by the Americans, the KDP were left in charge of previously PUK-controlled strongholds.

When I returned to Erbil in 1995 the parliament building was standing empty, its imposing exterior riddled with bullet holes. Civil war had broken out between the rival KDP and PUK parties and the dream of an independent Kurdistan had turned sour. Having fought so bravely against Saddam, the Kurds were now fighting each other. It was so tragic. Sanctions were hurting but now the Kurds were also hurting themselves. In Sulaimanyah the hospital ran out of medicines. For the parents of a young child with pneumonia the choice was stark. Antibiotics were only available on the black market, so it was pay up or let the child die. Another great irony of war: black-market goods make it through embargoes, legitimate ones do not. The city also recorded some 700 cases of cholera. If families had money they could escape to Tehran. If they did not, they stayed in Kurdistan and died.

In 1996 I visited Iraqi Kurdistan again. Free of parliamentary pressures and accompanied by Clive Furness, then Secretary of CARDRI, I hoped to use my personal standing with both leaders to bring them together, offering to act as an intermediary. When I arrived, I found a region crisscrossed with checkpoints and both sides holding opposition soldiers captive. It was hard to understand why two parties with a common enemy failed to work together. My first call was to Massoud Barzani, and although he greeted me warmly enough he refused point blank to meet with Talabani, despite openly recognising the damage the civil war was doing to his people. Things were no better on the other side of the mountain. We travelled for hours to get to the PUK's stronghold at Sulaimanyah, where Talabani expressed similarly entrenched views.

Both sides were guilty of human rights abuses and, as CARDRI had campaigned against abuse of human rights by Saddam for over sixteen years, you can imagine my distress to observe the Kurds degenerate into factional fighting which claimed over 3,000 lives. I pulled no punches in my conversations, even using emotional blackmail to remind them of my long-standing commitment to the Kurdish cause. I was blunt in telling them of the pain they were now causing their own people. I demanded, and received, access to their prisoners of war, which began an intense wave of shuttle diplomacy between the two sides.

I visited a prison right out in the countryside, a disused farm. I had a list of 300 names on Talabani's list; some had been there months, some over a year. Windows were blocked and they were in total darkness. With no mattresses, the men had to sit on bare ground or straw. One old man, of about seventy years old, had been there four months or so. Rather dramatically, in hindsight, I told him he was going home. Meanwhile Clive was on the opposite side of the divide, where he had ninety-one names on Barzani's list. It was impossible to free 400 men in one go, the distances were too great, but I hoped this would be the first step to peace.

We travelled back and forth across rutted, winding mountain roads. It was bitterly cold and wet and we worked from dawn to midnight before being advised to return to base to avoid being shot at. Eventually, we gained the agreement of both leaders to a prisoner exchange and that independent observers would monitor the handover. Then the problems really started.

It was a far-from-straightforward process. There was virtually no telephone coverage in the high mountains and we had to rely on telex and messengers. The KDP had identified twenty-two prisoners from the PUK list and the PUK agreed to release thirty-three KDP prisoners as a token of good faith. The exchange was to take place at armed checkpoints between Erbil and Salahuddin at midday.

A small convoy of land cruisers, coaches and pickups packed with Peshmerga drove down mountain roads; our convoy came in the other direction in poor visibility. Of course, nothing went smoothly. Each bus pulled up some two miles from the 'no go' zone and soldiers would not let either of us go any further.

The KDP smelt a rat and held the coach at the checkpoint while we checked the names on the PUK transport; only one of the men was on the KDP's list. There was lots of tension as several more hours of fruitless negotiation led nowhere, except us getting colder and wetter. As darkness fell we agreed to extend our stay another twenty-four hours and try again the next day.

That night, after a number of sharp telephone exchanges, I went on a late-night visit to Talabani. I confronted him with the KDP allegations and he was deeply upset that I would doubt his word. However, he committed to freeing all the agreed KDP prisoners the next day and also to renewing efforts to find the other named prisoners.

The next day dawned and the rain had been replaced by bright sunshine. I told the KDP that it was up to them what they were going to do with their prisoners but those held by the PUK were being released. There were emotional scenes as prisoners' names were called out, the men looking drawn, pale and malnourished as they were loaded on to a bus. I can still remember their faces looking at me out of the back window as it drove off. One elderly man was found to be from Kakho, a five-hour drive away, and was just bundled into the car of a passing motorist heading in that direction.

It was a relief that some PUK-held men went home that night and the KDP released its prisoners the next day. I think that it was only fifty or so prisoners released on this occasion, about a tenth of the total held captive. It was a small step towards peace. I felt that at least I had been able to use my personal standing with the two leaders to do some good. The following year an uneasy cease-fire was established and then, in 1998, the US mediated a peace treaty.

In politics, personal relationships can never be underestimated, especially in the Middle East. It takes time to build up positions of trust but, once established, they can often be called on to solve seemingly intractable problems. I had a constituent from the Cynon Valley who was taken off a tourist bus in Turkey by the PKK which was in long-standing conflict with the Turkish government. His relatives got in touch with me to ask for help. The PKK was on relatively good terms with the PUK so I phoned Talabani, asking for his help. I said I understood that it was not his people who had taken the man, but hoped he would be able to intervene and get a message through as I had a responsibility to my constituent. He said he would see what he could do and eventually a clandestine meeting was set up in a community hall down a backstreet in Tottenham, London.

I took Jim Mahon, an INDICT researcher, with me and we arrived to find the hall packed full of foreign-looking men. We sat down and waited for someone to approach us but for a long time no one took any notice, although I was the only woman in the room. Eventually, we were taken through to a back room and faced a group of men across the table. They were intimidating, even sinister, and looked like battle-hardened warriors. I made my case, talked about my concern for a constituent who had simply been a tourist. Through an interpreter they denied any knowledge of the event, but I stressed that all I was asking was for them to get in touch with anyone who might have contacts with someone who knew something about it. It was all very cloak and dagger. They talked among themselves and then we were dismissed. I did not know if they were going to do anything or not.

We heard nothing for two or three weeks then I got an anonymous phone call late at night. The voice said simply, 'Your man is out.' I was given a location in Turkey where he could be picked up and I arranged for some Kurdish contacts to meet him and take him to the airport. But he did not want to come home, he was happy there! I spoke to him and told him in no uncertain terms that he had no choice, he had to come back. I never actually met him although I did get a massive bouquet of flowers from his family in the Cynon Valley.

The incident took a further twist when, on holiday, I told the story to some Finnish friends. They knew someone, a government minister, who had a close relative who had also been kidnapped by the PKK and asked if I could help. I met with the minister and told her I would see what I could do. I made another appeal through the Kurdish PUK and the Finn was released as well.

CHAPTER SEVENTEEN

CLOUDS OF WAR

B y the late 1990s the international community was getting pretty fed up with Saddam and the Baghdad regime. The previous Bush administration in America had been pursuing a covert policy of regime change to the tune of $40 million a year without success. Neighbours in the Middle East were hugely embarrassed by Saddam's excesses but did not have the appetite for direct confrontation given the tensions throughout the region. The UN, which should have been taking the lead, was impotent. UN member states had signed a Convention on Genocide but over half a century later it remained unused. Although the end of the Cold War had brought hope that action would be taken, in practice the UN was found wanting in Bosnia, Rwanda and Kosovo. Even the situation in Rwanda, where some 1 million Tutsi were killed by the Hutu, did not warrant being defined as 'genocide'. So there seemed little hope for Iraq.

In September 1996 I had argued in the *New Statesman* that, although it was too late to indict Pol Pot for his crimes in Cambodia, it was not too late to indict Saddam Hussein. Ahmed Chalabi and Professor Chibli Mallat came to visit me in Cardiff and asked if I would chair a new organisation seeking to prosecute members of the Baghdad regime for war crimes, much in the way Slobodan Milošević had been prosecuted for his activities in former Yugoslavia.

I knew them both through CARDRI and had found Ahmed Chalabi a colourful character; a dynamic personality, a charismatic mover and shaker. He had left Iraq for Jordan in 1958, eventually becoming chairman of the Petra Bank there, before being accused of financial irregularities and allegedly fleeing the country in the boot of a friend's car. In 1992 he set up the Iraqi National Congress (INC), a coalition consisting of the Kurdish KDP and PUK as well as many of the major Shiite groups. The INC was to become the main vehicle for the US's covert activities and Chalabi knew his way around Washington's corridors of power. He had been *persona non grata* there for a while. The INC's continual infighting, together with the Baghdad regime's brutal repression, frightened the new Clinton administration into changing policy from 'regime change' to 'containment'. Now though, Saddam's obstruction of UN weapons of mass destruction inspections was mobilising Congressional support for the regime's overthrow – a climate in which Chalabi felt funding would be available again.

In general, when weighing up whether or not to lend my support to causes and campaigns, I have learnt to make decisions based on what I believe is the right thing to do rather than the personalities involved. At times this makes for some strange bedfellows: I do not know the reality of Chalabi's financial background, but we shared a passion to see Saddam brought to justice. I do not share Donald Rumsfeld's politics, but I shared his desire to rebuild Iraqi society after the war; I disagree with much of what David Cameron stands for but I was happy to become involved in an inquiry he set up into the NHS complaints system. At the end of the day, I am prepared to stand up and be counted for my actions, however uncomfortable that makes me and other people. Especially those who see politics as tribal and who believe that loyalty to the tribe overrides everything. Perhaps it is no wonder that I have always been seen as an awkward customer.

Over the next several years I got to know Ahmed Chalabi well. I found him fascinating, with a foot in many cultures, but, and like many others, we had our arguments. He divided his time between London and Washington and also had a home in Tehran. He was by no means universally popular; the left were particularly suspicious of his neo-con friends. An independently wealthy man, on one occasion in Cardiff we went at his request to see the impressive collection of Impressionist paintings at the National Museum of Wales. As we walked past the renowned Brangwyn Panels, painted by Sir Frank Brangwyn, Ahmed pointed at them and said casually: 'I bid for those at auction.'

Others involved in the formation of INDICT were Hamid Al-Bayati, later Iraqi Representative to the UN; Dr Latif Rashid, who became Minister of Water Resources in the interim government; and US policy advisor and author Peter Galbraith, son of J. K. Galbraith, and himself a former US ambassador to Croatia, who had spoken out against the Halabja chemical attack in the US. I was persuaded to chair this burgeoning new organisation and INDICT was launched in the House of Commons in January 1997. Our objective was that Saddam Hussein should not continue to escape prosecution for his war crimes and crimes of genocide. We believed it was essential that he should not cheat justice. The event was attended by the great and good and boosted by messages of support from political leaders across the board; from Margaret Thatcher and John Major, to Tony Blair. It seemed as though we had caught the mood of the moment and further backing came from Sweden, Norway, the Netherlands, Denmark, Germany, Switzerland and Czechoslovakia.

The original intention was to set up an ad hoc tribunal. Under the statute of limitations, the Americans could not pursue legal cases against the Iraqi regime but, it was believed, such prosecutions would be possible in Europe. Ahmed Chalabi was confident that we could access funds from the US State Department and we spent days holed up in his home in Washington working on an INDICT prospectus and our funding submission. It was a very intense time: hours of discussion and argument with the sense of a clock ticking in the background. Eventually we pulled a compelling case together, much of it focusing on the taking of British hostages during the invasion of Kuwait, and the big day dawned.

As with all our dealings with the State Department, there was a rather surreal feeling that we were caught up in some movie plot. We were presenting to a group of about ten people on Capitol Hill but we were only allowed to know the names of some of them and I had a strong impression that the Secret Service was vetting us. Then there was Kathryn Porter, wife of congressman John Porter, and apparently part of our delegation: although no one seemed to know who had invited her. We later found out that Tom Warwick, from the Office of the US ambassador for War Crimes, was anxious for her to be included on the INDICT board in her capacity as chair of the Human Rights Alliance, itself partly sponsored by the State Department. It was not a group I was familiar with and there was a certain vagueness when I attempted to get details of its work. In the event, Catherine was not invited on to the board.

It was a rigorous interrogation but the upshot was that the State Department agreed to fund us, subject to ratification by Congress. In May 1998 the US Congress agreed an appropriation of $2 million put forward by Jesse Helms, Chairman of the Senate Foreign Relations Committee. The money was earmarked for translating and publicising documented evidence of alleged Iraqi war crimes, some of which was to go to INDICT. US budget allocations are notoriously slow in coming through and by October we were still waiting for the contract to be approved and funds to be released. We also received a major contribution to our costs from the Kuwaiti government, which had an interest in locating Kuwaitis captured during the Iraqi invasion of Kuwait.

We found premises in the former London Docks Harbour Board building on the South Bank, opposite the House of Commons, and started our search for a chief executive. Although we had plenty of warm words, progress was slow. The builders renovating our new offices went bust, support in France evaporated, and the *Sunday Times* refused to carry our advertisement for the post of chief executive. I had briefed the Foreign Office on our plans and now asked them to push the US for release of the money. In February Peter Galbraith called from Washington to say that, subject to some administrative commitments, the money would be released. The first tranche of $500,000 arrived shortly afterwards, which was an enormous relief.

Meanwhile, in the absence of a chief executive, I was having to front much of the lobbying especially at the UN. I had positive meetings with the UN Special Rapporteur on Torture, Max Van der Stoel, the then UN High Commissioner for Human Rights Mary Robinson and Secretary General Kofi Annan. I also addressed an Inter-Parliamentary Union conference in Brussels, for which we prepared leaflets in multiple languages and a hard-hitting film on Iraqi atrocities. Despite the fact that each day the Iraqi delegation swept away our leaflets from the display table, the conference went well for us. In fact, pretty much everywhere, we were well received. There appeared to be a great deal of goodwill and sympathy for the cause – but, sadly, little action.

By the mid-1990s a body of law existed that could bring human rights abusers to court. Development of international law was slow; even though the law existed its application was dependent on institutions that had their own political agendas. A new ruling by the International Court of Justice blocked indictments of ruling heads of state. This meant that, as the President of Iraq, we could not indict Saddam Hussein. However, that still left key members of his regime open to legal action and we drew up our 'most wanted list'. We had a great deal of evidence against Foreign Minister Tariq Aziz. Then there was Chemical Ali. We had plenty of evidence against him.

Our objective was to gather proof that would stand up in court. Under the guidance of a top human rights barrister, Clare

Montgomery QC of Matrix Chambers, our researchers worked hard interviewing thousands of people to collect the testimonies. Once the evidence had been gathered and analysed by our legal team my role, along with other board members, was to persuade the law makers in the relevant country that there was enough evidence to indict the people concerned.

One of the reasons the Americans were funding this campaign in Europe was that prosecution would not be possible under US law, but in the UK, Belgium, Switzerland and Norway we were confident we could be successful. We came very close to a prosecution in Belgium, but at the last minute they changed their laws because someone else tried to indict Israeli leader Ariel Sharon. We turned our attention to Switzerland, where Hussein's half-brother was living next door to the British ambassador. Local intelligence was that he had large black sacks full of money, which he distributed liberally round the place. Anyway, the Swiss authorities did not want to know. We had a good case in Norway and I travelled there to meet with their senior law officers but, just like Britain, there were lots of warm words but no action. They just prevaricated and the issue dragged on without actually getting anywhere.

Meanwhile our main paymasters, the Americans, were having a change of heart. The Clinton administration had originally been enthusiastic, wanting us to campaign in the US as well as in Europe, but suddenly they changed their minds. About two or three times a year I would be summoned to late-night meetings at the Royal Horseguards Hotel in Westminster where a senior-level State Department official, ex-military, would meet me. I never knew if they were aware of the irony that the building used to be home to the British Secret Services! We would spend an hour or so, with me listening to his viewpoint and nodding a lot. Towards the end, the change of heart in the US became clear and he would advise us to back off, cue lots more nodding, and then I would leave and forget all about it. It was all a bit like a Hollywood movie; the 'heavy' would make his case and I would very politely listen. Given they had funded us I had to tread carefully, but I made it clear that INDICT was a UK-based organisation and they could not dictate to us. We would persist in trying to get indictments.

In the UK, we focused our attention on Tariq Aziz because of his involvement with the taking of British hostages. During the first Gulf War Saddam had, in contravention of international agreements on warfare, taken civilian hostages. Thousands of Westerners, mainly American and British, had been captured in Kuwait when Iraq invaded, including the passengers of a British Airways flight to India which had been refuelling. They were taken to Iraq and held in appalling conditions at key installations, such as power stations and military bases. It was an attempt to provide a 'human shield' to prevent bombing by coalition forces. The hostages were subjected to continual intimidation, even torture, and paraded for propaganda purposes. Some died in captivity, many had their health ruined, and even after release the suffering continued, with reports of post-traumatic stress, wrecked careers and even suicides.

Our researchers unearthed direct evidence that implicated Saddam Hussein and Tariq Aziz in the hostage-taking and our counsel advised us that both could be charged in the UK with the offence of hostage taking. Under the Taking of Hostage Act of 1982, the offence was prosecutable in the UK regardless of where the crime had been committed or the nationality of the offender. I wrote to the Attorney General, Lord Williams of Mostyn, in September 2000 asking for him to consent to a prosecution. As a member of the Labour Party, and also from Flintshire, I knew him fairly well. I had several meetings with him and continually pressurised his team to take action as we felt they were not moving fast enough. I would spot Lord Mostyn in the corridors at Westminster and take off after him to check on progress, chasing him down corridors. He would frequently joke that he was forever having to duck into the gents to avoid me.

Six months later, his reply arrived. He refused to grant consent to the prosecution on the grounds that there was no realistic prospect of conviction. The whole team was devastated and I can only imagine how the former hostages felt. Our barrister was bewildered, believing we had as much evidence as you could possibly need.

One day, Lord Mostyn told me he had good news for INDICT. 'Put out a press release,' he said. He was, at last, going to refer the case against Tariq Aziz to Scotland Yard. I looked at him and said, 'You're kicking it into long grass.' But he denied that was the case. We duly visited Chief Superintendent Bunn at New Scotland Yard and talked about the evidence we had, and offered our help with providing additional evidence, but we never heard a word from him. It is understandable in some ways, it was not their remit. They had neither the resources nor expertise and certainly not the interest. INDICT came in for much ridicule in the UK media – typical tabloid fare, with cartoons of British bobbies apprehending Saddam, one of which still hangs in my home.

We could not give up and we stepped up our efforts to gather further evidence and shore up our legal case. By now, Lord Mostyn had been replaced by Lord Goldsmith. Eighteen months later we submitted further advice seeking to prosecute Saddam and Tariq Aziz, but also adding the names of Chemical Ali and Taha Ramadan, Vice President of Iraq. As Claire said at the time: 'Short of getting Saddam Hussein to sign a confession in his own blood, you've got everything you need.' It was another six months before we had a reply; again we were turned down.

I still feel it was a really good opportunity missed and that, if the major powers had made a concerted effort at that point, then war might have been avoided. Iraqis do not like to lose face, particularly in front of other Middle East leaders. It was all very frustrating. So many people put in such a huge effort over the years to reach this point. Military intervention seemed to become more of an option, as we grew increasingly desperate, watching time slip by. We knew people in Iraq were being tortured and killed in large numbers and could not understand why others did not feel the same sense of outrage.

The campaign became all-consuming. Owen always encouraged me; there was never any begrudging the time I spent on it or the toll it often took, leaving me drained. He always used to tell me that one day I should write a book about my experiences.

I was bitterly disappointed that, when Saddam's cohorts eventually stood trial, they were not made to answer for this particular crime. The victims had a traumatic time and many had great difficulty in recovering from their ordeal. They deserved the opportunity to hold those responsible to account. The only consolation came when I was attending the trial of Saddam Hussein in a special court in Baghdad, and a group of American lawyers took me to an ante-room behind the court and showed me the files marked INDICT, and said they were using them as evidence. It gave me some satisfaction that our work had not been completely wasted and was finally being used to bring this tyrant to justice.

By 2003 the clouds of war were gathering in both Washington and London. The UN was proceeding with its weapons inspections but the world had finally stopped believing anything Saddam Hussein said. There had long been a school of thought advocating Saddam's forcible removal by Western forces, but it was not one I had subscribed to. I had always favoured non-military solutions. Yes, the Kurds and Shi'a had sought to topple the Baghdad regime, but that was a very different matter to foreign intervention and British soldiers on the ground. We desperately stepped up our work at INDICT. I met my fellow countryman Rowan Williams, the Archbishop of Canterbury, canvassing him to support INDICT as an alternative to war in Iraq. He was charming, he listened, but he did nothing. It was a massive blow and, I believe, a moral abdication.

Meanwhile I had been invited to open the Kurds' genocide museum.

I had seen genocide museums in Rwanda, Cambodia and, of course, in Europe, but nothing had prepared me for this. The museum had been set up in an old torture centre where thousands had died. There were bullet holes in the cells and pictures, drawn in blood, by the children imprisoned there. Former prisoners showed me around. On the walls were hundreds of photographs of piles of clothing, mass graves and skulls. There were pictures of prisoners, just before they were executed, grinning at the camera: the guards tickled them to make them laugh. The day I opened the museum it was snowing, grey and icy. Hundreds of relatives of the dead and victims queued up to watch and tell me their stories. One old man showed me a photograph of fifteen members of his family; he was the only survivor. I was asked to cut the ribbon, but I could feel my voice breaking. I have given thousands of speeches but I simply could not speak. I started walking round the room, trying to compose myself, but when a Kurdish cameraman asked me how I felt I burst into tears. I had never cried in public before. As I stood in that museum I just thought, 'Why didn't we carry on to Baghdad? Why did we let this keep happening for another twelve years?'

The next day I felt so embarrassed. The Kurds were so composed and I had not even suffered and I was sobbing. But when I went to the market with a Kurdish friend, all the shopkeepers were coming up to offer me gifts. One explained, 'We saw you crying on TV last night. Thank you. My mother cried for the first time in ten years when she saw you. She finally felt she could grieve for her lost husband and brother. Soon my whole street was crying.'

The suffering of the Kurds and Iraqis has touched me more than any other human rights issue. It was not all doom and despair, however. When I got to Kurdistan in 2003 I hardly recognised the place. It had become self-governing and semi-autonomous. There was a university, libraries and schools and even three women judges. The Kurds had achieved so much but it was now under threat again. Their intelligence indicated an imminent attack by Saddam Hussein. Hero

Talabani took me to Chamchamal and pointed out rocket placements on the hillside overlooking the town. 'That's where they're going to fire their chemical weapons from,' she told me, before we beat a hasty retreat. Everywhere we saw people heading out of the towns and cities to seek refuge in the open countryside. In the markets I saw women queuing up to buy disposable nappies, believing they would be able to use them as face masks when the attack came.

Jalal Talabani asked me to pass on a request to the British government for chemical-weapon protection suits. We discussed again the need to remove Saddam, but what was different this time is that they called for foreign intervention, for war to topple the dictator. It was the first time I had ever heard them say that, and I had had a long association with them. It was not easy for proud Peshmerga to ask another army for help, but no one could face the thought of another Halabja. There was a sheer feeling of desperation among them: once again they were going to be annihilated.

I returned to London and spoke in the House of Commons about this new turn of events. Several people told me that my speech changed their minds, but it was not an easy one to make. It was a difficult position but we had tried everything else. I felt desperately sad but it was the end of the road, there was no other way of removing Saddam and I was absolutely clear that it was necessary. The chemical attack at Halabja, war crimes during the Iran–Iraq war, the genocidal al-Anfal campaign, the invasion of Kuwait and killing of over 1,000 Kuwaiti civilians, a further 30,000 civilian deaths in the Kurdish uprising, the draining of the southern marshes and summary executions of thousands of political prisoners. Saddam Hussein's was an evil and fascist regime. But despite passing over seventeen resolutions, the UN did nothing about it. Why, Iraqi friends would ask me, did the West celebrate intervention against Pol Pot in Cambodia and Idi Amin in Uganda, but refuse to take action against Saddam Hussein in Iraq? Yet again, the UN had been found wanting in the face of genocide.

Agreement on a resolution to invade simply was not going to happen, so waiting for one was not an option.

I found myself aligning with people I never had before, while long-term friends on the Labour left were on the opposing side. I felt very isolated. My close colleagues, such as Alice Mahon, respected my position; they understood that this issue was important to me and that I had not arrived at my position lightly. Sadly, others such as Brian Sedgemore, simply could not accept my position and we became estranged. There was a noticeable coldness from some colleagues, who pointedly ignored me in the tea rooms. At Swansea, while attending a Welsh Labour conference, I was openly jeered and called '*Bradwr*', 'Traitor'. Somehow it sounded so much worse in Welsh. Meanwhile I was told that Tony Blair, in a bid to get his backbenchers on side, mentioned me at every opportunity. He had forgotten all about the fact that I was the first person he sacked from his front bench team, ironically for visiting Iraq.

I had tried my best to explain my position in the Commons and in the media. On the morning of the debate that would ascertain whether Britain would go to war in Iraq, I wrote an opinion piece for *The Times*. It was not my natural constituency, but all my attempts to write for *The Guardian* had been rebuffed in the name of political correctness by Seumas Milne, who went on to become Jeremy Corbyn's communications director. Seumas may have his strengths but an open mind and a tolerance of opposing views are not among them. Meanwhile Alastair Campbell, Tony Blair's communications guru, was being portrayed as the Prince of Evil. Personally I thought Alastair achieved a great deal for the Labour Party, and if at times he could be heavy-handed, I guess the job demands that. I pulled no punches in my *Times* article, shamelessly highlighting some of the worst atrocities committed by the Saddam regime to underline why the world in general, and his own people in particular, deserved to be rid of him. Chief among these was a well-researched piece that came through INDICT about dropping men's bodies, screaming, into a plastic shredder.

On 20 March 2003, the British and American coalition forces finally went in to Iraq, with live wall-to-wall news coverage of the unfolding horror. As the Americans put it, 'Shock and Awe'. I watched the saturation coverage, it was impossible to avoid it, in my office at the House of Commons. Unusually, very few people put their head around the door and I felt quite self-conscious in the tea rooms. I was out of step with my natural bedfellows and felt uncomfortable with the macho revelling displayed by some people who should have known better. I was not having regrets or cold feet, but as someone who had always been committed to peace, it did not make for easy watching. I was buoyed by the constant ringing of my telephone, as Iraqi friends from all over the world were calling with a running commentary on what was happening. They could not quite believe that, finally, the years of repression were nearly over. There was a fear that, somehow, the regime would unleash one last catastrophe. There was speculation as to the whereabouts of Saddam and his key henchmen. There was celebration when his statue was toppled.

The regime fell in six weeks, much more easily than anyone had ever imagined. Saddam's brutal and evil reign over the people of Iraq was over. There was a cautious optimism for a better tomorrow but a realistic acceptance that the rebuilding of the nation was not going to be easy.

The Iraq debate continues to dominate British politics and foreign policy. For me the most striking thing about the debate, past and present, is how little of it had to do with conditions in Iraq or the views of Iraqis. The debate prior to war, which contained many divergent views, has been narrowed down to a single argument about weapons of mass destruction. As the debate has evolved, what has been notice-able is the lack of Iraqi voices. If I was voting again today in the same circumstances, I would vote the same way. I knew that I could not face the Iraqi people if I voted against intervention.

CHAPTER EIGHTEEN

REBUILDING

The atmosphere in post-war Baghdad was febrile. Everything and everyone was in a state of flux. Rumour and counter-rumour. There was a huge amount of energy, enthusiasm and apprehension. In the streets, among the ruins, shops and market stalls were reopening and people were beginning to get used to some normality again. Shopping, drinking coffee, playing chess and debating. But underneath the surface, the threat of violence still loomed.

One day I was at the Central Criminal Court when bombs exploded nearby. We ran down the stairs and out of the building, bundled into flak jackets and helmets. As we left there were many people taking cover, some in tears. There was confusion, a level of panic and fear. But it did not remain like that for long. One woman said, 'We had the windows blown out of our flat the other day but we got them put back in and carried on.'

I was struck by the determination shown by everyone I met that these attacks must not stop progress. Ministers would tell me what measures were needed to prevent these incidents. Other politicians wanted answers on how such things could still happen. Ordinary people picked up their lives and got on with things. They were angry and wanted more done to protect them. But they were not sympathising with the bombers, who favoured death and mayhem over the rule of law and a representative political process.

The challenges now facing Iraq were immense. This was a country which had been brutalised for over thirty-five years. Its infrastructure had been collapsing before the war, now what had been left had been bombed to smithereens. There was no unified opposition; politics here was tribal and fractious. There was suspicion everywhere you looked, particularly at the members of the Ba'ath party who had pretty much run everything in living memory. It was a country that needed to learn how to do everything from scratch: a Civil Service, judiciary, media. Iraq needed help. But much of the world was washing its hands. The attitude was one of 'this is America and Britain's show, let them get on with it', or so it seemed. The international community, at different times, and through different agencies, had failed the Iraqi people during the years of dictatorship and now it looked as though it would fail them again.

The priorities for the coalition were not always the same as for the Iraqi people. The frantic hunt was on to find the WMDs that had become the predominant justification for war. With ever-increasing desperation, leads and rumours were pursued until the final realisation dawned that they could not be found, even if they had once existed. And now the Western powers, who had staked everything on this piece of intelligence, were left with egg on their face.

Wars do not end cleanly. The occupying forces were faced with a complex security situation of rounding up the remnants of the opposition and also evaluating the population. They were suspicious of everyone. The Iraqi police force was in a mess; seconded British officers observed that it was ill equipped, badly trained and systematically corrupt.

We waited for news of the capture of Saddam, Chemical Ali and others, knowing that only when the Iraqi people saw them in court would they be able to move on. But Saddam and his cronies had planned for this moment and were on the run. A former General in the Iraqi army, no supporter of Saddam, pointed out that many former officers would have been happy to help the coalition hunt him down. Had they been allowed to, the capture of Saddam would have been fairly quick, rather than the nine months it eventually took to catch him.

The coalition administration was not inclined to trust anyone associated with the former regime and had a major issue of what to do with the former Ba'athists. All sectors of society had been controlled by Ba'ath party members: the military, police and government agencies. Anyone who wanted advancement had to join the party – it was always said that a Ba'athist builder would earn ten times as much as a doctor who was not a party member. That did not mean that every member of the party was guilty of the regime's excesses; in reality there were probably twice as many pragmatic members as ideological ones. After the war it proved difficult to get the balance right. The party itself was banned, but it would not have been possible to sack all its members because there would not have been anybody left with experience to run anything. I still thought there were far too many former Ba'athists in the transitional authority and, as soon as I arrived in Baghdad, the Kurds and the Shi'a representatives were quick to bend my ear on the matter. Eventually the pendulum swung the other way and then the Sunni community, from which most of the Ba'athists came, felt deeply marginalised. I think my old friend Latif Rashid, by then the Minister of Water Resources, got it about right. He explained how, when he took over his new department, there was great concern among the 600 staff who were worried they would lose their jobs. He got rid of the top two or three senior managers then called all staff together and told them that as long as they worked in the interests of the new Iraq their jobs would be safe.

It was against this turbulent background that I was appointed Tony Blair's Special Envoy on Human Rights in Iraq in May 2003. Tony was more than aware of my commitment to a free Iraq; I had been badgering him at every opportunity for years! I had had regular contact with him and I always took what opportunities I could to talk to him about the work of CARDRI and INDICT, and always found him interested and engaged. He was particularly concerned about the human rights issues and would interrogate me on the detail of INDICT's research. You could tell he was a former lawyer. I got the impression he appreciated eyewitness accounts; the human interest stories which no amount of FCO or military briefings were able to give him. It was not a cosy relationship; I was not part of the inner circle. I came from a quite different wing of the party, but I got the feeling that, on this issue at least, I had his ear and his respect, and the feeling was mutual. I thought the decision to go to war in Iraq had been a brave one and said so at the time and since.

Over the next six and a half years I would travel to Iraq twenty-one times in the role of Special Envoy, as well as to New York, Washington and Geneva. I had one dedicated member of staff and also access to the resources of the Iraqi desk at the Foreign Office and the British embassy in Baghdad. Of course, I could draw on the resources of INDICT and over the years I had built up many personal contacts in the various opposition groups. I had been there for them when the world was not looking and they now trusted me and felt able to speak openly about what was going on and their hopes for the future.

Juggling this commitment with that of a constituency MP was a challenge and as a result I rarely stayed more than a few days which made each trip very intense and exhausting. A typical four-day trip could involve more than twenty-five different meetings ranging from ministers to NGOs; British secondees; ambassadors; members of the Coalition Administration; media interviews; visits to schools, hospitals and mosques; and official lunches and dinners. All these spread out over huge distances and on poor roads.

While Tony was Prime Minister I would report in person each time

I came back and if I came across something that needed urgent action he would always take my calls, usually on a secure line from the embassy. Towards the end of my time as envoy Gordon Brown became Prime Minister and those years were much more difficult. He did not seem to have much interest and certainly did not have the same commitment. Just getting to see him was difficult and my office would have to get into long, protracted discussions with his office. Eventually I would insist; on occasion resorting to bullying tactics by threatening to publicly reveal we had not met. That usually worked.

My physical attendance in the House throughout this period was my lowest over my thirty-plus years as an MP. The dedicated work of my offices in Aberdare and Westminster, and the technical wizardry of email and the internet, made it workable and I was able to keep on top of both roles. This did not stop some people in my Cynon Valley constituency complaining. Someone wrote to the local paper, accusing me of being 'the MP for Baghdad', but I was buoyed by the following week's postbag which was overwhelmingly supportive. Jean hated my trips to Iraq, not because she felt the pressure of my absence from the constituency but because she was frightened for my safety.

I would not say I was cavalier about my personal safety because that is not true: I always took sensible precautions. But I think I just have a very philosophical nature; when my time's up, it's up, and worrying about it is not going to change anything. So, it's a quick safety checklist and then get on with things. Having said that, if you were of a nervous disposition the military-intelligence briefing before flying out there would not have steadied the nerves. As well as advice on what to do if caught in cross-fire, or if bombs go off (get out of there quick!) we were advised that, if captured, we should eat whatever they gave us because we would never know where the next meal would come from!

Obviously we could not fly directly to Baghdad in the immediate aftermath of the war, so it was a commercial flight to Kuwait and then a military flight (UK or US) into Iraq. Even I was shaken, even

frightened, on one of these flights. I was accompanied by staff from
my office and a representative of INDICT who was to liaise with the
prosecutors on the upcoming trials. I think a female member of staff
and I linked arms throughout our descent into Baghdad on that flight,
as the plane took diversionary manoeuvres to avoid the tracer fire and
explosions outside. We were all shaken up, but the next morning I
had forgotten about it when I was approached by a member of the
security team at the British compound. He told me another colleague
who had been on the flight had been found wandering around in the
dark, having experienced some kind of breakdown. Although he did
recover it was very sad and goes to show that what had become normal
to some of us, was plain terrifying to others.

A more joyous experience was my first-ever visit to Baghdad. It was
May 2003, only weeks after the liberation, and I was accompanied by
an Iraqi Kurd, Shanaz Rashid, on her first visit to her homeland in
over thirty years. When we came down the steps of the aircraft at the
military airport in Baghdad she fell to her knees, sobbing.

That trip was emotional for me too. When I met the Iraqi Governing Council for the first time it was as though I had come home. So
many of them had been involved in CARDRI and I had known them
for many years. There were smiles and tears all round as we hugged
one another in joy. My welcome was so incredibly warm, almost em-
barrassingly so. They talked about naming a square after me, perhaps
a statue or university chair but, thankfully, we moved on swiftly to real
business. I was genuinely astounded at what appeared to have been
achieved in such a short period of time, as much in eight weeks as at
least two years in Afghanistan.

It quickly became clear that in those early days the coalition authority
was missing an opportunity to win the hearts and minds of the ordinary
Iraqi people. That goodwill was essential to rebuild the country and,
even then, I felt there was a narrow window available to us to build the
basic foundations for a democratic civil society. In the end, the window

turned out to be narrower than anyone could have anticipated. Insurgents, supported by surrounding countries, entered very quickly and the security situation deteriorated as terrorists sought to undermine attempts to create a new democracy. In the immediate aftermath of the war the American-led coalition administration was making life difficult for itself by frequent, if unintentional, insensitivity. For example, a Sunni was appointed mayor of Najaf, a major holy city for the Shi'a. A military camp was built on ancient Babylonian ruins; US troops shaved men's heads at checkpoints and used male soldiers to search Iraqi women. Again and again my contacts would complain to me and I would try and explain, directly in meetings as well as in my reports, that ignoring cultural sensitivities was just stacking up problems.

The coalition did not put communication high on its list of priorities either. This was something I felt was a major mistake, and it became a recurring theme in my reports. Attempts were severely hampered by the lack of available Arabic speakers, but there was also a tendency to be dismissive of the Iraqi people. People needed to hear the messages from their own people not 'the occupiers'. This approach was exemplified by a toe-curling electoral registration advertisement made by Bell Pottinger, the US advertising giant. It was dreadful, comparing unfavourably with later ones made by an Iraqi publicity firm.

Many of these insensitivities were born out of pure ignorance. At Abu Ghraib, though, matters were far more serious. The prison had been symbolic of all that was wrong with Saddam Hussein's regime. Torture had been rife there in the past, now it was the main prison for those detained by the coalition forces. In 2004 Amnesty International published a report, 'USA: Pattern of Brutality and Cruelty: War Crime at Abu Ghraib'. It highlighted violations by American personnel, including sexual abuse, rape and torture. When I first took up the role detention issues were not part of my remit, but everywhere I went people wanted to talk about what was happening, and the issue was rapidly becoming an own goal for the coalition. I took my case to Tony

Blair and he agreed that I should add this to my remit, despite opposition from the FCO. The number of detainees was large but inevitable given the security issues. On the other hand the cases of mistaken identity, the heavy-handedness of the Americans and the lack of transparency, were ringing alarm bells. It was taking the authorities too long to process suspects. It even took the ambassador four weeks to locate one prisoner. I was concerned at the lack of legality in many of the cases and stressed to the Prime Minister that the primacy of law was being undermined. The US authorities even denied the Iraqi Minister for Human Rights access to Abu Ghraib.

There was an ongoing reluctance by the British military to tackle sensitive issues with their American counterparts on the ground. I had no such compunction and on a visit to Washington DC I raised the detainee issue – including the abuses at Abu Ghraib – in a meeting with Paul Wolfowitz, US Deputy Secretary of Defense. He had a formidable reputation as a Republican hawk, but it emerged that he had a long-standing association with human rights issues, dating back to his time as ambassador to Indonesia. Surprisingly, we hit it off. He told me he had been horrified by the alleged abuses and was committed to a full investigation. That eventually led to courts martial. At our meeting he was also keen to canvass my opinion on personalities within Iraq and mentioned a few names in the context of an Iraq President. Then followed a conversation on who that person should be – I spoke strongly in support of Jalal Talabani, since I felt that he had the ability to draw factions together, in other words he could provide the glue. At that point Donald Rumsfeld came into the room, and Wolfowitz said, 'Tell him what you just told me.' We discussed why I was against some of the names he had mentioned and why Talabani would be such a strong candidate, and I was delighted when Talabani did indeed land the job as interim President of Iraq. I felt he would be able to bring people together. He had been a leader of the Peshmerga and had fought Saddam; he was a man of stature.

Despite the attention of Tony Blair, Paul Wolfowitz and others, the situation in Iraq's jails worsened and on returning from a trip in May 2004 I told Tony that the moral authority of the entire coalition was being undermined by the continuing abuse of Iraqi prisoners. I stressed that the UK government had to have access to information on the treatment of all detainees; we could not and should not bury our heads in the sand. We were part of the occupying power, under a unified command, and early warning might help prevent abuses and avoid us looking as though we were part of a cover-up.

I continued to have concerns about bad practice. Two years after raising issues with the Americans, access to lawyers and families had not been resolved. The embryonic Iraqi justice system was overwhelmed and I urged the British authorities to persuade the US to slow down the transfer of prisoners into Iraqi jails. They had neither the capacity nor the training to deal with such volumes and their likely response would be to keep them imprisoned without trial, or introduce extra-judicial procedures. Neither was a good legacy to leave behind. In their own camps, the American policy under Major General Douglas Stone had become enlightened. He promoted an imaginative approach, offering courses on bricklaying, calligraphy and moderate Islam, using the detainees' time productively and preparing them for a law-abiding life after release. Elsewhere though there was a disproportionately high number of Sunni prisoners, who increasingly felt they were not protected under Iraqi law and were humiliated by detention practices. We were inadvertently radicalising these young men and sowing the seeds for civil war.

An area that had not only been included in my original remit, but one which the Prime Minister had made it clear was to be my priority, was to report back on the excavation of mass graves. These were important in many ways. They illustrated the scale of atrocities carried out by the regime, provided forensic evidence which could be used at trial, but most importantly of all, they would allow the families of those buried there to achieve some form of closure. The first sites to be excavated were those at Al-Hillah near Babylon, where it was estimated some 10,000 bodies were buried. Witnessing the work there was a traumatic experience for everyone involved. I certainly found it extraordinarily grim.

The killing fields themselves looked unremarkable. Shepherds tended their sheep, children rode past on bicycles. But on their knees, sifting through identity papers, coins, human bones and teeth, a team of forensic scientists examined evidence. In another area of the field a lonely woman dressed in black was on her knees, rifling through row after row of plastic bags.

The scale was something wholly unimaginable to ordinary people. Spades cut into the ground, hitting another skull or rib bone. Thousands of men, women, sometimes with babies in their arms, and children lay here. Some were blindfolded, others had their hands tied behind their backs. Some wore everyday clothes, others military dress. Alongside the corpses lay cigarettes. Sometimes bullets were found in the skulls.

Every so often the digging would stop and, in silence, the bodies would be brought up. Perhaps it was apt that this setting, the Babylon of my childhood Sunday school, should now bear witness to suffering of such biblical proportions.

As the bodies came up they were checked for any identification so that, where possible, they could be returned to their families for burial. The thousands that remained unidentified were reburied carefully in individual unmarked graves, waiting for someone to recognise a ring, a watch, a piece of cloth or a faded identity card.

In the searing, dusty heat, elderly black-clad women painfully combed the rows of graves where the excavation teams had placed the deceased's possessions in drawstring bags on top of the graves. I found it quite shocking, watching the women open these little packages to see if they could find anything that might identify their lost husband, son or daughter. Surely there had to be a more humane way of doing this.

Al-Hillah was not the only site and the work to excavate them all was overwhelming. It was important that the exhumations were to a standard that would stand up in an international court and the FCO seconded British forensic scientists to advise the local teams on protocols and practicalities. For example, it was important to use non-invasive methods for identifying sites; remove skulls upside-down to prevent the teeth falling out; and keep bones inside clothes to preserve them. But all this took time and for the families, enough time had already passed and they were desperate to bury their relatives with dignity. It had to be a balance between their needs and those of the investigators and in the end we were able to agree that graves of legal significance were ring-fenced and overseen by the British advisors, whereas the others could be managed locally and excavated more speedily.

As the security situation in Iraq deteriorated, it became dangerous for the British teams to spend long periods on-site and they were withdrawn in April 2004. I had first-hand experience of the dangers when a convoy I was in was ambushed by bandits. We were returning from a visit to a mass grave near Kirkuk, escorted by US military and Peshmerga fighters, when we narrowly avoided driving straight into an ambush. I was travelling with some INDICT researchers and we were talking about the day's findings when all hell broke loose. Our convoy was fired on and we were told to stay in our vehicles while our escorts called up reinforcements and chased the gunmen away. Luckily no one was hurt, but only because of the military escort. Our forensic teams would have been far more vulnerable.

There were plans to train the Iraqis but there appeared to be a lack of funding, and possibly of will, to continue the work. There are still tens of thousands of unidentified bodies in mass graves in Iraq but the ISIS insurrection has halted the remaining work and, indeed, is contributing to the problem with more mass graves.

I have travelled the world to areas devastated by war and in all of them the plight of widows is heartbreaking. In Iraq there was the enormous emotional pain of not knowing what had happened to their husbands, sons and relatives. In addition, there was the very practical problem of not being able to claim compensation or a pension unless they could prove their husbands were dead. In so many cases that was impossible.

One of the things I did find inspiring in that period was the Iraqis' appetite to establish their own organisations. One of the most striking was the Free Prisoners Association, set up in a room in a Baghdad house in April 2003. For them, and for the families of prisoners who had disappeared, finding out what had happened dwarfed every other issue. The association's members were all former prisoners of the regime and they went into schools, hospitals, prisons and anywhere where records might have existed, and picked up everything they could find such as files and record books. They had already collected some 150,000 names by my first visit but they only had one computer, no camera, no storage facility and no security. They had also been attacked four times by former Ba'athists.

It was total chaos. There were queues of Iraqis snaking down the street outside the office, waiting for hours, trying to find out if a missing husband, son or daughter was alive or dead. You would have had to be made of stone not to have been moved by the desperation of these people, who always arrived with a glimmer of hope that their relative had survived. There were heart rending outbursts of wailing when they finally came across the family name and often details of the most gruesome death. I remember walking in one day and a woman grabbed me. She told me she was a dentist and that her husband had disappeared. She showed me a photo of him and begged me to try and find out what had happened to him. You wanted to find out – for all of them – so I lobbied everyone I came across for help. I mentioned it to Jalal Talabani and the Kurdish government donated desks and computers. By my next visit funding had come through and the organisation was able to be far more effective. Nothing changed the facts, but knowing had become the driving imperative. Until people knew what had happened they could not move on.

I still keep an eye on the plight of the widows and chased our ambassador to follow up on the issue. Even though there are other enormous geopolitical challenges and crises, someone must keep track of these things. It infuriates me that the turnover of staff in the FCO means that things do not get followed up. Some ten years after the liberation I told the head of the Iraq desk about the problems the widows continued to face and he looked bemused. I will keep pursuing this. The widows deserve justice.

For many of my colleagues at CARDRI and INDICT, the work of the Free Prisoners Association finally vindicated our campaigns by substantiating the lists of names we used to publish before 2003. Further vindication came from an unlikely source. Fox News had obtained a book containing documents from the director of the Execution Department. There really was someone with the job title of 'official rapist'. The book listed different methods of execution and, along with hanging, shooting and electrocution, it also noted the use of a 'mincing machine'. My opinion piece in *The Times* in 2003 on the eve of Parliament's vote on war, highlighting the worst atrocities of Saddam Hussein's regime, had attracted a great deal of controversy. Some people queried the validity of the account of the use of a human shredder.

I will always remember 14 December 2003, hearing the news that Saddam had been captured the previous evening. It was a wonderful early Christmas present. An Iraqi Kurd friend called me at 8.45 on the Sunday morning; the news was just breaking. I immediately called Barham Salih, the Prime Minister of Kurdistan, and he confirmed it. It was quite hard to make out what he was saying, there was so much shouting and cheering in the background. Then, later that morning, Tony Blair called me from his car on his way back to London from Chequers to make the public announcement. After that the phones went mad for the rest of the day as friends in Iraq, Cardiff and all over the world called in to share their joy and television, radio and press called for interviews.

The Iraqis made it clear that they did not want Saddam to take centre stage and play to the galleries. On the other hand, the international community had different standards of due process and it was important that the trial was fair and seen to be fair.

INDICT's meticulous research and cataloguing of the regime's abuses would prove invaluable when it came to trying and convicting Saddam Hussein. He, and his key associates, were indicted on counts of war crimes, genocide and crimes against humanity. It was unlikely that the UN would approve an international criminal tribunal so it was decided he would be tried in Iraq by his own people. In the lead-up to the trial the UK played its part by training the special tribunal judges in London and after it was all over I received a personal email from the presiding judge, thanking us for our help, saying that without it the conviction would not have been possible.

I attended the trial, squeezing into the narrow gallery above the courtroom, only a few feet away from the man who had dominated so much of my political life. Although I could see him, he could not see me. Yet I still felt a shiver down my spine.

On the whole I found the court dignified and well controlled, but I was concerned about rumours that Prime Minister Maliki was interfering with the process, trying to exert political influence on the judges behind the scenes. Amnesty International shared these misgivings, claiming it was a flawed trial.

A further problem for a human rights campaigner was the issue of the death penalty. The Iraqis were determined on this outcome whereas I was with the UK government in opposing any form of capital punishment. In November 2006, Saddam Hussein was found guilty of crimes against humanity and sentenced to death by hanging within thirty days. He was refused leave to appeal and the sentence was carried out on 30

December 2006. It was a botched event, which the chief judge at the trial described as 'uncivilised and backward'. The hanging took place during a religious festival, breaching one of the legal conditions. Videos of the event later surfaced, showing hooded Shiite guards mocking and jeering the former dictator. The proceedings outraged the Sunni minority and did not bode well for a new Iraq. However, finally, his brutal and evil rule was well and truly over.

When I talk to people about my role as Special Envoy they assume it was all doom and gloom, but that was far from the case. The energy and optimism of the people trying to rebuild their country was infectious. And we did a lot of good work – training people in basic practical democracy, from running elections to investigative journalism. UK government departments seconded specialist teams to help their Iraqi counterparts and NGOs also did some great work. The Institute for War and Peace Reporting, based in Islington, went out to train Iraqi journalists who had no experience of a free press. The Iraqi media had previously reported Saddam Hussein's words in publications owned by members of his family. Now, some twelve months after liberation, new publications were appearing almost daily; satellite dishes sprouted on Baghdad's rooftops and internet cafes linked Iraq to the outside world. There was a thirst for information, for discussion and these youngsters saw journalism as a possible career.

One evening I was invited to talk to them in my role as Special Envoy and I was quick to remind them that I started my working life as a journalist. I talked about how it was in that role that I had met the Iraqi students that formed the basis of my interest in Iraq and how, for the next twenty years, I had campaigned for the end of Saddam's regime. I told them that the role of the journalist was to ask difficult questions to those in power. A hand shot up. Raising the issue of regime change, the student asked: 'Why did it take you so long to get here?'

In November 2004, I reported to Tony Blair that civil society was flourishing but remained under threat from terrorist elements.

Elections were planned for January and there was debate as to whether
they should be put back until the security situation improved. The impression I received from across the political spectrum in Iraq was that
the elections had to go ahead. They might be imperfect because of
security issues but they were essential to the morale of the people and
to undercut support for the terrorists. Iraq needed a democratically
elected Iraqi government at last and who could argue with that?

When election day finally arrived, on 30 January 2005, I was in
the south of the country in Basra. There were large queues at all the
polling stations I visited; it was obvious that the people of Basra could
not wait to get out and vote. The atmosphere was one of measured
elation. 'I have waited all my life for this,' was a frequent comment,
reminding me of monitoring the first free elections in South Africa.
At the first polling station we walked past security up the long drive to
a school, decked out in ribbons the colours of the Iraqi flag, and two
queues, one of men and one of women. The queue of women waiting
patiently to vote stretched down the road as far as I could see, perhaps
one of the happiest sights I saw over the course of the day. They were
all smiling, chatting and waving, handing out sweets. Earlier in the day
one of the centres had been shelled, but the women waiting to vote
simply responded with songs of defiance. The process appeared to
work efficiently, with a discreet but reassuring security presence, and
posters on the wall with pictorial instructions on how to vote. After
voting, people had their fingers dipped in ink and purple fingers were
held up everywhere with pride. Whole families turned out to vote and
they told me it was a day of celebration for them. They said it was 'like
going to a wedding'. Elderly and disabled people were brought into the
polling stations, sometimes on makeshift wheelchairs.

The next year, following ratification of an Iraqi constitution, a further general election was held. Again turnout was high and violence
low, leading to a belief that Iraq might, just might, manage a peaceful transition to democracy. Jalal Talabani had become the interim

President of Iraq and after the introduction of elections he was subsequently twice re-elected. He was the unifying figure we had all hoped
for, trying to integrate the various disparate groups, reduce sectarian
violence and corruption and mending relations with Iran and Turkey.
It was not an easy role and he often felt undermined by the Prime
Minister Nouri Maliki. To my great distress Talabani had a massive
stroke in 2012, just a fortnight after telling me he was going to get rid
of Maliki. 'I can't trust him, he says he's going to do things and never
does them,' he told me.

One of the things that Maliki did not do was pursue a human rights
agenda. I had continually raised the issues in meetings with him and
his ministers as well as in my reports. We should have done more, for
example, to lobby the Iraqi government to establish free trades unions
and pursue the rights of women. The latter was always a delicate issue
in Muslim countries but I do not see that as a reason to turn our backs
on issues that need addressing. Nowhere were the double standards so
vividly demonstrated than on a visit to a women's prison in Kurdistan.
'What have these women done?' I asked. The reply was 'adultery'.
I asked whether their partners were in prison too but was told 'it's
different for men'.

In many parts of the country, however, the lives of women were
improving and they were able to take part in the political life of the
country. Under the constitution 25 per cent of the Council of Representatives were women – better than many Western democracies.
The women MPs whom I know had built a strong caucus within the
Council of Representatives and played an important part in shaping
the future of their country. Those who undermine them do so at their
peril, as the Speaker of the Iraqi parliament was to discover. In one
speech he inexplicably attacked women for not having suffered enough
during the war. All the women MPs walked out in response, forcing the
Speaker to stand down.

In 2010 Gordon Brown lost the general election and my time as

Envoy came to an end. Since then British and American troops have been withdrawn and the situation on the ground has deteriorated. I have continued my association with the Iraqis and the Kurds and am very aware of their problems, particularly the continuing threat from ISIS Daesh. These are not new threats, they existed before the war. In Kurdistan, for example, they went by the name of Ansar al-Islam. I believe we should continue our engagement with the Iraqi people whose needs are great. We need to help protect the many minorities in the country, I believe we have a moral responsibility to do so and will continue to speak out on their behalf.

In July 2016 the long-awaited Chilcot inquiry eventually reported on the war in Iraq. I am out of step with the prevailing political view that the war was a mistake. I do not believe that. I never made the argument about weapons of mass destruction; my concern was always Saddam's human rights abuses. And in the clamour of voices seeking to put their spin on the events, I note that little has been heard from the Iraqi people themselves.

Dr Latif Rashid, a Kurd who became the senior advisor to the Iraqi President, points out that it must be remembered that at the time not only did Prime Minister Blair and President Bush wish to remove Saddam Hussein from power in Iraq, but so did most of the entire spectrum of the Iraqi opposition (including Kurds, Arabs, Shi'a, and all other minorities that make up Iraq) and most of the international community.

'The Iraqi opposition lobbied governments throughout the world, and we, as representatives of the Iraqi opposition, believe that Prime Minister Blair and President Bush were acting in response to the Iraqi people and to protect them, based on evidence available at that time. There was concrete evidence that Saddam Hussein was complicit and had instructed organised campaigns of genocide, torture, war, ethnic cleansing and use of chemical/biological weapons against the Iraqi population as well as neighbouring countries. We are still finding the mass graves of the nearly 1 million Iraqis murdered as a result of his actions.

'Although Iraq currently has its problems, I believe they are the result of Iraqis themselves. We will always remain grateful for the support shown by Tony Blair, and the British government and British Parliament at that time.'

CHAPTER NINETEEN

HEALTH

As a prospective MP I found the Denbigh Mental Hospital a forbidding place. Despite the manicured lawns and formal flower beds it was atmospheric in an ominous sort of way, as if decades of suffering had somehow seeped into its walls. As a child I, along with many other Welsh children, was threatened with being 'sent to Denbigh' when I misbehaved. The place not only housed desperately vulnerable people but many whom society had failed. Girls who had been incarcerated by their families for having illegitimate children, or unsuitable liaisons, were now elderly ladies but still here because it was deemed they were too institutionalised to live anywhere else.

In some ways, they were the lucky ones. I suspect those with severe difficulties had a much rougher time, often kept in their rooms, drugged or restrained, for most of the day. Many of the staff were caring, a few abusive, others simply indifferent. This was how mental health patients were treated in the 1960s and Denbigh was no different from other institutions.

I know because, in 1970, I was appointed to the Welsh Hospital Board in the wake of the Ely Hospital scandal.

The previous year the issue of mental health provision had caused a nationwide controversy, when a *News of the World* exposé revealed that inpatients at Cardiff's Ely Hospital were routinely ill-treated and abused. An independent inquiry was set up under the chairmanship of Geoffrey Howe and a whole host of abuses came to light. The hospital in Cardiff was run by doctors with no specialist knowledge of mental health; elderly and severely handicapped patients were condemned to 'back wards' which were virtually ignored; staff routinely ill-treated patients and, of course, there was a culture of cover-up. It sparked a nationwide outcry at the time, revealing systematic ill treatment of mental health inpatients.

At the time the Welsh Hospital Board oversaw health services in Wales and in the wake of the inquiry the Secretary of State for Wales asked the Board to submit a report on conditions in long-stay hospitals in Wales. The team's findings made for depressing reading, highlighting outdated facilities lacking toilet and bathroom facilities, with beds crammed together, offering little or no privacy for the patients. The service was also under-funded and there was a lack of appropriate training.

The Board took an enlightened approach and in addition to earmarking increased funding for the long-stay sector it worked to develop new policies for the mentally handicapped. My colleague, Bob Dumbleton, and I were co-opted on to a team and visited hospitals the length and breadth of Wales talking to patients, their families and staff. It provided a bleak picture.

I also travelled to Denmark with another colleague, Professor Margaret Stacey from Swansea, to look at provision of mental health services there. We travelled around Copenhagen by bike which was fun and quite an experience! We found their system innovative and exciting because it was not about locking people up in big institutions but, where possible, letting them live in the community in smaller units. People were able to be individuals and live in a home setting rather than a hospital environment.

It was cold in Denmark, so I took to wearing a fur coat. As a supporter of 'Beauty without Cruelty' it was a fake one, a very hairy thing that made me look like a gorilla. On one of our visits a patient grabbed me from behind and tried to give me a bear hug. When I realised what was happening I slipped out of the coat and left it on the floor and escaped. Everyone reassured me the patient had not been a danger, just attracted by the gorilla coat. Nevertheless, it was a nervous moment.

The principles arriving out of all this work were enshrined in a charter for the mentally handicapped patient, which was published in 1971. A cornerstone of the charter was 'normalisation', which advocated that mentally handicapped people should be helped to live as normal a life as possible. This was a big departure from accepted thinking in the UK and led the Board to decentralise services, begin running down large institutions and replacing them with new, smaller units. We even employed our own architect who pioneered a model of 'homely' accommodation.

Meanwhile, those working in the sector often referred to Ely as a watershed. It was presumed that provision and the quality of care improved from that date. Much did change, especially the move towards replacing large long-stay hospitals with smaller units and care in the community. The English regions eventually caught up with our work. Another major improvement was the establishment of a national inspectorate of hospitals, a proposal bitterly opposed by doctors, who were reluctant to have their clinical performances subjected to scrutiny.

None of this happened overnight. When I was a candidate in Denbigh four years later and walked through those imposing gates again I saw few visual changes. But I told myself it was early days; these things take time to work through the system.

Fast-forward nearly fifty years and I was sitting in the House of Commons listening to a debate on failures in the Southern Health Trust. The mental health trust had come in for damning criticism from the health watchdog, the Care Quality Commission. There were serious concerns about the safety of patients and a lack of response to concerns raised by patients, carers and staff. An eighteen-year-old man with a history of seizures had drowned during an unsupervised bath. More than two years later, procedures had not changed. There were risks of hanging found on acute wards and thousands of unexplained deaths had not even been investigated. It seemed as though, half a century after Ely, people with mental health issues were still considered second-class citizens. If things continue to move at such a slow pace we will be asking the same questions in another fifty years.

Reform of large institutions is never easy and, as every politician knows, reform within the NHS is particularly difficult. Not only is it the fifth-largest employer in the world, but it is a much-loved institution. There are many dedicated people working, under often trying conditions, to provide care. There are highly qualified specialists undertaking ground-breaking work. But the health service is often, literally, a matter of life and death. Getting things wrong can have disastrous repercussions.

Organisations and people make mistakes; successful ones learn from those mistakes and improve their performance. However, the NHS's resistance to change is matched by its defensiveness, a tendency to close ranks and reject all criticism, often manifesting itself as arrogance. Defend, deny and delay.

I first came across this professional arrogance as a member of the Welsh Hospital Board, when one single consultant sought to block our work because of his personal beliefs. It was the early 1970s and women were discovering their voice in the first wave of feminism. Many no longer wanted to raise large families and for some of those living in abject poverty another pregnancy could be ruinous, both to family finances and to the mother's health. Effective contraception was yet to be widely available, so some women resorted to the 'back-street' abortionist, often with fatal consequences. After extensive discussion we, the Hospital Board, decided to establish a termination clinic in Cardiff, giving women access to a safe service. Elsewhere, in the few instances where terminations were available, they were carried out in general hospitals where the patients were treated on the same wards as people who had miscarried or had fertility issues. We felt that having a dedicated clinic was the most sensitive solution for all concerned, including staff who would actively choose to work there.

It was a brave, progressive move by the Board but, unsurprisingly, a contentious one. One of its main opponents was Professor Brian Hibbard, professor of obstetrics and gynaecology at the University Hospital of Wales. Not only did he refuse to work in the clinic but he leant heavily on the rest of his team who, of course, were dependent on him for promotion. We had a long battle with the department but, in the end, had to set up the clinic in Newport instead.

Lord Gwilym Prys Davies was a motivating and inspiring chairman. He brought new, young blood on to the Board and encouraged us to be progressive. I had great admiration for him. He had been at university with the future Secretary of State for Wales, John Morris, and they were both proud to describe themselves as the original republicans in Aber! Under his leadership we saw ourselves as enlightened progressives, but the Welsh Hospital Board only lasted four years (1970–74) before the Tory government decided to scrap its powers and move them into the Welsh Office. It was a great mistake and the health service in Wales lost its focus. It was run by civil servants, whose concerns seemed to be balancing the books, rather than the welfare of patients. I think it was a retrograde step for health in Wales.

My time on the Board was a tremendous experience and I learnt a lot because of the people on it. People like Aneurin Bevan's sister, Arianwen Bevan-Norris, and his former agent and schools inspector, Archie Lush. They were both formidable characters. Archie was a puck of a man, very humorous, and could defuse any situation by getting everyone to laugh. Arianwen's approach was very different. She was a dynamo of a woman and people were in awe of her. I would sometimes go on hospital visits with her in her capacity as chair of the catering committee. On one visit to a hospital in Gwent she demanded to see the patient menu and exploded. 'Coley-fish!' she said in an outraged voice that would have done justice to Lady Bracknell. She demanded to see the catering manager. When the poor manager appeared, Arianwen got into her stride. 'Coley-fish is for cats,' she stated imperiously. 'Don't ever, ever let me see it on a menu for patients again.' It was an unforgettable and stimulating experience working with those two formidable and inspiring people.

It was an exciting time and I was bitterly disappointed when it came to an end. I continued my interest, serving on the Cardiff Community Health Council, and became a visitor at Cardiff's Whitchurch Hospital, another mental health institution, where I was forever making a nuisance of myself protesting about locked doors and so forth.

It was a stroke of luck then that, a year later, I was appointed a member of the prestigious Royal Commission on the NHS, established by Barbara Castle. I was the youngest member and excited about the prospect of playing a part in influencing the future development of the NHS, but I had not been there five minutes before I inadvertently caused a row. In order to sit on a Royal Commission, you have to be appointed by the Queen and I was asked how I wanted my name to appear in the *London Gazette* – Mrs Ann Clwyd or Mrs Ann Roberts? I did not want my name to appear as Mrs anything, it offended my feminist sensibilities that women had to be identified by their marital status. Apparently that was a massive protocol issue and there was much toing and froing between officials, but I persisted and eventually got my way, appearing simply as Ann Clwyd.

Once again I was fortunate to work with an inspirational chairman, Sir Alec Merrison, vice chancellor of Bristol University and an eminent physicist. He had a really fine mind. I remember his opening words to us: 'Unlike other Royal Commissions this one is not going to gather dust.' He and we genuinely believed that. But history played a cruel trick. Just as we reported there was a change of government and the recommendations landed on Margaret Thatcher's desk. The report did gather dust. It was a genuine shame because there had been a great deal of good work and some great ideas.

One of the areas we looked at was the underuse of pharmacists. Here were highly expert people, who often knew more about pharmacology than prescribing doctors, and yet they were often viewed as little more than glorified shop assistants. The pharmacists themselves were often frustrated at not being able to use their years of university study and the NHS was certainly losing out on a valuable resource which, used properly, could have lifted some of the workload from doctors. Unbelievably, we are still discussing whether pharmacists should prescribe antibiotics.

The Commission was ahead of its time in many ways. Things were different back in the 1970s; the concepts of consumers and service were in their infancy and, as far as the public sector was concerned, wholly irrelevant. Whether it was council tenants or patients, people were expected to be grateful and leave decision-making to those who knew best, an attitude that still persists in some parts of the health service. There were pockets of enlightenment such as the work of Dr Alistair Wilson in Aberdare. He was a local GP and a communist, who believed that patients needed to participate proactively in their own care. I brought members of the Commission to meet him and learn about the first patients' committee in the UK which he had established. Through listening to their concerns and issues, Dr Wilson felt he could provide them with a better service. It was radical thinking at the time and the Commission was sufficiently impressed to recommend financial support for establishing such committees in its final report.

We also visited Dr Julian Tudor Hart in Glyncorrwg, near Port Talbot. He was an extraordinary but unassuming man, a passionate advocate for the NHS and socialism, who became a renowned researcher, practitioner and author on epidemiology – the study of patterns and causes of disease. It is hard to imagine a more deprived community than Glyncorrwg, a tight-knit mining village whose population Dr Hart came to know well. He used his experience in practice to pioneer genuinely ground-breaking research. He was the first doctor in the country to routinely measure the blood pressure of his patients and, as a result, he was able to drastically reduce the number of premature deaths in his high-risk patients.

It was hard to attract doctors to communities like Glyncorrwg and deprived inner-city areas and not much has changed. On a fact-finding trip to America with the Commission I visited North Carolina, which had a similar problem. Doctors simply did not want to work in poor areas. But there the authorities, who had paid for the medical training, were able to direct newly qualified doctors into areas of need for at least two years after qualifying.

While in Chicago we visited the American Medical Association, the US equivalent of the BMA, and spoke to doctors in a large rheumat-ology hospital who had worked in both the British and American systems. I recall a senior doctor telling me that, in the American system, because it was fee-based, people delayed going for treatment until it was too late. Earlier diagnosis was possible in the UK, he said, and this meant more effective treatment.

The experience in Chicago took me back a decade or so, to when I had visited the US with the Fabian Society to discuss health matters with the Democrats. There was an enthusiasm, even a hunger, to consider a state-funded model. We met many high-level politicians, including Hubert Humphrey and Teddy Kennedy. The problems within the American model were blatantly manifest. Those in most need of help, such as the elderly and the poor, had virtually no access and many others were at the mercy of iniquitous insurance schemes. To me everything that was wrong with the system was encapsulated when, on the first day of our trip, a friend of mine, Elizabeth Anionwu, now a professor of nursing, and I were having breakfast in our New York hotel. Out of the blue, one of the hotel porters collapsed on the floor next to the breakfast bar. Elizabeth immediately jumped up to help.

Someone shouted, 'Stand back and leave him alone.' She insisted that she was a nurse. 'Look in his wallet, you don't know what insurance he's got,' they replied. We were both stunned and it really impressed on me how unfair and unjust their system was.

I returned from America more convinced than ever of the value of our NHS, proud that in the UK a person's ability to pay had no impact on their access to health services. Today Nye Bevan's vision is slowly being eroded as the service is gradually privatised. You cannot really blame people for turning to the private sector when faced with lengthy diagnostic waiting times, but it is indicative of an NHS that is failing its patients.

My time on the Welsh Hospital Board and the Royal Commission was to have a profound impact on me. I had always been interested in health matters and written extensively on them. The insight I gained from my colleagues and the people we met were to stand me in good stead in the future. I became convinced that, while our NHS might be the envy of the world and the quality of care generally excellent, the patient's voice was seldom heard. I banged this drum so often that, when the Royal Commission wound up and we were given badges to reflect our three years' work mine read: 'The Patient's Friend'.

Ask any MP and they will tell you – housing and health are the issues which dominate postbags and surgeries. When I became MP for the Cynon Valley, health was certainly one of the main concerns. Over the next couple of decades, a growing body of research pointed to a link between unemployment, poverty and poor health. There is evidence that impoverished people are more likely to have a poor diet, less likely to take exercise and generally lead an unhealthy lifestyle. As a result they are more prone to obesity, resulting in diabetes, heart problems and myriad other conditions. In my constituency you could add in industrial disease, poor housing and a polluted environment. Time and again I would raise the issue in Parliament, asking the Welsh Office to address the issue. Little was done.

As well as a built-in propensity for ill health in the South Wales valleys, my constituents also had trouble accessing adequate care. Do not believe anyone who tells you that the health service is the same country-wide. Whether it was GPs, consultants or nurses, local health services in many areas were, and are, woefully undermanned. When I raised the issue I would either be told there was insufficient funding or, where there was funding, that the area simply could not attract professionals. Since the semi-privatisation of dental services in 2006, trying to find a dentist with an NHS list has become virtually impossible. And with plentiful money to be made elsewhere, dentists avoid deprived areas where people can not afford to pay their fees.

Increasingly, I can see an American-style insurance-led system replacing the NHS. At first it was the peripheral services, although dentistry is hardly peripheral, but I now fear for the future of a health service 'free at the point of delivery'.

Every medical practitioner I have ever spoken to has stressed that early diagnosis is the single most important factor in successful health outcomes. And yet NHS waiting lists continue to grow longer and longer. As a result, the medical insurance industry is booming and elsewhere desperate constituents tell me they have had to cash in savings to buy private care.

I have been raising the issue of waiting times in Wales since I first became an MP, that's over thirty years. Not only has the situation not been addressed, things are getting worse. In almost every category, from A&E to cardiac, cancer and orthopaedics, Wales is consistently underperforming compared to England and Scotland. Let's face it, there is plenty of dissatisfaction with waiting times on the other side of the border too, but it is definitely worse here.

I used to come up against defensive Conservative Welsh Office ministers and was criticised for attacking the NHS. When, in 1996, I questioned Rod Richards on the chronic shortage of beds in the Merthyr and Cynon Valley area, he replied: 'I wish the hon. Lady would stop knocking the National Health Service.' Now I am attacked by the Welsh Assembly government, responsible for health care in Wales. They try and muddy the issue, pointing to differing evaluation systems. It is madness. You would think that an organisation committed to improvement, as the Welsh Health Service claims to be, would at least have a measurement system that it could use to benchmark itself with its nearest neighbours. But the defensiveness is too ingrained, and the public are being misled. The Royal College of Surgeons raised the alarm about diagnostic waiting times in Wales in 2013. The following year, *The Times* reported that ninety-nine people had died in the past five years while on waiting lists to receive cardiac surgery in South Wales.

Some of our hospitals in Wales are as bad, if not worse, than the English hospitals that triggered Sir Bruce Keogh's mortality review. I once asked Sir Bruce just to look at the diagnostic waiting times and mortality rates in Wales for me. He was aghast and called it a 'moral issue'.

I am not an opponent of the health service as some people would have you believe; I am a huge supporter and have been all my life. I want it to be better and I certainly do not see why my constituents should be more likely to die simply because they live in Wales.

Meanwhile an increasing number of people, not only the Royal Family, are turning to alternative therapies alongside conventional medicine. Perhaps it is part dissatisfaction with an interventionist health service and part new-age desire to return to more natural healing. Often it is a desperate search for a miracle cure. When Owen was first diagnosed with multiple sclerosis back in the 1970s we certainly explored alternative medicine. We travelled all over the country visiting practitioners who we hoped would be able to help. Owen even tried a gluten-free diet but, sadly, nothing worked. However, there are undoubtedly many people out there who have received relief from alternative remedies when conventional medicine could not.

Some forty years ago I damaged my knees quite badly skiing and have suffered recurring problems over the years. Twenty years ago I was told by a consultant that I would eventually need two new knees and a few years later I met an Iraqi professor of rheumatology and his wife at a dinner with friends. His wife spotted I was having a mobility problem and asked her husband to take a look at me. Professor Ali Jawad, originally from Baghdad, is a genius who did not have to resort to surgery. I have never looked back.

CHAPTER TWENTY

NHS COMPLAINTS

On 22 October 2012 I sat helplessly by my husband's bedside, stroking his arm and whispering to him while he died. We had been married for 49 years. He had been admitted to hospital for tests, contracted pneumonia in hospital, and now I was witnessing his re-markable life-force draining away.

Owen had been a young man, in his mid-thirties, when he had been diagnosed with multiple sclerosis following a car accident. Typically, he refused to let it dominate his life. He continued to work, going on to become Head of News for BBC Wales and Assistant Head of Pro-grammes. He bore the disease with fortitude and dignity. He could be totally pig-headed at times and that was how he approached his disease; he fought it every inch of the way. He fell over regularly, picked himself up, dusted himself off, and carried on. Two years earlier he had a partial hip replacement; after that his condition deteriorated and he became confined to a wheelchair. That still did not stop him. While I was away he would regularly make his way to the Cardiff & County Club for a good lunch and a gossip. He met up with old Oxford friends and had philosophical debates. He was always eager for my return at weekends with the Westminster news. After his death friends told me he was the only one among his dining pals who stood up for the Labour Party.

Twice in the last six months of his life he had fallen over and, seemingly on the brink of unconsciousness, his carers had called for an ambulance to take him to A&E. There, after an X-ray he would return home.

Just before his last admission into hospital one of his oldest and closest Oxford friends, John Fleming, professor of literature at Princeton, came to visit with his wife. John later recalled how grateful he was for that opportunity to spend time with his old friend. 'The wonderful qualities of his youth – gentleness, sharp intelligence, geniality and intellectual curiosity – had only matured over the long years,' he said, adding 'his response to adversity was magnificent'.

I was at home when he became unconscious but, as he went into the ambulance, he gave me a 'thumbs up'. I followed him and then sat with him for hours in A&E, waiting to talk to someone about his condition. I tried to speak to the nurses but they ignored us. A doctor came in with a check-list and then left without a word to either of us. Like most of my colleagues, I am always on my guard against throwing my weight around in these sorts of situations. So I sat it out.

Eventually my patience broke. I went outside to use my mobile phone to call Jean, and asked her to get an administrator to come and talk to us. Finally, two and a half hours later, a doctor came and said that Owen would be admitted to the respiratory ward for tests and suggested I went home for the night.

Owen was not happy, but I persuaded him to stay in and get a proper diagnosis. It was a decision I will always bitterly regret. Had he come home with me that night I am sure he would still be alive today.

I returned the next morning only to find Owen still in A&E. He was there for a nightmarish twenty-four hours before being given a bed.

To compound our difficulties, I went down with a severe chest infection and was told by the respiratory ward to stay at home rather than risk contaminating the patients. Our friends and family visited Owen, carrying messages between us. I did not like what I was hearing.

Owen, it seemed, was becoming irritable and dispirited. I phoned the ward daily for updates, but I was not allowed to speak to him. He was finally diagnosed with sleep apnoea, a condition that interrupts breathing, but a staff nurse reassured me that he was fine and cheerfully predicted he would be home the following week.

After twelve days in hospital came a bolt from the blue. The hospital called and said Owen had contracted pneumonia. I was stunned and rushed in to be at his bedside. I took with me a new catalogue of men's shirts and ties that had arrived that morning; Owen loved bright and stylish ties and I thought it would amuse him. But he was tired. '*Yfory*' – tomorrow – he said to me in Welsh and smiled. That was his last word to me.

I sat at his bedside, stroking his arm, desperately trying to reassure him. He was a tall man and he was squashed against the side of his bed like one of the battery chickens whose conditions I had campaigned against. I wedged a pillow between his legs and the bars. He was cold and shivering under a light blanket so my neighbour, who had driven me to the hospital, found a towel to put on top of him. He had an ill-fitting oxygen mask cutting into his face so I tried, unsuccessfully, to get him a larger one. His eye was infected, so I wiped it with a damp tissue. His lips were cracked from dehydration, so I used my lip-salve to give him some relief. There appeared to be an unbelievable lack of care or compassion.

For hours on end we saw no one. When a nurse did come down the corridor I asked her, 'Why is my husband not in intensive care?' She retorted, 'There are plenty of people worse off than him.' I asked when a doctor would see him. She replied that there was no need. 'The nurses know what they are doing,' she said, and turned on her heel, speeding on down the corridor.

Looking back, I should have stood in that corridor and screamed for help, but you assume the health professionals know what they are doing. This was a renowned University Hospital – we were not in a

Third World country. Gradually my friends and I realised that Owen was dying and Geraldine ran to get help. Suddenly, they took notice. There was panic as they tore the oxygen mask off him and started pulling drips out of his arms. They gave him an injection, but it was all too late.

I had never seen anyone die before. I was shocked, upset and above all angry. There was no need for him to have died then. Four years later I still feel he died from cold and a lack of attention, among health professionals who did not care.

In the following days, friends and family rallied round. We planned a traditional Welsh funeral, attended by people representing all aspects of Owen's life. It was comforting. He was buried on the side of a mountain in a peaceful graveyard in Aberdyfi, looking out to sea. It is where my parents and grandparents on both sides are buried and it felt right to bring him home.

I am not very good at being inactive, so I decided that the best remedy was to throw myself into work. The North Wales child abuse case was back in the news, so I returned to Westminster with every intention of getting back to normal as soon as possible. On my first day back Jeremy Hunt, the Health Secretary, was at the despatch box, talking about how poor standards of nursing care are one of the biggest problems facing the NHS. He said that in the worst cases, hospital staff are overseeing 'a kind of normalisation of cruelty'. I knew then that I had to speak out about what had happened to Owen.

I was broken-hearted about Owen's treatment and furious with the University Hospital of Wales in Cardiff. I decided that radio would be the best medium; I could not face appearing on television with my tear-splotched face. I talked to contacts on BBC's Radio Four and was subsequently interviewed by Martha Kearney for the *World at One* programme. Martha is a brilliant interviewer and she just let my words pour out. Afterwards, the programme was deluged with calls and correspondence from people whose relatives had also suffered similar fates.

The next day at PMQs I caught the Speaker's attention and rose to speak. I had not prepared anything; I was not certain I would be called or certain I wanted to be. 'There are increasing complaints about nurses who fail to show care and compassion to their patients. What exactly will the Prime Minister do about that?' I asked. It was a simple enough question, but I struggled to get my words out. Everything was still so raw and my composure went. I wept. Occasionally the House of Commons forgets to be a bear pit. MPs of all political persuasions knew what had happened in my personal life and showed compassion. It was too much and I retreated to my office.

My interview brought an avalanche of reaction. I even received support from within the health profession. A retired GP wrote movingly, 'I felt ashamed of my profession, I cried at your distress.' A former Director of Nursing wrote of the lack of care given to her mother leaving her 'ashamed of the profession I was once very proud of'. Another former nurse spoke of the 'indignity, abuse and misery' her father had received over three months at an NHS hospital.

The communication that affected me most was from members of the public. The letters came in their hundreds. My own grief was still raw and knowing that our experience was not an isolated incident, rather that it was an increasingly common occurrence, only fuelled my anger. I embarked on a round of media interviews, which, unusually for me, proved very difficult. Iain Dale, who hosts a live phone-in programme on LBC radio, had had a similar experience during his mother's final days. When I took part on his programme it left interviewer, interviewee and callers all in tears.

Before Owen's death I had only once cried in public, at the dedication of the genocide museum in Iraqi Kurdistan. Now, it seemed, it was to become an almost daily occurrence. There were people who accused me of using Owen's death for self-aggrandisement or political purposes – including the Welsh First Minister. No one would willingly reopen these wounds without good cause. They were too painful for that. I was doing it because I wanted to protect other people from a similar fate. Owen would have wanted me to.

A week after my question at PMQs, I stood up again in the House; this time I simply read out excerpts from my postbag and let the facts speak for themselves. It was the twenty-first century for goodness' sake and yet an elderly man had been left lying in his own faeces for hours. A former GP, whose arms had been paralysed by a stroke, had food left for him to 'look at'. No one fed him or held a cup for him to drink from. Another correspondent recounted a ward sister who said her job was too busy to allow her to talk to relatives.

An underlying theme in all the letters, apart from the pain and frustration, was the guilt at not complaining at the time. But, as one woman put it: 'I was fearful that an angry outburst from me would rebound on my poor mother.'

A clear picture was emerging of an NHS where nurses, once revered for their compassion and kindness, were now too often the cause of suffering and worse. Of course the health service was under-staffed and under-funded, but compassion costs nothing. Representatives of the nursing profession said they were pushing for an emphasis on compassion and consideration in nursing. Was it not already emphasised in their training? It is all very well providing nurses with university education, rather than on-the-ward training, but in doing so we may have lost many of the necessary practical aspects of nursing. We need nurses who do not mind wiping people's bottoms or holding the sick bowl under somebody's face. There are not enough of those any more.

Meanwhile the long-awaited report into Mid Staffs hospital was looming. As a result of 'patient power' from a brave lady called Julie Bailey – founder of 'Cure the NHS'– the abnormally high mortality rate at Stafford Hospital had been exposed. Several inquiries later,

Gordon Brown apologised to the families of the bereaved in the House of Commons. But despite severe criticism of the Trust's management, the individuals concerned continued to hold senior posts in the NHS or received handsome pay-offs.

The Nursing and Midwifery Council held its own hearings and several nurses were sacked and struck off the register. But the bereaved families remained angry; it seemed that lessons simply had not been learnt, nothing had changed. The lack of public confidence in the Trust led the then Labour Health Secretary Andy Burnham to order a public inquiry under the chairmanship of Robert Francis QC. By the time it reported, in February 2013, the Conservative/Liberal coalition was in power.

Francis found 'a story of appalling and unnecessary suffering of hundreds of people' and concluded that they were failed by a system which ignored warning signs and put corporate self-interest and cost control ahead of patients and their safety. He pointed out that complaints by patients, their relatives and staff had been ignored and concluded that a failure to listen to complaints meant early warning signs of systematic failures were missed and people's suffering aggravated.

Prime Minister David Cameron addressed the issue in the House of Commons, deploring what had happened in Mid Staffs and announcing a series of measures to prevent a recurrence. One of those was to be a review of the NHS hospitals complaints system in England – and I was to co-chair it.

I had been approached a few weeks previously and, although it only affected the NHS in England, I agreed to take on the role. I felt I owed it to the people who had come forward after they heard me speak, but also in the hope that improvements made in England would eventually work their way into the Welsh system too.

The political dimension was tricky. I was a Labour MP who would be chairing an inquiry for a Tory government. I asked for a meeting with my party leader, Ed Miliband. He said, 'Fine, go ahead and do it.' He was a totally reasonable man and said that it was a worthwhile thing to do. Of course, there was a backlash from elements of my own party, but I just ignored it. This was too important. My constituency party was supportive although one of my oldest supporters, an ex-miner, criticised me for working for the Tories. I put him straight. I said: 'I'm not getting paid for this, Dai, I'm doing it because it's a valuable thing to do.'

Valuable, but not easy. I was still having nightmares about Owen's death and also trying to work my way through a labyrinthine complaints system. There had been no communication from UHW in the weeks following Owen's death, despite my making a complaint immediately. When I went public they sent the Chair of the Board, Maria Battle, to see me and I made it very clear that I was furious at the callousness of the hospital. There were plenty of warm words, but nothing seemed to happen. I was still receiving letters from constituents and others in Wales of very similar cases. The hospital's internal review concluded that my words of criticism were unfounded. Even more astonishingly, it leaked its findings to the Welsh media.

UHW still refused to acknowledge what had happened and apologise. Like most relatives, it was the apology, and some reassurance that the same thing could not happen again, that were my main motivations. Neither has emerged in any satisfactory form – yet. I continue to push and have involved the Health Service Ombudsman. I will keep going until I get a satisfactory resolution but it has been a difficult process and the system forces complainants to relive the pain – often for years. Even with access to health experts, researchers and a specialist medical negligence lawyer it has been hard to navigate a way through the process. There has to be a simpler way.

The NHS Review was slow getting off the ground. A couple of months went by and nothing happened. The promised enabling resource was not forthcoming. It transpired that the planned support was to come from the complaints division in Leeds – hardly impartial. I insisted on independence.Meanwhile I saw next-to-nothing of my co-chair, Professor Tricia Hart, a nursing expert who had been a member of Robert Francis' inquiry team. In fact, during the whole year I only met her a few times.

For the rest of the team it was a hard-working period but also a fascinating and rewarding one. We received thousands of letters and emails, conducted public meetings across the country, and met with key individuals. We came across many examples of good work which we highlighted. At times, though, it became harrowing; having to listen to people talk while my own grief was still raw. But all that I heard confirmed my belief that there was quite a lot wrong in the system.

Our report, 'Putting Patients Back in the Picture', was published in October 2013. It recommended radical reforms to address both the common causes of complaints and the often shocking and distressing experiences of those who try and bring them. People who felt they had to fight the system for months, even years, to find out what had happened to their loved ones. For too long hospitals had been 'marking their own homework'. Truly independent investigation of serious complaints should be routine.

The complaints system itself was far too complex and ineffective. Patients and their families were often unaware of how to complain and feared reprisals if they did. There was little confidence that anything would actually be done as a result. The report's recommendations included an advocacy service to provide impartial help and guide people through the complaints procedure. I also recommended a national branding for the service, something I felt was common sense but which was turned down flat by the Local Government Association. As a result, the service that is provided is ill-defined, of uncertain quality and badged differently in each area. Few know it exists.

I wanted to go further and felt there should be an Independent

Commissioner for NHS Complaints. I was persuaded by health officials that it was not necessary and that the role could be incorporated
into the Care Quality Commission's remit. I now wish I had insisted.
The CQC has added complaint handling as an indicator in its inspections, but it is not a priority.

The review was a huge time commitment, over a year of work, but
it was worthwhile and every single recommendation was accepted by
the government. That was only the first step, the battle ahead is to
get them implemented. Things have improved, to a point, but complaints still keep coming in and lessons are not learnt. The overriding
culture within the NHS Trusts is one of defend, deny and delay. Until
the complaints procedure is fully independent I cannot see much
changing.

Of course, with health being a devolved power, the review only
covered the NHS in England. When I agreed to take it on I had hoped
that its recommendations would also be considered by the bodies in
Scotland, Northern Ireland and, in particular, Wales. People across
Wales, including my own constituents, had written in their hundreds
with heartbreaking tales of lack of compassion and care, and poor
communication.

The Welsh Assembly Government was not interested. The leadership were living in a bubble where they believed there was no problem.
It is insanity to think that what happened at Mid Staffs was an isolated
incident and could not happen anywhere else. In December 2013 I
met the First Minister, Carwyn Jones, and the Health Minister, Mark
Drakeford, to raise my concerns and I can only describe their attitude
as polite hostility.

The English NHS had at least acknowledged there was a problem,
but Wales was in denial. Elin Jones, Plaid Cymru's Health spokeswo-
man, tried to issue an invitation for me to come to the Assembly to
share the evidence I had received from Welsh patients. Welsh Labour
were clearly embarrassed and managed to block the invitation, twice.

Leighton Andrews AM claimed it was unconstitutional. Why, for goodness' sake, when national leaders are frequently invited to appear in other country's parliaments, can an MP with a Welsh constituency not give evidence to a Welsh committee?

There was uproar, with all the other parties demanding to hear my evidence. At last, a Welsh woman representing a Welsh constituency was allowed into the Welsh Assembly to address the Health and Social Care Committee.

The issues raised in Wales were, unsurprisingly, exactly the same as in England. Patients and their relatives believed their care would be affected detrimentally if they complained. When you are lying alone in a hospital bed you are vulnerable and dependent, often on the very people you want to complain about. Members of staff were also afraid that if they spoke out about colleagues they would lose their jobs.

Complainants wrote of insensitive, often callous and unsympathetic, responses. The system itself was difficult to navigate and lacking in independence. Many people felt complaints did not result in any change. Hardly surprising perhaps when hospitals are investigating themselves.

Hospital trusts are, quite simply, missing the opportunity to learn from experiences of complainants which means they are doomed to keep repeating the same mistakes, causing even more distress to an ever-growing number of people. With no regulator in Wales, no equivalent of the CQC, the only redress is the Ombudsman – I feel complaints reaching the ombudsman is a condemnation of a system which should be able to address issues locally.

In addition to comments on the complaints service, the letters revealed yet more examples of a lack of compassionate care. We all know that, thankfully, the care received by most people in the NHS is appropriate. When I had to go into the Prince Charles Hospital, Merthyr, for tests I was keen to observe how staff treated people generally and was heartened to see nurses showing tenderness and compassion and doctors communicating quite naturally with their patients. Yes, it is the minority of cases that attract the attention, but that does not make them any less serious. For the people concerned they are immensely important, even life-changing, and they are also indicative of a problem in the system that needs addressing.

People wrote in with very personal stories.

'My mother had two broken wrists. No one would feed her when meals were delivered despite the fact she had two arms strapped up in the air.'

'I went to the nursing station on one occasion to see the entire team bidding at the end of an eBay auction. I was kept waiting and ignored until it was ended.'

'When visiting my wife … after an operation to mend her broken hip, I asked a nurse for help as she was being very, very sick. She announced, "I am a graduate. I don't do sick."'

I despair. These sorts of issues need to be addressed, which is why I would love to see a wide-ranging inquiry into standards in the Welsh NHS – similar to the Professor Sir Bruce Keogh Review in England. But saying so publicly caused a storm of protest.

The First Minister's response to my evidence and ensuing publicity was a public attack in the Welsh Assembly, claiming I was only interested in Welsh health issues because of a grievance over my husband's death. 'I'm afraid Ann has based her allegations on the way her husband was treated,' he said. It was a despicable personal attack which horrified so many in the Labour Party that Ed Miliband intervened. Carwyn dismissed the evidence I presented to him, in the form of extracts from letters, on the grounds they were non-attributable. This despite my explanation that due to data protection rules I could not reveal anyone's identity.

Lynne Neagle, Assembly Member for Torfaen, illustrated the myopia of Welsh Labour on this issue by saying, 'We have all had cases of problems with poor care, but I do not believe that gives Ann Clwyd the right to denigrate the entire Welsh NHS, and I wish she would stop it.' To put the record straight, I have never denigrated the entire NHS but, where care falls below the required standard, I believe I, and every other elected member, have the duty to speak out. However inconvenient that may be to the ruling party.

CHAPTER TWENTY-ONE

POLITICAL MELTDOWN

The summer of 2016. British politics was sucked into a whirlpool of tragedy and intrigue of Shakespearean proportions. The 24-hour news services were struggling to keep up, news flashes being interrupted by news flashes. At times it seemed surreal. No one could predict what was coming next. In over thirty years as a Member of Parliament I had never known anything like it.

It had all begun three years earlier when the Prime Minister, David Cameron, called a referendum on Britain's membership of the European Union. It was a bad call.

I have never been a fan of referenda. They are too simplistic, too prone to emotional rather than considered judgement. On the surface the European referendum seemed straightforward, a simple in/out vote. In reality it was a highly complex issue and I believe it should have been left to elected representatives. It is what we were paid to do.

The vast majority of my parliamentary colleagues, and those in other parties, were in favour of remaining. I was not surprised when Labour MPs Gisela Stuart and Kate Hoey became prominent Brexiteers, but neither was I concerned. This, we all believed, was primarily an internal battle within the Tory party. And there is little the opposition enjoys more than civil war on the government benches.

It was a poor campaign, full of false promises and disinformation. The Remain campaign focused heavily on scaremongering rather than on the benefits of membership. The Leave campaign was 'economical with the truth'. People were seduced by promises of £350 million a week into our NHS. In reality it was what informed people knew full well, a load of old baloney.

I am a member of the Foreign Affairs Select Committee that heard evidence from both sides of the argument in order to produce a report into the pros and cons of membership. Even we struggled to reach consensus. Opinions were polarised and exchanges were unusually bad-tempered. In the end we lined up with the Conservatives on one side, the SNP and us on the other, and a split report. The chairman, Crispin Blunt, had not called for a vote, knowing he could not get a consensus. In effect we agreed to disagree, the process leaving us all feeling irritated and angry. I became even more annoyed when I had to watch Crispin Blunt taking to the TV studios with unseemly haste to support the Brexiteers.

Meanwhile, the country at large was snowballed with claim and counter-claim. The media hardly helped by focusing on personalities rather than information. Much of the media had its own agenda and skewed its reporting accordingly. To be honest, I do not think many people understood the issues they were voting on. The complexities of how Europe worked are difficult to grasp. When I stood as an MEP there was so little useful information I had resorted to an excellent Penguin book by Tory Robert Jackson, who himself became an MEP. Thirty years later things had not improved.

The campaign dragged on and, it seemed to me, people didn't care. In Wales the focus was on the Welsh Assembly elections. I would ask the local party what it was doing to campaign on the referendum and be greeted with apathy. The Labour Party was not mobilising its troops. I was concerned that it would result in an appallingly low turnout. I asked to meet Alan Johnson who was one of the leaders of Remain.

He and Harriet Harman were doing a great job but others on our side were simply not engaged. Jeremy Corbyn, for example, made few speeches on the subject and those he did make did not fire enthusiasm in anyone. Alan and I met over coffee in the House of Commons and I shared my concerns about the apathy within the party. He too was concerned, although neither of us was sufficiently worried to imagine actually losing the vote. He cited Wales as one of the most difficult areas to get the campaign rolling. We agreed that once the Assembly elections were out of the way we needed to go in hard and I pledged to do what I could.

Once Parliament broke up I spent time out on the streets of my own constituency. Again, it seemed that people were pretty apathetic. Also very badly informed. Many seemed unaware of how much of the Valley's infrastructure had been funded by Europe, how much assistance actually came in. They thought that voting Leave was a vote against Cameron and Osborne. 'Oh,' they would say when I talked to them. 'If you think we'd be better off staying in then we will vote yes.' Nevertheless, the South Wales valleys – one of the biggest beneficiaries of European funding – were to vote overwhelmingly to leave.

Amid so much claim and counter-claim by the rival campaigns, many people latched on to the thorny issue of immigration. For most politicians it is a delicate issue, as Gordon Brown can testify following his gaffe in branding a Labour supporter a 'bigot' over her views. Many people's views are emotional and irrational, fired up by the tabloid press. In the Cynon Valley some people would come up to me and say they were voting Leave because of the immigration problem. I would look round and ask, 'What immigration problem?' They would then look shame-faced and mutter something about Cardiff or London. They would rarely articulate a coherent argument as to how it affected them.

However, there are clearly problems in some areas of the country that need to be addressed. We in the Labour Party, including myself, have buried our heads in the sand because the issue is morally very complex. We pride ourselves on being internationalist, of caring for human rights. We measure ourselves on how we look after people most in need. And yet, in some areas people are frightened. You just have to look at history to see that when people are scared they lash out at minority groups.

All the facts in the world about how we need people to come here to work are no good when people are scared. You can't counter emotion with facts. What we have to do is deal with the underlying problems. Not just of employment but of infrastructure. In those areas with a high influx of migrant workers we have to provide funds to local authorities, in order to provide the necessary homes, surgeries and school places. The migrant workers are paying taxes into the Treasury after all. What is required is leadership, not jingoistic manipulation of the issue for nefarious purposes, which is what I think Michael Gove, Boris Johnson and co. were guilty of.

Then, just a week before the vote came the first bombshell of the summer. I was campaigning in the Cynon Valley when I heard on the radio that MP Jo Cox had been attacked outside her constituency office. Although she had only been an MP a short time, you couldn't help but notice Jo. Her energy and passion singled her out in the House. Her years with Oxfam had made her very knowledgeable about many issues and we shared many similar views, especially on Syria and refugees. So I immediately tweeted 'get well' wishes and said, 'We are all praying for you'. Soon afterwards I heard she had died. I was stunned.

So were all my colleagues in the House, regardless of party. Tributes came in thick and fast, which was hardly surprising. Parliament reconvened so that we could mark the occasion in the Chamber and at a service of remembrance. We put aside the bitter divisions of the referendum campaign and mourned together. Her cohort of new MPs made powerful and emotional speeches and then we all paired with someone from a rival party to walk across the road to the memorial service in Westminster Abbey. It was Westminster at its best. Multicultural Britain was also shown at its best in her Yorkshire constituency, as people of all faiths and backgrounds grieved over the loss of their popular MP. It was a fitting tribute, marking a tragic loss to public life. Above all, though, our hearts went out to her husband, Brendan, and their children.

People in public life are vulnerable. This had been brought home to me when a vicar in my constituency, Father Paul Bennett, was tragic-ally murdered by a mentally ill man in 2007. His shocked wife saw him slaughtered on the steps of the vicarage. In 2000 Lib Dem MP Nigel Jones was attacked by a constituent – also someone suffering mental health problems – at a constituency surgery in Cheltenham. A local councillor colleague was killed.

Such violent attacks against MPs are thankfully extremely rare, but hostile behaviour is becoming increasingly common. In 2010 a Labour colleague, Stephen Timms, was savagely stabbed at his constituency surgery. His assailant had wanted to punish him for voting in favour of the Iraq war.

A survey by *The Independent* shortly before Jo's murder suggested that one in six MPs had either been attacked or threatened with attack. In the aftermath of Jo's murder, the Speaker insisted that security should be tightened at MPs' offices and homes. The question of security at constituency offices is a difficult one; MPs do want to be genuinely available to their constituents. Since my earliest days I have had a panic button in the office and, although I have never had to use it, it is a reassuring presence especially when Jean has been alone in the office. Now our offices are in a secure block. But nothing is foolproof; Jo was not murdered in her office but outside it.

The referendum campaign was halted for a few days out of respect for Jo, but then it stepped up again as polling day dawned. Those of us who had hoped the tragedy would give people cause to reconsider, who would look at Jo's own work on integrating communities, were to be disappointed. The Leave campaign, its UKIP arm in particular, stepped up its barely disguised messages of intolerance.

In the early hours of 24 June I sat in bed in the dark, half-listening to television pundits in disbelief, trying to make sense of what they were saying. I felt like crying. Britain had, it seemed, voted overwhelmingly to leave the European Union.

I struggled to believe that so many people had fallen for the easy rhetoric of the Brexit campaign. Until the very last I had thought they would see through the lies, the undeliverable promises. Within twenty-four hours of the result, even Brexit campaigners were forced to admit that the savings they had quoted were misleading and, along with promises of cuts to immigration, undeliverable. At a Foreign Affairs Select Committee in November I challenged David Davis over the infamous Vote Leave poster. The one that Boris Johnson had posed in front of. The one promising £350 million a week extra for the NHS. 'I made no such pledge,' he said smugly. 'Some did, and if you want to argue the case you should invite them here.'

After weeks of campaigning I was tired and had not intended to stay up for the results. Then I thought I would watch the first result come in. Then the second. As the news came in I kept thinking the tide would turn. It did not. Eventually I fell into a fitful sleep. Perhaps I would wake in the morning and find it had all been a nightmare. Instead I woke to the gloating rhetoric of Nigel Farage. How had it come to this?

The morning after the night before I was in shock: I simply had not seen it coming. Like many others, I had assumed that Cameron and Osborne would not call a referendum until they had polled extensively and were certain of the outcome. Promising one in the first place had been irresponsible – gambling the country's future for short-term political advantage over UKIP. It was a terrible and devastating mistake.

With the results in, David Cameron immediately announced his decision to step down as Prime Minister, triggering a leadership battle within the Tory party. I think that was another instance of lack of judgement. He had got us into this mess and while he probably would have to stand down eventually, he should have been steadying the ship, not jumping overboard. What was needed now was a period of calm as Britain came to terms with the verdict of the British public and worked out how best to proceed.

Instead we had a farcical couple of weeks, which illustrated just how ruthless politics can be. There was Michael Gove's Brutus moment against his old pal Boris Johnson, then former Welsh Secretary Stephen Crabb throwing his hat into the ring before withdrawing after a sexting scandal. Normally a party's leadership contest, especially in the midst of angry recriminations like this one, would have been manna from heaven to the opposition.

But the Labour Party chose to up the stakes by launching its own, even bloodier battle. The day after Cameron resigned, plunging the Tories into turmoil, Hilary Benn asked for a meeting with Jeremy Corbyn and told him he no longer had confidence in his leadership. Jeremy duly sacked him, prompting a wave of front bench resignations that soon became a tide. More than two dozen MPs resigned, triggering an urgent meeting of the parliamentary party. I have no idea why Hilary chose to act when he did. He is an honest, unassuming man and I am sure it had less to do with ambition than frustration. He and Jeremy had very different views on most matters of current foreign policy and in this I was firmly with Hilary. When he made his emotional and masterful speech in favour of intervention in Syria back in December he alienated himself from Jeremy. Afterwards I bumped into him in the corridor. 'You spoke for me, Hilary,' I said.

But now, he had plunged the party into chaos. I was not surprised. There had been murmurings for some time; Jeremy was not everyone's cup of tea, and the European referendum provided an excuse for mutiny. It has always been a feature of the Labour Party. As Chair of the PLP I had seen it all before, when there were attempts to unseat Tony Blair and then Gordon Brown. There are always undercurrents of dissatisfaction with the leadership, stirred up by those who imagine things would be better under a different leader. I had not nominated Jeremy for the leadership; I chose Yvette Cooper who was extremely able, with front bench experience, and whom I had worked with on the Coalfield Communities Committee. But Jeremy had been voted leader with an overwhelming mandate from the wider party. I believed we had to respect that.

I considered Jeremy a friend. We had once shared office space, had worked together on many human rights campaigns and I had a lot of respect for him. He was a man of integrity and had never been afraid to speak out for unpopular causes. Now he was the leader and I believed he deserved loyalty and time to settle in. At the same time, I could understand the frustration felt by colleagues, particularly those on the front bench, who complained they were unable to meet him and discuss policy. People like Seumas Milne formed an inner group around Jeremy and were hell-bent on isolating him from the parliamentary Party. I remember Seumas well when, as Features Editor of *The Guardian* during my time as Special Envoy to Iraq, he had refused to carry a single line from me on the Iraq conflict. Now Seumas had isolated Jeremy from his own shadow Cabinet. It all became a shambles. People were resigning; others were appointed in their place and then they too were resigning.

Life in Parliament had become a whirlpool of seething frustration on both sides. I tried my best not to get sucked in, but it was unpleasant. Everyone was plotting and lobbying and at times I just wanted to lock myself in my office and avoid the lot of them. Jeremy's team was desperately trying to find people to fill the vacated shadow Cabinet positions, but although I was approached I felt strongly that it would be inappropriate because I would not be able to see it through.

Margaret Hodge called for a vote of no confidence in Jeremy by the parliamentary party. I did not agree but most of my colleagues did. Jeremy, however, made it clear that he believed he had a mandate from the party at large and would not stand down.

Meanwhile I had other things to occupy me, such as the long-awaited publication of the Chilcot report on 6 July. Some weeks previously Tony Blair had asked to meet me. He looked tired and strained; the pressure was clearly taking its toll. I reiterated my view that toppling Saddam had been the right thing to do. I do not think he ever doubted that my views would be consistent. We talked for a while about people we knew, about political topics, and I knew he would come out fighting over Iraq; he had no doubts. I had, and still have, the utmost respect for him. He was a good and brave leader and Prime Minister.

As publication day drew nearer everyone involved was getting nervous. There were no substantive leaks but endless media speculation. The inquiry and report had been a long time coming. Gordon Brown had instigated it in 2009. I was always sceptical: Parliament had voted for the war, so why dig it all up again? But Gordon was being pressurised by people who felt strongly that it had been wrong and he was trying to distance himself from Tony. He had initially intended the proceedings to be heard in private but, of course, the whole thing had gathered momentum and there was a clamour for public hearings.

The inquiry ran from November 2009 to February 2011. It was undoubtedly thorough. It heard from civil servants, military and intelligence chiefs, diplomats and politicians from home and abroad, as well as from Cabinet ministers and Tony Blair. I was one of the many witnesses called to the QE2 Buildings opposite Parliament to give my testimony. When I arrived on the appointed day I was taken aback by the protestors outside, and at the level of hostility. But inside what was tantamount to a courtroom, all was calm. Sir John Chilcot put people at ease and was an excellent chair and proceedings moved along smoothly. I had spent months preparing for the hearing, going through old papers and correspondence to ensure my memory was accurate. As I took my seat I was nervous, anxious to get my points across. Most of my testimony related to the work of INDICT and human rights. I was reassured when the panel members made open recognition of the work I had done in lobbying for the Kurds and against Saddam's human rights abuses. After giving my testimony my part in the inquiry was over. Like everyone else, I would have to wait until 2016 to hear the conclusions of the report.

So it was that less than three weeks after Jo died, two weeks after Britain voted to leave Europe, and one week after the PLP's vote of no confidence in Jeremy, the political world tuned in to Sir John Chilcot's report on the Iraq inquiry. The report was published on a Wednesday morning and, as a prominent campaigner for the war, I was sucked into a round of media interviews. As I told Andrew Neil, the interview was easier for him than for me because he had seen the report beforehand; politicians had not. I continually repeated my view that the war had been justified on human rights grounds and that I was pleased the report exonerated Tony Blair from deliberately lying to Parliament. I was shocked at the amount of bile shown by some people, and at the very personal nature of their attacks on what had been a decision by Parliament. To some extent I could understand criticism from those who had vociferously campaigned against the war, but for those who had backed Tony at the time and now turned against him, I felt nothing but disgust.

Jeremy was one of those people who had consistently opposed the war. After he spoke at the first parliamentary hustings before becoming leader I went up to him afterwards to tell him he had spoken well, but that he had lost me on his position on the Iraq war. He smiled and said, 'I know.' Now he stood up in Parliament and apologised on behalf of the Labour Party – a party which had backed the intervention. I was horrified.

The Chilcot report reserved most of its criticism for lack of post-war planning, something I had spoken out about on a number of occasions. I felt the Americans, in particular, had been cavalier in this aspect but we were not that much better. At least with the publication of the report I felt we now had some closure and could move on. Hopefully, lessons had been learnt.

The following day at Westminster the battle for the Conservative leadership, and therefore our next Prime Minister, was narrowed down to two women candidates: Theresa May and Andrea Leadsom. The party at large would vote in the autumn. Within a week Leadsom had withdrawn from the contest. Theresa May became Prime Minister the next day. The surprises were not over as Boris Johnson, to everyone's astonishment, rose Lazarus-like from his political grave to become Foreign Secretary.

The same day as Leadsom announced her withdrawal, Angela Eagle ended weeks of speculation and challenged Jeremy for the Labour leadership. As Theresa May was sworn in as PM, the Labour Party was embroiled in an argument as to whether Jeremy would have to secure a nomination from the parliamentary Party. This was ruled unnecessary by the National Executive and, although challenged in the High Court, the decision stood. What a farce. Before the month was out Pontypridd MP Owen Smith had announced his candidature and Angela stood aside. As Jeremy and Owen took to the hustings, Parliament went into recess and I headed for Aberdyfi for some rest and to switch off.

The election eventually delivered Jeremy an overwhelming majority, which partially silenced his internal critics. Jeremy has re-energised parts of the party that were previously feeling disenfranchised. Many of his supporters are new members; they may have voted Labour previously, but were not sufficiently inspired to become active members. He has enthused them to join and be active. Certainly what he has to say is going down well at those rallies. We need to learn from that, to bring the excitement and passion back into the Labour movement. Jeremy isn't an orator, not a Foot or a Benn, but he is saying things that some Labour Party supporters desperately want to hear. I've been to three rallies and he fires people up. They have the feeling of an old-style religious revival.

Meanwhile we need to find a way of reconciling the parliamentary

Party and the membership. There is a lot of talent in the parliamentary party but at the moment a lot of it lies outside the shadow Cabinet. Yvette Cooper is focusing on the refugee crisis and chairs the Home Affairs Select Committee and Hilary Benn chairs the parliamentary Select Committee on Exiting the European Union, for example. There are mutterings about the wholesale deselection of sitting MPs, but I do not think that will happen.

The issue that came to dominate British politics, and which I believe will do so for a generation, was our exit from the European Union. Prime Minister Theresa May may have said that 'Brexit means Brexit' but that grossly oversimplifies matters. There was an electoral mandate to withdraw from the European Union but, for example, no one was asked about the single market. In fact, Brexit campaigners regularly cited Norway as a success story; a country out of the EU but in the single market.

Brexiteers also claim that other member states will want our trade at any price. I know from my own time as an MEP that they will not be kind to us. They have their own problems and will need to make a scapegoat of us. Farage's contemptuous speech at the European Parliament, a real embarrassment, will not have helped.

I sit on the Foreign Affairs Select Committee where we have heard evidence that we have neither the lawyers to redraft legislation nor enough qualified people to negotiate our exit. It is also estimated the Foreign and Commonwealth Office will need to double in size to deal with Brexit. The whole thing is a frightening mess and the public mood is beginning to change as the reality becomes clear.

Of course, the government, anxious to pre-empt any public change of heart, sought to start negotiations as soon as possible. Theresa May summarily announced that she would not be seeking to remain in the single market and published a timetable for exit that circumvented the House of Commons. Her attempt to introduce Article 50 without an Act of Parliament was thwarted by the Supreme Court but it only delayed the inevitable. On 1 February a Bill allowing the Prime Minister to trigger Article 50 was passed. I was one of forty-seven Labour MPs who voted against the Bill and a three-line Labour whip.

The leadership's handling of the Bill – and of the Brexit issue in general – has been a real let-down. Although I was not one of Jeremy Corbyn's intital supporters for the leadership, I like and respect him. We have worked together on many human rights campaigns, East Timor in particular, and I know him to be a principled man. When he won the leadership election with an overwhelming mandate I believed we all owed it to him to support him, and I said so publicly and did not support Margaret Hodge's vote of no confidence in him in the PLP.

However, his performance over Europe has been disappointing, with his support of the Remain campaign lukewarm at best. Since then our strategy has been incoherent. It did not need to be like that. He could have accepted the referendum mandate and still fought on the detail, such as membership of the single market. Instead, he failed to mount any meaningful opposition and split the party. We even had whips voting against the whip.

It could have been so different. We could have come up with a co-herent position that allowed us to work with the SNP, Lib Dems and others – including some Tories – to stop the triggering of Article 50. I thought Ed Miliband and Nick Clegg's speeches were excellent. There could have been a cross-party coalition, but Jeremy did not even try and explore this avenue.

Unfortunately, it is not an isolated incident. There is a vacuum where the official opposition should be and that has distressed me. I dislike the constant plotting against the leadership that is so prevalent in the Labour Party, but it appears as though we may be saddled with this until after the general election.

My parliamentary career has been marked by rebellions but, what-ever my private misgivings, I have always supported the elected party leader. Now, nearing the end of my political career, there may be one more rebellion. It is not one I relish.

ANN CLWYD'S HONOURS

Elected as a Member of the European Parliament for Mid and West Wales 1979–84

Member of the Executive Socialist Group in the European Parliament

Elected as Member of Parliament for the Cynon Valley since May 1984

First woman to be elected chair of the Tribune Group, 1986

Chair of the All-Party Parliamentary Group on Human Rights since 1997

Appointed Special Envoy on Human Rights to Iraq by Prime Minister Tony Blair in May 2003

Appointed to the Privy Council on 9 August 2004

Vice-chair of the Parliamentary Labour Party, 2001–05

Chair of the Parliamentary Labour Party, 2005–06

Appointed by Prime Minister David Cameron to report on complaints in the National Health Service in England, February 2013

Former chair of the British Inter-Parliamentary Union Group

Honorary doctorate of Laws from Trinity College, Carmarthen, for her contribution to politics and as a human rights campaigner

Honorary fellow of the University of Wales, Bangor

Honorary degree from the North East Wales Institute of Higher
   Education
Awarded Communicator of the Year at the Wales Yearbook Political
   Awards 2005
Admitted to the White Robe (which is the highest order) of the Gorsedd
   of Bards at the National Eisteddfod of Wales 1991
BBC/*The House* magazine and *Spectator* Awards for Backbencher of
   the Year 2003
Channel 4 Political Award for Campaigning Politician of the Year 2004
Centre for Kurdish Progress Award for Extraordinary Contribution to
   the Kurdish Cause
The Churchill Award 2014 for Politics
Member of the Arts Council of Great Britain 1975–79 and the vice-
   chair of the Welsh Arts Council 1975–97.
Member of the Royal Commission on the National Health Service
   1976–79

INDEX